Teetering on

•

Teetering on the Rim

●

Global Restructuring, Daily Life, and the Armed Retreat of the Bolivian State

Lesley Gill

Columbia University Press
New York

▰

Columbia University Press
Publishers Since 1893
New York   Chichester, West Sussex

Copyright © 2000 Columbia University Press
All rights reserved

Parts of chapter 3 were first published as "Relocating Class: Ex-miners and Neoliberalism in Bolivia," *Critique of Anthropology* 17, no. 3 (1997):293–313. Copyright © 1997 Sage Publications, Ltd. Reprinted by permission of Sage Publications, Ltd.

Parts of chapter 4 were first published as "Neoliberalism and Public Education: The Relevance of the Bolivian Education Reform Law and the Teachers' Strike of 1995," pp. 125–40, in Lynne Phillips, ed., *The Third Wave of Modernization in Latin America: Cultural Perspectives on Neoliberalism* (Wilmington, Del.: Scholarly Resources Press, 1997). Copyright © 1997 Scholarly Resources Inc. Reprinted by permission of Scholarly Resources Inc.

Parts of chapter 5 were first published as "Creating Citizens, Making Men: The Militarization of Masculinity in Bolivia," *Cultural Anthropology* 12, no. 4 (1997):527–50. Copyright © 1997 American Anthropological Association. Reprinted by permission from *Cultural Anthropology.*

Parts of chapters 6 and 7 were first published as "Power Lines: The Political Context of Nongovernmental Organization (NGO) Activity in El Alto, Bolivia," *Journal of Latin American Anthropology* 2, no. 2 (1997):144–69. © 1997 American Anthropological Association. Reprinted by permission from the *Journal of Latin American Anthropology*, by permission of the American Anthropological Association, Arlington, Va.

Library of Congress Cataloging-in-Publication Data
Gill, Lesley.
    Teetering on the rim : global restructuring, daily life, and the armed retreat of the
  Bolivian state / Lesley Gill.
      p. cm.
    Includes bibliographical references and index.
    ISBN 0-231-11804-X (cloth) — ISBN 0-231-11805-8 (pbk.)
    1. El Alto (Bolivia) — Economic conditions. 2. El Alto (Bolivia) — Social conditions. 3. Bolivia — Economic policy.   I. Title.
HC183.E4 G54 2000
338.984'12—dc21   99-055581

Casebound editions of Columbia University Press books
are printed on permanent and durable acid-free paper.
Printed in the United States of America
c 10 9 8 7 6 5 4 3 2 1
p 10 9 8 7 6 5 4 3 2

To Art, with affection

Contents

Acknowledgments

This book is the product of the support, advice, friendship, and hospitality that I have received from a great many people in Bolivia and the United States. I could never have written it without their interest and forbearance, and the personal and intellectual debts that I have accumulated are substantial. It is therefore with great pleasure that I thank them for their support.

In Bolivia I am grateful to Pablo and Felicidad Huañapaco, Marcela Lema, and Clara López for their generous hospitality. My stays in El Alto and La Paz would have been much less comfortable and enjoyable without them. A number of people also helped me with my research as it took different twists and turns. Leonidas Rojas and many of his former workmates from the mining area Catavi-Siglo XX helped me to understand the social consequences of the neoliberal assault on Bolivia's state-owned mining sector. Berta Chuquimia taught me a lot about the public school teachers' struggles to avoid the same fate as the miners', and Luis To explained much about the shady world of real estate development and land speculation to me. Juan Ramón Quintana's fascinating insights into the workings of the armed forces were central to the formulation of my analysis, and Gueri Chuquimia and the late Roberto Santos assisted me in comprehending how the complex social relationships among ordinary men and women shape the ties between poor Bolivians and the army. I owe special thanks to Cecilia Araujo and Claudia Hanagrath, who combed newspaper archives and arranged some key interviews.

I would also like to thank the numerous people who elucidated the complex world of nongovernmental organizations for me. These men and women really are too numerous to name individually, but to all of them I am deeply grateful. I am particularly indebted to Juan Carlos Balderas, who was always generous with his time and knowledge. Guillermina Soria guided me on numerous trips around El Alto and shared her knowledge of the city with me. Genoveva Villarreal, Ineque Dibbits, Felix Muruchi, and Emilse Escobar were always willing to help. My biggest debt, however, is to Xavier Albó, who has always been a major source of ideas, analysis, and inspiration. In one way or another Xavier has provided important insights, contacts, and suggestions for all the research projects that I have undertaken in Bolivia since the early 1980s, and this one was no exception. His intimate knowledge of nongovernmental organizations was a major resource for me, and his jokes and endless good humor were always reinvigorating.

In the United States a number of people read the entire manuscript or portions of it. Gerry Sider commented on the completed project, and he waded through crude versions of articles and papers that form the basis of certain parts of the whole. I learned a lot from him, and the book is much stronger as a result. Leigh Binford, Marc Edelman, and Adam Flint read different chapters and offered helpful advice. The members of the Columbia University Cultural Pluralism Seminar listened to portions of my argument over the last several years. I am particularly grateful to Linda Green, Carolle Charles, Tony Lauria, Johanna Lessinger, Susan Lowes, Nicole Polier, and Janet Siskind for sustaining a supportive scholarly community that, despite its outdated name, manages to stay focused on what really matters.

I conducted the research for this book during 1994 and 1995; it included one-month visits in 1996 and 1997. It was supported by generous grants from the American Council of Learned Societies, the Aspen Institute, and American University. A research leave from American University in 1994–1995 gave me the time to carry out most of the fieldwork on which I based the book. And finally, I would like to thank John Michel of Columbia University Press for his enthusiasm for this project.

Teetering on the Rim

•

1 · Introduction

Behind the abstraction known as "the market" lurks a set of institutions designed to maximize the wealth and power of the most privileged group of people in the world, the creditor-rentier class of the First World and their junior partners in the Third.

—Doug Henwood, *Wall Street*

The State is . . . in every sense of the term a triumph of concealment. It conceals the real history and relations of subjection behind an a-historical mask of legitimating illusion; contrives to deny the existence of connections and conflicts which would if recognized be incompatible with the claimed autonomy and integration of the state.

—Philip Abrams, "Notes on the Difficulty of Studying the State," *Journal of Historical Sociology*

Poised on the rim of a steep escarpment, high above the canyon that protects the Bolivian capital, La Paz, from the cold winds that blow off the Andes, is a second city—impoverished, rapidly growing, and neglected by the state. Here, in the immigrant city of El Alto, many victims of Bolivia's ongoing experiment with free-market reform teeter on the edge of survival. Recently arrived peasants clad in tire-tread sandals look for work. Women sell fruits, vegetables, and a variety of trinkets on the streets, and they are frequently accompanied by small children. Others—domestic servants, gardeners, shoe-shine boys, and part-time handymen—travel in the early morning to jobs in the capital. Most of these people are indigenous Aymara, immigrants from the countryside.

The lure of employment opportunities generated by new forms of capital accumulation cannot explain their presence. The international investors and multinational corporations that transformed Pacific-basin nations and changed the face of neighboring Chile and Brazil are not attracted to Bolivia in large numbers. And the cocaine traffic—Bolivia's most lucrative, albeit illegal, source of foreign exchange—remains concentrated in the eastern lowlands. Nor have migrants come to El Alto because of the devastation unleashed on a peasantry caught in the whirlwind of expanding agrarian capitalism. For decades the Aymara peasants who populate the rural hinterland have faced the steady deterioration of any possibility to create viable small-scale agricultural activities, because inheritance has fragmented their small holdings, and soil erosion, drought, and overexploitation have further diminished productivity. To make matters worse, the relative worth of agricultural commodities has declined in relation to the chemicals (e.g., fertilizers and insecticides) necessary to produce them, and the state has willfully ignored the plight of poor rural cultivators.

The influx of rural immigrants to El Alto and to its wealthier sister, La Paz, represents a desperate search for a livelihood by people with few other options. Those who have fled the effects of economic restructuring elsewhere, such as thousands of former miners, find little relief in El Alto, where stable forms of employment have been disappearing and living conditions are not always better. In addition, budget agreements between the state of Bolivia and the International Monetary Fund (IMF) preclude additional spending to improve the quality of urban life. Unemployment, nonfunctioning schools and health clinics, and the dearth of adequate infrastructure attest to the massive and deepening impoverishment. One consequence is the expansion of a vast reserve army of unemployed or marginally employed people, also conceptualized as an "informal economy," from which a few emerge as incipient entrepreneurs but in which the vast majority experience new and old forms of oppression.

Traveling down the canyon to central La Paz, one encounters smartly dressed people who are primarily "white" and who have weathered Bolivia's turn to free-market policies or benefited from them. These individuals are government technocrats—the so-called Boys—who spearheaded the free-market transformations.[1] They are also importers who profited from lower tariff barriers, and Bolivian entrepreneurs who feared the effects on their business of hyperinflation, labor militancy, and a resurgent Left more than the effects of trade liberalization. Others are professionals of various sorts who have inserted themselves into new circuits of global power via, for example, a burgeoning number of international development organizations.

Cellular telephones are a new status symbol for these individuals. The proliferation of cellular telephones dates from 1996, when the state dismantled its telecommunications company, and foreign firms moved in to compete for the spoils. The cell phones symbolize one of the divergent social and economic pathways that accompany the economic transformations reorganizing Bolivia. Depending upon their position in society, Bolivians alternately celebrate and condemn these transformations, which are widely referred to as neoliberalism.

Broadly conceived, neoliberalism, like its older nineteenth-century variant, is an economic, political, and moral doctrine that posits the individual as the fundamental basis of society. More specifically, this ideology is rhetorically antistate and places unlimited faith in the "magic of the market" to resolve all social problems. The most compelling aspect of this ideology lies in the conceptualization of the market as a neutral, even beneficent, arbiter rather than a metaphor for capitalist processes. Neoliberals see the state, in comparison to the market, as a bumbling, inefficient, and frequently corrupt actor whose presence constantly encumbers the market's unselfish actions. As E. P. Thompson has observed, "Market is indeed a superb and mystifying metaphor for the energies released and the new needs (and choices) opened up by capitalist forms of exchange, with all the conflicts and contradictions withdrawn from view. Market is . . . a mask worn by particular interests, which are not coincident with those of 'the nation' or 'the community,' but which are interested, above all, in being mistaken to be so" (1993:305).

The transhistorical notion of market as beneficent mediator is not what requires explanation. Such ideological assertions are compatible with a variety of capitalist projects that achieve dominance and then portray themselves as the necessary and foreordained outcome of history or simply declare the "end of history." Neoliberalism is one such project. What needs explaining are the rather more specific ways that contemporary capitalism is transforming particular markets for labor while depriving ordinary people of access to the means to satisfy their most basic subsistence necessities. For these people, the market is less a neutral regulator than an imperative—a demand, or requirement—to constantly reconfigure an entire array of social relationships to ensure the basis of their material existence. This imperative intensifies as heightened competition for the basics of subsistence fractures social life among the poor while broadening the huge gulf between them and more powerful groups.

Policy makers in Latin America, where diverse administrations have been implementing reforms based on right-wing and centrist economic principles, accept the market imperative. Their reforms include public spending cuts and the privatization of state enterprises, the reduction of tariff barriers to encourage foreign investment, the "freeing" of financial markets, and debilitating attacks on labor; the IMF champions these reforms and uses them to evaluate a nation's financial health and loan eligibility. The effect of these reforms on daily life is profound.

After more than a decade of neoliberal economic restructuring in Bolivia, more people have become irrelevant to global and national processes of capital accumulation, while they have been losing other means of supporting themselves. At the same time, the provision of social welfare services by the state has diminished, and vulnerable low-income people are increasingly exposed to economic forces biased against them. One consequence is that social life has grown increasingly precarious for the majority of Bolivians. As June Nash (1994) has suggested, Bolivia has a subsistence crisis. Exploitation has also become more rooted in the fabric of daily life, as poor people are forced to compete with each other for the diminishing returns generated by insecure part-time jobs. Yet the general deterioration of living standards means that the space—social, political, and economic—in which impoverished people can maneuver is increasingly circumscribed. In addition, the weakening of the labor movement—symbolized by what has happened to the Central Obrera Boliviana (COB), a national umbrella organization of workers and peasants—has made the articulation of popular demands in national and international arenas more difficult.

This book offers a critique "from below" of what has been called neoliberalism, and it examines how changing forms of state rule are affecting the lives of vulnerable people in El Alto. To this end, it focuses on the ways in which neoliberal policies reorder men's and women's relations to each other and the kinds of alliances, opportunities, and collusions that become possible and impossible. How, it asks, are changing forms of domination both creating and destroying various kinds of relationships, understandings, and intimacies among ordinary men and women? How too are these changes reorganizing relationships between increasingly impoverished peoples and dominant groups? And how are these changing social relationships transforming people's sense of what they can do by themselves and with others and of what is improbable, unimaginable, or simply absurd? Addressing these questions allows us to explore the ways that diverse peoples are making claims on the present and the future in the context of painful social and economic changes.

Focusing on these issues is particularly important in cities, where the contradictory tendencies of neoliberal capitalism are most apparent. In Latin American cities, and in most large urban centers of the Americas, the concentration of wealth and the expansion of poverty take place side by side, belying any facile assumption that there is no alternative to the misery that so many people experience in their daily lives. Cities are also places where the power and reach of the state are most developed. Consequently, they offer good settings to explore how neoliberal state policies, and the reconfiguring of the state under neoliberalism, are affecting the lives of ordinary people. Finally, the enormous social and cultural diversity of major metropolitan areas—itself the result of shifting forms of class formation—

provides an opportunity to examine new and old processes of differentiation among people who are being incorporated into draconian forms of national and international regulation.

Cities and the Changing Politics of Struggle

As the pace of urbanization intensifies at the turn of the century, the future of the world's peoples increasingly appears to lie in cities. Urban peripheries not only house newly marginalized workers expelled from declining Fordist production systems but receive others—such as ruined peasants—displaced by the dramatic shifts in global capitalism. Cities in Latin America contain 80 percent of the 78 million "new poor" who emerged in the region between 1980 and 1990 (ECLAC 1992). Not surprisingly, cities are often vast regions of unemployment and oppression with weak or nonexistent class-based organizations (D. Harvey 1993; Bourgois 1995; Seabrook 1996). They contain people with different histories and often deeply disparate beliefs and cultural understandings. How, this book asks, are these people dealing with exploitation and domination?

In answering this question, the centrality of class, and particularly class struggle, are important analytic concepts. Although they have fallen out of fashion in much contemporary scholarship, these concepts have guided the work of a generation of social historians influenced by the work of the late E. P. Thompson, who insisted on the centrality of struggle to any conceptualization of class. According to Thompson, the prosaic struggles of work and daily life give rise to class and class consciousness. Classes do not exist sui generis; they are born of strife and contention. For Thompson the struggles that generate class take place primarily between groups with differential access to power and wealth, but some scholars, influenced by Thompson's work, have suggested that important struggles also take place among people who are very much alike. Although rooted in changing forms of domination, these tensions have a dynamic that is partially autonomous, and they shape to a considerable degree the ways in which subjugated people understand and fight against oppression (Sider 1993; Linebaugh 1992; Lagos 1994).

Although class is not the only reference point for understanding social processes, it is important to bear in mind that a variety of forms of identification shaped the historical emergence of class in different places.[2] Class, argues Carlos Vilas, "doesn't replace these other identities, nor does it necessarily take precedence over them. Rather, it organizes them" (1993:39).

Yet despite these caveats, some analysts often oversimplify and reduce to an undifferentiated essence a diverse tradition of Marxist scholarship.[3] Scholars who acknowledge the importance of class are often criticized for using the notion in crude economistic ways that fail to account for cultural complexity and the gender and ethnic diversity of social processes. This process of marginalization is occurring at precisely the moment that global economic reorganization is widening the divisions between the haves and the have-nots. Social life at the bottom of this deepening divide is changing in extremely problematic ways, and realistic alternatives to a triumphalist capitalism are increasingly hard to imagine.

El Alto is a good place in which to explore how ordinary men and women continue to update a long-established tradition of popular struggle that is at times a class struggle and at times a struggle that moves on the edges of other categories—some as yet unnamed. Like many Third World cities, El Alto is not a center of labor exploitation of the easily recognizable sort. Some light manufacturing industries employ a small percentage of the work force, but trade liberalization has eroded this limited industrial base. Unemployment and underemployment are the dominant features of the city; this forces many different kinds of people to contend with each other for an increasingly precarious existence. They include Aymara-speaking peasants and urban-born or urbanized mestizos—the so-called *cholos*—who speak Spanish, have some education, and have distanced themselves from rural life.[4] They also consist of thousands of Quechua-speaking former miners. Together these people shoulder the brunt of unemployment and public sector cutbacks, although they do so in different ways and to different degrees.

By attending to the fractures and disjunctures that shape, and emerge from, the struggles of poor *alteños* (residents of El Alto)—with each other, with the state, and with an array of international organizations—we can appreciate how multiple and uneven processes of differentiation simultaneously create and undermine various kinds of beliefs and social relationships.[5] Such an appreciation is important not only for understanding how particular forms of identification, such as class, gender, and ethnicity, emerge and become salient politically. It is also crucial for comprehending how these affiliations shift and how they shape political choices in different ways in particular places and at specific times.

One might reasonably ask what, if anything, is new about the concentrated poverty, unemployment, malnourishment, and chronic diseases that afflict so many Bolivians and the social discontent that arises from these conditions. Contemporary capitalist restructuring is more than a little reminiscent of life in Bolivia at the turn of the century, when Liberal Party re-formers "opened" the economy, privatized public resources—especially land—and subjected poor and indigenous peoples to multiple forms of state and market discipline. One has only to read Jaime Mendoza's *En las Tierras de Potosí* (1911) to appreciate that the misery, social dislocations, and health threats generated by the transformations of global capitalism are nothing new to many Bolivians.[6] Yet the condition of working people has under-gone a key shift: labor redundancy, rather than labor scarcity, distinguishes contemporary Bolivia from that of the nineteenth and early twentieth centuries, and the state's approach to social and economic problems differs as well.

Nineteenth-century Liberals wanted to build a modern (i.e., Euro-peanized) nation-state based on capitalist relations of production. They mobilized a labor force for the tin mines and haciendas by attacking com-munal property, and they imposed order by implementing vagrancy laws and sanctioning various forms of unpaid labor in what was then a pre-dominantly rural society. The Liberals also hoped to transform La Paz into a cosmopolitan urban center modeled after the great cities of Europe. To this end, they addressed urban problems that not only imperiled the poor but threatened the health, power, and aesthetic sensibilities of the wealthy. They did so by investing in extensive public works projects in La Paz, in-cluding sanitation, lighting, and infrastructure construction, such as the stately Prado boulevard (Klein 1982:169).

The nation-building project continued after the 1952 revolution. The government decreed a far-reaching agrarian reform, nationalized the major tin mines, abolished unwaged labor, instituted universal suffrage, pro-moted public education, and opened a series of teacher-training institutes. Leaders of the revolution and their successors wanted to dismantle the bar-riers that precluded the full integration of indigenous peoples, such as yeoman farmers and waged laborers, into the project of capitalist modern-ization. They also downplayed the invidious racial distinction that had long divided Bolivian society and promoted a nationalist discourse that ex-horted all people to identify as Bolivians.

In addition to agrarian reform, public education was key to the creation of a national citizenry: students received instruction in Spanish, mastered the facts and dates of a standardized history, and learned the national an-them and the significance of national symbols. Compulsory military ser-vice was also crucial to the integrationist project. Military instructors la-bored to convert "Indian" conscripts into "citizens" and linked beliefs about masculinity to patriotic duty. The United States, which financed the expansion of the post-1952 armed forces as the cold war heated up in the Americas, assisted their efforts.

Today, however, turn-of-the-century neoliberals are less concerned with nation building than with managing the country's balance of payments and maintaining the order necessary to create a favorable investment climate for foreign companies. Rather than promote broad initiatives that aim to build consensus for state rule, they either ignore social policy completely or limit it to specific schemes for containing social tensions. This approach is evident in cities, where neoliberals isolate themselves in exclusive suburban enclaves and prescribe exploitative food-for-work schemes or infusions of microcredit for the poor. Their indifference is particularly striking given the enormity of urban distress. A majority of Bolivians (60 percent) live in cities (ECLAC 1996), where the general quality of urban life is declining. Central La Paz and El Alto, for example, are clogged with traffic; pollution is becoming a problem; diseases like cholera have made brief reappearances; and the metropolitan area is increasingly balkanized between wealthy enclaves and vast areas of poverty.

The state, and the changing relationships between state institutions and ordinary people, must necessarily become a focus of analysis. Major shifts in the organization of worldwide political and economic power—for example, the ceaseless transformations of global capitalism, the Third World debt crisis, and the end of the cold war—are undermining the ability of states to maintain the political, economic, and cultural conditions that are crucial to the unity of the nation-state. In the wake of the debt crisis, multilateral financial institutions have arrogated the right to design state policies and to make crucial decisions about the living conditions of some people. States and their institutions, in turn, are increasingly less accountable to citizens than to powerful international agencies (e.g., Held 1991; Conaghan and Malloy 1994).

This matrix of political and economic power—reminiscent of earlier forms of colonial and neocolonial domination—creates complex problems for the nominally democratic Bolivian state and other Latin American states that have ostensibly made a "transition to democracy." As policies enforced by states drive more people into poverty, "governability" increasingly becomes an issue for national and international policy makers, who must devise methods to manage the tensions that erupt among the legions of unemployed and underemployed. These methods frequently rely on the use of force. Consider, for example, the Mexican government's militarization of the state of Chiapas, where peasant rebels have been demanding changes in neoliberal policies (N. Harvey 1998), or the use of the military for police functions in El Salvador and elsewhere. Similarly, Carol Smith (1990a) demonstrates how the Guatemalan state, in the aftermath of civil war, is dealing with unresolved conflicts and declining living standards by expanding its security apparatus and encouraging military-backed "development" programs. Indeed, as Jennifer Schirmer (1998) describes in compelling detail, the Guatemalan military has incorporated counterinsurgency structures into the heart of the state. Thus, as Linda Green (1999) argues, fear pervades the daily lives of rural Guatemalans.

In Bolivia, before thousands of unemployed miners resettled in El Alto, the closure of state-operated tin mines prompted massive protests and moved the government to declare a state of siege. The government also repeatedly used force to quell the opposition to a 1994 educational reform law that threatens the livelihoods of thousands of public school teachers. And the increasing militarization of the coca-producing regions attests to the intractable dilemma posed, on the one hand, by peasant cultivators, who militantly assert their right to grow coca, and, on the other, by the United States, which advocates the eradication of this lucrative cash crop. The exercise of force, however, is problematic for nominal democracies, because military and police repression undermines the legitimacy of states and minimizes the frequently limited consensus upon which their authority rests.

States must therefore attempt to balance, or eliminate, the use of force with the deployment of political strategies and discourses about inclusiveness. In Bolivia discourses about "popular participation" and "empowerment" surround the promulgation of new laws designed to deepen the neoliberal project. The 1994 Popular Participation Law, for example, mandates the administrative decentralization of the country, devolves certain decision-making powers to local entities, and acknowledges the pluriethnic, multicultural nature of Bolivian society. The law speaks to the cultural sensibilities of many Bolivians and to their deeply felt desire to be free of oppressive state rule. But despite the discourse on multiculturalism and popular participation in local decision making, the law does not necessarily promote greater equality and autonomy among local people. It is notably silent on the deepening class divisions that characterize Bolivian society.

Critics argue that the Popular Participation Law seeks to contain protest and prevent conflict from reaching and disrupting the central state and that it effaces growing class differences by undermining broad-based alliances. Popular participation thus becomes the "niche" for politics at the local level, where elites may dominate it, while politicians at the national level concern themselves with the demands of global financial institutions.[7] Therefore, how local people engage the meanings and organizational forms imposed on them—how they struggle within and against domination— once again becomes an important consideration.

Contradiction lies at the heart of the state's activities and reveals the conflicting pressures that shape its ability to rule. A focus on contradiction encourages us to explore the multiple measures—discourses, political practices, laws, and, of course, repression—that the state uses in attempting to resolve the tensions between its economic policies and the political necessities that arise from them. Such an approach does not presume the unity and coherence of the state but seeks to explore the conflicting criteria that define its effectiveness in the volatile political and economic context of global capitalism. It allows us to investigate how contending social groups are shaping, understanding, and legitimizing new forms of rule and how alteños are participating in this process.

Central to this endeavor is a consideration of the organizations that local people seek out, create, and work to maintain in their efforts to press popular demands in local, national, and international arenas. Prominent among these are a plethora of internationally financed nongovernmental organizations (NGOs) dedicated to a variety of development issues.[8] Although some NGOs pressure states to respect human rights or adopt environmental conservation measures (Clark 1995), in this book I consider only those institutions that are commonly referred to as "development" or "intermediary" NGOs (e.g., Bebbington and Thiele 1993; Carroll 1992), because they are the organizations that predominate in El Alto. Development NGOs are understood as nominally private, nonprofit agencies that act as intermediaries between international financial donors and local residents and whose function is to implement projects favoring the so-called popular sectors (Landim 1987) or to provide services to grassroots constituencies. They are thus not state institutions, nor are they institutions *of* the poor, because they are not based on membership. In addition, unlike the miners' union, peasant organizations, and some neighborhood associations, NGOs do not allow constituents to represent and defend their political and economic interests vis-à-vis the state, employers, and international organizations.[9] However, as we shall see in chapter 8, the distinctions are not always clear.

Development NGOs in El Alto are far from homogeneous. They emerged in different historical contexts and with distinct political agendas. Although their programs and relationships to political projects have in some cases changed over the years, certain NGOs offer some groups the opportunity to obtain resources and advance their concerns in transnational arenas. They also extend the tantalizing possibility of bypassing the Bolivian state and establishing ties to international aid agencies. Other NGOs, however, are intent on deepening the neoliberal project at the local level. State administrators and other international institutions, such as the World Bank and the U.S. Agency for International Development view some of them as effective private-sector actors, capable of palliating the city's wretched poverty without state intervention, and encourage their limited growth. State officials have encouraged the partial transfer of social welfare services, formerly assigned to state agencies, to some NGOs. Establishing an NGO has also provided middle-class professionals with novel employment opportunities as the state agencies that employed them retrench. All this creates new tensions and opportunities, as a variety of people and organizations resituate themselves within a changing field of global power. Not surprisingly, considerable debate surrounds the activities of NGOs in El Alto, and scholars differ about whether the NGO phenomenon is best understood as facilitating the process of privatization (Cernea 1989), evidence of strengthened democracy within civil society (Bratton 1988; Fowler 1991), a potential resource for alternative development practices and discourses (Fisher 1997), or part of a new repertoire of changing tactics of collusion and accommodation with international domination (Arellano-López and Petras 1994; Lofredo 1991).

This book considers how NGOs are opening up arenas for struggle, as well as alternative routes to class mobility. And, more generally, it examines how the rise of NGOs is changing the relationship between poor urban constituencies, the Bolivian state, and dominant groups. How, it asks, has the proliferation of NGOs affected the dynamics of local political organizing and the kinds of alliances that people create and discard? An analysis of this sort requires a detailed consideration of the obstacles and opportunities that are shaping daily life in El Alto. It is clearly not a matter of documenting the demise of the state, the rise of the market, the spread of NGOs, and the concomitant implications for social life. The key issue is how new institutional relationships reflect changing forms of engagement, accommodation, domination, and immiseration at the local level.

The Neoliberal State and Daily Life in a Changing Global System

The neoliberal transformations that have swept Bolivia, and particularly El Alto, mirror forms of capitalist reorganization that are underway throughout the world. The ways in which these processes unfold are not the same everywhere, and the meanings that ordinary men and women attach to the attendant changes in their lives vary as well. In the United States, for example, the reigning political and economic wisdom is called *neoconservatism,* although some people called it *Reaganomics* for most of the 1980s. Unfortunately, such labels have not always elucidated the complex processes that disrupt and reconfigure people's daily lives.

Many poor alteños have a basic understanding of the economic transformations buffeting their lives and label these processes neoliberalism. This label, of course, can obscure as much as it reveals, just like neoconservatism and Reaganomics. But neoliberalism—the concept and the slogan—has also enabled some alteños to focus debate and resistance. They understand neoliberalism to be a series of policies and practices that express contemporary forms of class and national oppression. Most people locate the ultimate source of oppression in the workings of the IMF, whose severe fiscal austerity measures and intransigence are understood well among broad sectors of the population. Disparaging references to the IMF pepper the speeches of the leaders of popular organizations, and several alteños, in response to my questions, lectured me about the IMF and U.S. imperialism, a concept that has not yet been displaced by squishier notions like "globalization."[10]

They should be excused if they sometimes overemphasize the made-in-the-U.S.A. quality of neoliberalism. Not only is the United States a major power within the IMF, which has its global headquarters in Washington, D.C., but many U.S. politicians and economists—from Ronald Reagan to Milton Friedman—have been the world-class cheerleaders of neoliberal orthodoxy. We must also keep in mind that Bolivia's mid-1980s plunge into neoliberalism was advocated locally by Harvard economist Jeffrey Sachs and designed by then–minister of planning and later president Gonzalo Sánchez de Lozada (1993–1997), whose heavy American accent, acquired from a childhood in the United States, made him the brunt of constant jokes.[11]

According to popular memory, neoliberalism arrived in Bolivia on August 29, 1985. That was the day that President Víctor Paz Estenssoro (1985–1989) launched Supreme Decree 21060, the opening salvo in an assault on the poor called the "New Economic Policy." The New Economic Policy—labeled a "structural adjustment program" in the innocuous language of the IMF—was one of the most draconian economic and social engineering initiatives launched in any Latin American country, and it represented much more than an adjustment. The policy reforms took aim at the public sector and strove to radically reconfigure the Bolivian economy. The curtailment of state subsidies, the elimination of much public sector employment, wage freezes, and the retrenchment of state agencies dedicated to social welfare activities such as health and education, and the privatization of their services, exposed the poor and sectors of the middle class to severe hardships. Supreme Decree 21060, for example, enabled the government to close state-operated tin mines and fire about thirty thousand workers during the mid- and late 1980s. Miners lost not only their jobs but an entire way of life, because the firings forced desperate workers and their families to leave the mining centers and find work elsewhere. The government targeted the miners because they represented the most militant, well-organized opponents to IMF-backed economic reform, and for years they challenged the power of the state and mobilized popular resistance to state policies. Their defeat and debilitation as a viable political force effectively hobbled a major source of opposition to the government's ongoing program of free-market reforms.

Paradoxically, Paz—a recent convert to neoliberalism—had created a large public sector after the 1952 national revolution. But only two weeks after returning to power in 1985, he imposed Supreme Decree 21060 to cope with a mounting economic crisis. Yet despite all the antistate policies and rhetoric associated with the New Economic Policy, the reform program was less an effort to diminish the power of the state than an attempt to reorganize it and redefine the actors who would be the primary beneficiaries of state intervention (Conaghan, Malloy, and Abugatas 1990; Dunkerley 1992). Commenting in the mid-1980s on the fragility of the recently democratized Bolivian state, Minister of Planning Sánchez de Lozada—who was becoming the architect of Bolivian neoliberalism—remarked that "one comes to the conclusion that the state is practically destroyed. The fundamental institutions of the state's productive apparatus have been feudalized, corruption has been generalized . . . , and the mechanisms of control and oversight have stopped operating. . . . Therefore, the first political goal consists of reestablishing the authority of the state over society" (Conaghan, Malloy, and Abugatas 1990:18).

Indeed, in 1985 a national economic crisis was spinning out of control, and Paz's predecessor, Hernán Siles Suazo (1982–1985)—the first democratically elected president after nearly eighteen years of military rule—had been completely unable to manage it. Massive foreign debt, accumulated during years of fiscal mismanagement by military regimes, consumed declining export earnings; inflation devoured wages overnight; tin production—Bolivia's major legal source of foreign exchange—had stagnated; and cocaine had replaced tin as the country's primary export commodity. Dominant groups, which had timidly embraced the nation's return to democracy, feared that they would lose control to a newly empowered Left. Extremely dissatisfied with the statist policies of the Siles administration and attentive to changing domestic power relationships, key business sectors argued that drastic solutions were necessary to stem what appeared to be a process of total social and economic disintegration. Neoliberalism took hold in the country because these groups saw it as a solution to some of their problems. Although differences frequently divided them and unity had to be continually manufactured (see Conaghan, Malloy, and Abugatas 1990), they managed to suppress or marginalize the protests of labor and popular organizations, and they found a powerful ally in the International Monetary Fund and its affiliated institution, the World Bank.

We would be mistaken, then, to assume that the United States and the IMF simply imposed neoliberalism on Bolivia, even though we should never underestimate their power to discipline a Third World country. Similarly, the advent of neoliberalism has not portended the disappearance or decay of the state. Marc Edelman has suggested that "to analyze neoliberalism only in terms of the market's corrosive effect on the public sector, or to talk incessantly about a generic 'neoliberalism' or 'globalization,' obscures the way that state institutions continue to figure in real political-economic processes" (1997:4). Indeed, as Edelman points out, the IMF depends on state officials to draft letters of intent, make decisions about how to reconfigure the state apparatus (e.g., whether to close hospitals, schools, or army bases), and control domestic opposition. It is important, therefore, to appreciate how neoliberalism has developed, and continues to develop, out of political struggles that take place within Bolivia.[12]

Far from shriveling away, the state apparatus is being reorganized and transformed, and state institutions are figuring in this process in different ways: the military, for example, has defended its budget more successfully than those agencies charged with social service provision (Franko 1994), and as poverty intensifies for those on the bottom, many people are asking the armed forces to attend to the needs of the poor. In this way, poverty becomes the wedge the state uses to extend its repressive control over society. And, by advocating development and civic action programs, the armed forces are attempting to use poverty to redefine themselves in the post–cold war era (see chapter 6). "Reestablishing the authority of the state over society" means other things as well. It entails curtailing corruption, reinforcing claims to private property to encourage foreign investment, and strengthening the power of the state to tax citizens. Tax reforms target consumption, and they are aimed primarily at the middle class, which, in the words of Carlos Vilas, represent "the turkey at the neoliberal banquet" (1997:25). Unlike the poor, who have increasingly less to extract, and the wealthy, who resist taxes on their income and property, the middle class still has resources, which the government targets through value-added taxes and other forms of indirect taxation.

Most important, however, is that reinforcing state power meant disciplining organized labor, particularly the Central Obrera Boliviana, and the tin miners' federation (Federación Sindical de Trabajadores Mineros de Bolivia–FSTMB), the COB's most influential affiliate. No one understood the importance of controlling the tin miners better than Gonzalo Sánchez de Lozada, a wealthy mine owner who became president. By breaking up the mining communities and dealing a heavy blow to the miners' union, the government demonstrated to international financial institutions that Bolivia was prepared to pay its foreign debt and was ready to compete for investment with other states by enforcing strong labor discipline and driving wages into the ground. Although Supreme Decree 21060 and subsequent policy measures facilitated the miners' defeat, a precipitous drop in the international price of tin in 1986 provided the government with a rationale for the massive dismissals.

The decimation of the mining communities was the most sensational and contested feature of Bolivia's plunge into neoliberalism. But the neoliberal attack on the labor movement continued into the 1990s. In 1994, faced with the Education Reform Law, which critics argued mandated the de facto privatization of public schools, public school teachers took up the banner of resistance to neoliberalism. State security forces responded by repressing the teachers' demonstrations. Yet despite the continuing power of states to dramatically affect the lives of subject peoples, much recent academic research downplays the significance of states and state institutions, focusing instead on nations and nationalism. This is partly the result of the popularity of discursive approaches in the social sciences that have diverted attention from the concrete material aspects of state formation. In an instructive essay Stoler and Cooper argue that "twenty years ago, the colonial state and the imperial economy would have been the point of departure [for a study of European colonialism]. . . . Their importance has not diminished. Current academic fashions risk privileging the idea of nation over state institutions" (1997:18).

Consider, for example, recent studies of transnationalism. Much of this research assumes the existence of states and borders, and these studies often call attention to the ways that states' ability to act in domestic and international arenas is either changing or has never been effectively consolidated. Yet with the exception of Gledhill's research on Mexico (1995), transnational studies are frequently less concerned with the reorganization of political and economic relationships within and between states than with deterritorialization, identity, cultural flows and "hybridity," migration and the social "imaginaire" (Appadurai 1990; Glick-Schiller, Basch, and Blanc-Szanton 1992; Kearney 1991, 1995; Hannerz 1992). These studies are disturbing because they do not fully analyze the extent to which states are implementing and presiding over painful social dislocations and the cultural conflicts that attend them. Clearly, as Stoler and Cooper (1997) indicate, studying the state and the nation is not an either/or matter; the changing relationships of states and ordinary people in an increasingly interconnected global capitalist society merit more attention at this time.[13]

An influential essay by Corrigan and Sayer (1987) provides a useful starting point. Both Sayer and Corrigan view the state as the primary agency through which a capitalist society organizes social power and cultural forms, and they explore state formation in England as a process by which "the state lives in and through its subjects" (Sayer 1994:337). They call this process "moral regulation": a project of "normalizing, rendering natural, taken for granted, in a word 'obvious,' what are in fact ontological and epistemological premises of a particular historical form of social order" (Corrigan and Sayer 1987:4). Moral regulation takes place through state institutions that encourage certain forms of identification and behavior while marginalizing or repressing others, and it is manifested through laws, rituals, census classifications, military service, public education, and so forth. This process of regulation and social integration relies on a mixture of coercion and consent, although Corrigan and Sayer emphasize the way in which force regulates "consent."[14]

Corrigan and Sayer's study is instructive, because it attends to the multiple and complex ways in which state and society are mutually constituted. And it helps us appreciate how the domain of daily life is never completely separate from the realm of domination and exploitation. Unlike many contemporary theorists, Corrigan and Sayer avoid romanticizing the autonomy and egalitarian qualities of "civil society." In a variety of guises this concept has been much in vogue since the fall of the Berlin Wall and the collapse of communism in Eastern Europe. It has also generated enthusiasm among Latin Americanists in the years after military dictatorships gave way to civilian rule and generated so-called new social movements.[15]

Yet the process of moral regulation, or the manufacturing of consent and the legitimation of state power, becomes problematic in the neoliberal

Bolivian state. The state's ability to encompass and control the wide-ranging activities of daily life depends on the activity of numerous powerful and effective state institutions, such as those that emerged in England. The presence of such tightly organized, efficient, and interconnected state institutions is rare in Latin America (Roseberry 1994; Nugent 1997). In El Alto—as in many poor urban and rural areas of the region—the military and the police are the most visible signs of the state's presence, whereas other institutions are notable for their absence. Although the armed forces, through the practice of compulsory military service, play an important part in organizing consent, they are also actively involved in repressing the protests of subordinated people who view state policies as illegitimate (chapter 6).

More important, the notion that consent legitimates government and the state becomes questionable as soon as we consider the shifting ties between local constituencies, state policy makers, and international financial institutions. Whose consent is necessary for the implementation of unpopular IMF-backed economic reforms? Who should participate in the selection of beneficiaries for development programs sponsored by internationally financed NGOs? Who has to agree for the de facto privatization of public education to take place? Many individuals and institutions involved in these decisions are not accountable to people in El Alto; moreover, they operate beyond the boundaries and the control of the nation-state, which has, in any case, shown itself to be increasingly unwilling to regulate the private sector. The implications are far reaching, not only for conceptualizing consent and legitimacy but for the nature of political organizing and the capacity of the nation-state to control subjects and create citizens.[16]

Given these problems, it is important to keep in mind that domination in Latin America is often less a matter of consensus than coercion. Ordinary men and women often reject, sometimes violently, the relational forms, beliefs, and rules that the state and international entities impose or encourage (e.g., Gould 1990; Womack 1968; Winn 1986; Levenson-Estrada 1994). This situation forces us to consider the social and political disjunctures, where common understandings cannot be achieved, and where domination is accomplished by the overt use of force.[17] To this end, it is important to keep in mind the ways that power unleashes turmoil in peoples' lives—for example, the power to impose and enforce draconian economic reforms, the power to demand military service, and the power to suppress or forbid acts of protest. Power is, according to Sider and Smith, "as much the precondition for continued accumulation, both of goods and further power, as is any transient, apparent or even actual order that may emerge from the exercise and 'legitimation' of power" (1997:12). It does not only define the terms on which people *have* to behave. Power can so disrupt daily life that the social relations and understandings that informed popular struggles in one historical moment may be of little use in another. Mounting any realistic challenge to power under such circumstances is also extremely difficult. It requires that oppressed peoples constantly reestablish and recreate their relationships to each other and the institutional forms that represent these ties. This is a complex process that relentlessly forces people not just to struggle to get by from one day to the next but also to reconceptualize the past and the present in order to create different kinds of futures.

Poverty and the Politics of Representation

Depicting social life in El Alto and describing the devastating poverty of the city inevitably force one to confront the contentious politics of representation. The scholarship on poverty in U.S. cities, where minorities have long been the target of state efforts to regulate them, poses the difficulties most starkly. Much of the public policy debate about urban poverty turns on racial stereotypes and beliefs about individual merit, which stigmatize the poor, blame them for their suffering, and portray them as violent deviants. Social scientists have fueled this debate with demeaning concepts and characterizations, such as Wilson's "underclass," and Oscar Lewis's "culture of poverty."[18]

Because of the highly politicized, unnuanced, and polarized context in which debates about poverty frequently take place in the United States, many North American anthropologists have, according to Philippe Bourgois, produced overly sanitized accounts of impoverished urban neighborhoods (1995:11–18). Such accounts strive to protect defenseless constituencies from victim-blaming ideologies and portray the humanity of oppressed peoples. Yet by avoiding serious discussion of the harsh conflicts that frequently shape daily life in these settings, and that are rooted in the very process of domination, these scholars eschew a deeper understanding of the dynamics of oppression. The condemnation and the praise that have greeted the publication of Bourgois's ethnography on Harlem crack dealers—*In Search of Respect*—gives some idea of the intensity that shapes the debate on urban poverty in the United States.[19]

This kind of debate has been less intense in Latin America, where the "agrarian question" has dominated scholarly and public policy debates for decades.[20] Nevertheless, a spate of urban research during the 1960s and early 1970s found urban "marginals" in a backward, wholly autonomous "informal economy." These studies reflected a broader pattern of characterizing poor people—peasants and urban immigrants alike—as atavistic and resistant to change. As Latin America has grown increasingly urbanized since the 1980s, scholarly attention has shifted from a predominant concern with agrarian issues to include more varied and nuanced consideration of changing urban life. Several Bolivian scholars have produced some fine studies of migration, ethnic struggle, and economic survival.[21] And North American academics have written thoughtful accounts of working-class neighborhoods in Managua under the Sandinistas (Lancaster 1992), child death in urban Brazil (Scheper-Hughes 1992), trade union struggles in Guatemala City (Levenson-Estrada 1994), and changing understandings of masculinity in Mexico City (Gutmann 1996).

Despite these sensitive portrayals of urban poverty and social life, some social scientists and international development specialists nonetheless have a tendency to applaud uncritically the courage and fortitude of impoverished residents of the Third World for creating lives for themselves amid incredible adversity. Such celebratory depictions are particularly widespread among international development sycophants who ignore class oppression and champion the democratic virtues of an autonomous egalitarian "civil society." They are also evident in the enthusiasm for NGOs expressed by world bankers eager to develop the private sector.

Calling attention to a people's capacity for self-help and community organization is by no means invalid. It challenges the views of local elites, who perceive poor urban neighborhoods as eyesores and threats to social peace, and it corrects a bias in some of the social science literature, which portrays these neighborhoods as sites of hopelessness and despair. Yet too much emphasis on the positive aspects of social life in destitute communities can be extremely dangerous during a period of neoliberal restructuring, especially when the toadies of leading global financial institutions promote this viewpoint. It opens the door for the withdrawal of state support and investment from impoverished communities and, in the end, worsens the already precarious position of the poor.

The real story of El Alto is not about self-help and community empowerment. It is about the disruptions to people's lives and the new kinds of collusions and accommodations that emerge from them, as people struggle within and against the imposed disorder. It is about how people contend with the state and international organizations, as well as with each other, to simply continue their lives from one day to the next. Hope is often their greatest resource, and it is supremely exploitable.

The City in Global Perspective

To understand how neoliberalism and its associated forms of power are transforming the relationships among ordinary alteños, as well as between them and the state, I had to grapple with the difficulties of studying a city of 500,000 people. When I arrived in El Alto in 1994, I planned to embark on a much more modest research project that examined the relationships between NGOs and popular organizations in one of El Alto's many villas, or neighborhoods.

During the next several months, however, events and conversations with a variety of people nudged, encouraged, and forced my attention into different areas. A dramatic public teachers' strike sparked by the state's educational reforms disrupted the city and moved the government to declare a state of siege. The "relocation" experiences of former miners in the aftermath of Supreme Decree 21060 forced me to consider the changing forms of popular struggle in Bolivia. And the experiences of many young men with compulsory military service piqued my interest. Why, I wondered, were men so eager to serve an institution that oppressed them, and why did they consider themselves to be more complete men and "citizens" after military service? Their experiences raise issues of participation and citizenship in an ostensibly democratic society, where citizenship rights guaranteed by the state via the military are juxtaposed against deepening immiseration and cultural degradation. How are neoliberal policy reforms, which are changing geopolitics in the wake of the cold war and exacerbating poverty, reshaping the relationship between the armed forces and ordinary people? None of this fit neatly with my carefully laid research plans. What follows, then, is an account of neoliberal urban Bolivia that moves restlessly around El Alto and makes forays into the countryside and La Paz. It frequently zooms in to consider people and events in considerable detail but also periodically steps back to examine social processes more abstractly.

This book departs from the approach adopted by most urban ethnographies, which focus on a specific neighborhood or group of neighborhoods. Despite the considerable strength of traditional urban fieldwork, which relies primarily on participant observation, this approach cannot always capture the political, economic, and cultural processes that enmesh cities and the people who live in them. I pay particular attention to what Thompson (1978) describes as a "field of force" and conceptualize El Alto as the nexus of a series of contentious and wide-ranging social relationships of inequality. Unlike Thompson's metaphor, which draws on the idea of a bipolar magnetic field, the arenas of domination and forms of popular experience in El Alto are various. They are crucial to understanding neoliberal restructuring, and, unlike the field of force metaphor, they are dynamic (see Roseberry 1994).

My research therefore demanded that I include a variety of people and localities and adopt a methodology that George Marcus (1995) has called "multi-sited." The importance of multisited ethnography lies in the opportunity to follow the changing relationships of diverse people in particular times and places and not, as Marcus suggests, to analyze the circulation of culture in "diffuse time-space."[22] To this end, traditional participant observation occupied much of my fieldwork, but I also interviewed immigrants and longtime residents about their experiences of migration and dislocation. These interviews served several purposes. First, they enabled me to better appreciate the growth and development of El Alto, a city for which few archives are available. Second, the stories of societal rupture, migration, and unemployment helped me to understand the radical disjunctures that constantly undermine the relationships and cultural understandings through which working people make their history. Old strategies and forms of identification may, at times, be of only limited use to these people, as they set about the task of reconstructing a whole series of social relationships that they need to craft a minimally comfortable life in the city. Their accounts helped me to grasp how they struggle both within, as well as against, particular relationships and how these struggles shape understandings of the past, present, and future.

Finally, a concern with conflict and contradiction was also central to my field research as it evolved. How, for example, were the residents of El Alto attempting to control and participate in the NGOs that had proliferated throughout El Alto by the mid-1990s? And what kinds of relationships existed between the included and the excluded, as well as between alteños and the well-paid NGO staffs (chapters 7 and 8)? Similarly, how were people understanding new reform laws that the government was emitting in the mid-1990s? By following the conflict that emerged around the 1994 Education Reform Law and the people engaged in this controversy, I was able to partially address this question. I attended street demonstrations, clandestine union meetings, and the gatherings of parent associations during an eight-week strike in 1995. I also interviewed parents, teachers, and students in schools and homes and met with the jailed leaders of the teachers' union in La Paz (chapter 5). This fieldwork not only enabled me to see how parents and teachers were understanding and attempting to deal with the state's neoliberal reform program. It also highlighted for me the disjuncture between NGO claims to "strengthen civil society" and "empower local people" and NGO practice when some people actually challenged the state.

In part 1 (chapters 2 to 6) I explore the new and old forms of oppression that shape the changing relationships between the state and ordinary alteños, as well as between local people. Specifically, I consider some of the different ways that the state is intervening in, and vanishing from, the lives of city residents, as the state itself is simultaneously reconfigured. Chapters 2 and 3 describe El Alto and the broad effects of neoliberal restructuring on the legions of Aymara immigrants and longtime urban residents who populate the city. Chapter 4 focuses on the particular experiences of "relocated" tin miners with neoliberalism. It examines the decimation of their communities in the wake of the structural adjustment reforms of the mid-1980s and charts their arrival in El Alto at a time when the city was ill prepared to receive them. The chapter also considers how the vastly different living and working conditions of El Alto challenged the miners' understandings and practices associated with a long tradition of class struggle. Chapter 5 takes up the topic of public education and particularly the struggles of schoolteachers, who have moved to the forefront of popular resistance to neoliberalism. The chapter explores the prolonged teachers' strike of 1995, when teachers challenged the recently enacted Education Reform Law, a central pillar of the state's neoliberal agenda. It also examines the conflicts between parents and teachers that intensified with the passage of the law. Chapter 6 targets military service. It discusses how poor urban and rural men are drawn to the army to deal with their deepening poverty, as the state withdrew from its social welfare responsibilities. It also considers how the disorder generated by state policies ensures a continued role for the armed forces in the maintenance of the status quo. The chapter lays out a complex matrix of gendered alliances, oppositions, and collusions that the practice of military service creates among ordinary people.

Finally, part 2 (chapters 7 to 9) examines how a diverse group of nongovernmental development organizations have partially filled the vacuum left by the retreat of the state in El Alto. It considers the new possibilities that the organizations offer to some people, who are able to use the NGOs to bypass the state and incorporate themselves into new global networks. It explores the frustrations of others who are left out of NGO initiatives altogether. The NGOs, I argue, are aggravating patterns of social and economic differentiation in the city, and they are providing cover for the withdrawal of state agencies by appearing to offer solutions to the worst effects of neoliberalism on the poor. The conclusion summarizes the argument and discusses the broader implications of my analysis.

Part I

•

Ruptures

2 · City of the Future

The rising sun momentarily illuminates a peeling billboard on the road from the airport to La Paz that reads "El Alto: City of the Future." The early morning rays bathe the distant peaks of the Andes in an almost preternatural golden glow. A cold wind stirs, picking up dust and pieces of trash. A street vendor wraps a shawl more tightly around her shoulders as she serves a steaming beverage to commuters en route to La Paz. Farther along, young fare collectors hang from the doors of minibuses, shouting out prices and soliciting passengers for the trip to the Plaza Pérez Velasco, the first stop for many minibuses traveling from El Alto to La Paz. "A La Pérez un boliviano, La Pérez un boliviano," yells one boy, who struggles to fill a minibus with two more riders before departing. The fare, however, abruptly drops to 70 centavos, when another minibus pulls alongside. "La Pérez 70, La Pérez 70," he bellows, trying to lift his voice above the competition but pronouncing the words so rapidly that they run together in an almost unintelligible slur.

We are in "La Ceja"—literally, "the Eyebrow"—the nerve center of El Alto, more than two miles above sea level on the Bolivian high plateau, or *altiplano*, and the gateway to La Paz, several thousand feet below. El Alto has grown on the western edge of Bolivia's capital city, where the broad expanse of the altiplano meets the rugged canyons that shelter La Paz, which was founded in 1548. This is an area of cold winds, low temperatures, searing sunshine, and scant vegetation. Night-time temperatures frequently drop below freezing during the coldest winter months of June and July. Although the cold is alleviated in the daytime by a brilliant sun that burns

Ayamara countryside, ten to fifteen miles outside La Paz

down from a crystalline blue sky, bone-chilling winds often cancel the sun's warmth. The winds abate when the frosty dry winter gradually gives way to the summer rainy season (November–March), but heavy showers that cast a damp chill over the city often preempt the more clement weather.

When El Alto separated from La Paz in 1988 and became a city in its own right, municipal boosters erected the billboard that so enthusiastically heralds the birth of the new metropolis. But why, a visitor might reasonably have asked, did they find so much reason for optimism? The country, and particularly El Alto, was in the grip of a wrenching crisis. Social indicators—unemployment figures, infant mortality rates, housing statistics, and public access to social services—suggested that living conditions were getting worse, not better. The city's spectacular growth only aggravated these problems: the annual rate of expansion hovered around 9 percent in the late 1980s and early 1990s, which contrasted with a 4 percent rate of population growth nationwide (INE 1992).

By 1995 nearly a half-million people lived in the city. Although many in the city's younger population cohort were born in El Alto, most of their parents emigrated from the rural Aymara hinterland of La Paz department; indeed, 92 percent of El Alto's residents were born in the city or the surrounding countryside (INE 1992). High prices and unaffordable rents in

La Paz drove another big group into El Alto, and thousands of Quechua-speaking miners resettled in El Alto after state mines shut down in the 1980s.

What the "City of the Future" represented to the people who encountered it—as native sons and daughters, longtime residents, recent arrivals, temporary sojourners, or passing motorists—varied tremendously. For affluent residents of La Paz, El Alto was stillborn from the very beginning; indeed, the very suggestion that El Alto could be the future—their future—struck them as a sick joke. The economic depression of the 1980s had already shaken them to the core, and imagining their destiny intertwined with El Alto's was more than they could tolerate. From the comfort of their homes in the warm low elevations of La Paz, El Alto appeared to overflow with filth and contagion. Its destitute indigenous inhabitants fed their more affluent neighbors' fears of crime and rebellion, and El Alto's expanding perimeter—pushed steadily by legions of new immigrants—evoked images of a permanent stain (*la mancha urbana*) that would spread inexorably across the flat treeless landscape and threaten to engulf them. Well-heeled *paceños* (residents of La Paz) therefore entered El Alto only when absolutely necessary, such as when they were on their way to another destination. Some had to go to the airport, located in the center of El Alto. Others sped through on the Panamerican Highway, heading to weekend redoubts on Lake Titicaca. Most never stopped in El Alto.

Standing in El Alto on the rim of the canyon overlooking La Paz and contemplating the steel-and-glass skyscrapers that rise from the city center below puts the crushing poverty—and the abundant wealth—of metropolitan La Paz in stark perspective. Symbolic of the increasing concentration of wealth in Bolivia, many of these gleaming monoliths are the product of "free" financial markets, which have allowed cocaine traffickers to repatriate their profits and launder them in the construction industry. The urban tableau, etched against the backdrop of the majestic snow-capped Mount Illimani, is extraordinary, but it is also an affront to those who must endure the indignities of daily life in El Alto, Bolivia's fourth largest city.

If one ventures down the canyon from El Alto, past the city center, to La Paz's Zona Sur at the opposite end of the metropolitan area, one sees the extreme measures that the rich are taking to protect themselves. Here lies the exclusive neighborhood of Aranjuez, a gated community of large garish houses. Security guards strictly control entry, allowing only residents and their visitors past the gate. When I entered the neighborhood one day without permission, a nervous guard told me to leave, because, he said,

Minibuses in El Alto provided transportation for urban residents.

"People are very touchy here." (La gente se pone muy susceptible aquí.)[1] Other neighborhoods in the affluent Zona Sur are increasingly constructing their own shopping centers and restaurants so that residents do not have to venture into the city center for these services.

Despite the growing disparities between rich and poor, "the City of the Future" still means something important to many people who settle in El Alto. It represents their hopes and dreams of a better life, or, at the very least, of another chance. Recent immigrants often complain that urban life is no better, and sometimes even worse, than in the countryside. Yet the city does hold certain attractions for them. In rural areas schools do not extend beyond the third grade, so El Alto offers immigrant children more educational possibilities. It also lures people with the hope of jobs—any

Aranjuez neighborhood, Zona Sur (southern zone), La Paz

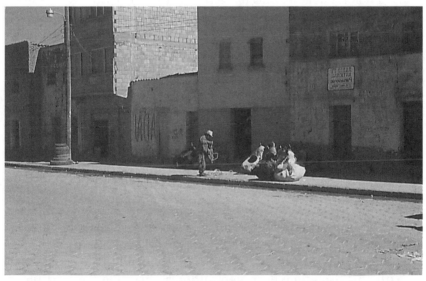

Central El Alto

job—that will allow them to pursue dignified lives and attain the modicum of subsistence security that was wrenched from their grasp in rural areas and mining centers. Running water—even if only from a distant public spigot—and cooking on a gas-fueled stove can also ease the domestic burden of women, who walk long distances in rural areas to obtain water and firewood. But these minimal services and opportunities have grown more restricted since the mid-1980s.

Of course, everyone in El Alto does not succeed; a great many never do. But even though living conditions have worsened, some people acquire part of what they want for themselves and their families, and a few consider themselves quite successful. These people are a source of inspiration to others, which is one reason that people with few other options keep coming to the city. The pride that so many people have, either in their accomplishments or about their lives, belies the notion of El Alto as a cold forbidding slum.

Slum is a pejorative that devalues the lives of people in poor urban neighborhoods, and it is misleading for several reasons. For U.S. suburbanites, slum provokes fears of street violence, and it conjures up images of decay: decrepit tenements, leaky pipes, cockroach-infested apartments, and crumbling public housing projects. These images tell us little about the ways that residents of poor U.S. neighborhoods struggle to live dignified lives and build meaningful relationships with each other. And they completely misrepresent El Alto. Although dilapidated buildings do exist and most housing is inadequate, El Alto is a new city: the people have built most of the dwellings with adobe or kiln-fired bricks and corrugated metal roofs, and, because of the high altitude, El Alto has very few insects.

Similarly, crime certainly exists, and many people will tell you that it is getting worse.[2] Yet compared to New York, Los Angeles, Detroit, Medellín, Rio de Janeiro, San Salvador, and other cities of the United States and Latin America, El Alto is a relatively peaceful place. Few people own guns, and the homicide rate in El Alto, and Bolivia in general, is low. Equally important, the police do not regularly use deadly force against criminal suspects.[3] This is not to say, however, that people are content with the police force. Complaints of police ineffectiveness are widespread, and many people believe that police officers are less interested in protecting citizens than in separating them from their money through fines and the extraction of bribes.

Explaining the comparative tranquility of El Alto is not easy; indeed, the poverty and social inequality are so severe that one might ask why people do not own guns. Part of the explanation may be that the drug traffic has largely bypassed El Alto, and the gang warfare and police violence associated with it elsewhere have not become major problems. Another explanation for El Alto's low levels of violent crime is, perhaps, the intricate network of grass-roots associations (e.g., mothers' clubs, neighborhood committees, civic associations, labor organizations, soccer leagues, and folkloric groups), some nongovernmental organizations, and churches that struggle against considerable chaos and disarray to sustain a modicum of economic security, decency, and social solidarity.

The Catholic Church is a major presence in the city. An imposing cathedral looms above humble adobe homes on the western edge of El Alto, and a variety of less ostentatious local churches house numerous neighborhood congregations throughout the city. More than half of El Alto's residents (71 percent) profess adherence to Catholicism, and many priests, religious, and lay catechists do their best to minister to the needs, both spiritual and material, of this population. For example, Father Vitaliano Choque—a Bolivian Aymara—meets periodically with a number of Christian base communities to read the Bible and discuss its implications for people's daily lives. Christian base communities are Catholic congregations that emerged in the 1960s from reforms in the Catholic Church and the desire to encourage progressive social change. Their expressed purpose is to bring together small groups of people for reflection, the formation of social awareness, and the struggle for social justice. Father Vitaliano, who receives little encouragement or support from the Catholic hierarchy, works with these groups to build a sense of community and forge a critical understanding of the social problems that weigh heavily on them.

Yet many of El Alto's residents are Catholic in name only, and the city has considerable religious mobility. Many professed Catholics rarely, if ever, attend mass, and limit their dealings with the church to baptisms, funerals, and other major life passages. These individuals, together with about forty-two thousand others who express no religious preference, are frequently drawn to a variety of evangelical churches that are mainly Protestant and have sprung up across the city in recent years. The churches include the Baptists, the Jehovah's Witnesses, and the Seventh-day Adventists, but the Pentecostals represent the majority of new denominations.

Pentecostal *cultos*, or worship services, are ecstatic events characterized by music, singing, and praying. They are intensely participatory occasions in which congregants receive the healing power of the Holy Spirit by collectively cleansing themselves of sin. The cultos occur several times a week and provide residents—particularly new immigrants and women—with an institutional setting in which to build and reaffirm new social relationships. Unlike the Catholic base communities, which focus on social inequality, the Pentecostal culto concentrates more closely on the individual and self-sacrifice as a means of personal improvement. A growing number of people are experimenting with Pentecostalism and other forms of evangelical Protestantism as they search for new solutions to their problems, and as established institutions, particularly state agencies, fail to adequately address their suffering.

In addition to the churches, 285 neighborhood committees, or *juntas de vecinos*, operate around the city, and together they form the Federación de Juntas de Vecinos de El Alto (FEJUVE). These local groups seek to improve the quality of life in particular urban neighborhoods by channeling the demands of residents for electricity, sewerage, potable water, land titles, and other social services to state officials. The most dynamic neighborhood committees are those that struggle to represent rural immigrants on the expanding urban periphery. Unlike residents in older, more established neighborhoods, where a minimal urban infrastructure exists, people in outlying areas lack all basic services, and unscrupulous land speculators frequently prey upon them. Thus new immigrants usually initiate the formation of a junta de vecinos to obtain title to their property.

Forming a neighborhood committee is a complicated matter. Local groups receive legal recognition only after the state approves an urban settlement plan. For the state to grant this approval, which paves the way for land titling and the provision of services, a minimum of two hundred families must inhabit a designated area. Yet many lot owners are unable to move immediately into the new settlements, because they lack the funds to build a home or because they have not established the urban contacts that are crucial for a successful move to the city. Land speculators may also simply retain empty urban lots until real estate values increase and they can sell the land at a higher price (Sandóval and Sostres 1989). To make matters worse, the state cannot keep pace with the demand for services, and as neoliberal restructuring further reduces its budget, providing social services to new neighborhoods is usually a painfully slow process.

As state agencies have retrenched under neoliberalism, a plethora of nominally private nongovernmental organizations (NGOs) have proliferated across El Alto and partially taken the agencies' place. These grassroots development institutions do not engage in large-scale urban infrastructure projects, such as constructing sewage systems or installing electricity. They do, however, attempt to provide urban residents with some relief from the city's grinding poverty through a series of small-scale projects funded by organizations in North America and Western Europe. Such projects include adult literacy classes, small business development, home construction loans and support, day care centers, seminars on gender and sexuality issues, and health clinics.

By the mid-1990s conservative estimates put forty NGOs in El Alto. Some NGOs concentrate their projects exclusively in particular neighborhoods of the city, but others operate programs in La Paz and other parts of Bolivia as well as El Alto. Many NGOs maintain their headquarters in La Paz, where most of the professional staff lives, but a few are headquartered in El Alto, primarily in the commercial neighborhoods of La Ceja and Villa 16 de Julio. The largest NGOs employ thirty to forty people, but a great many operate with staffs of five or six and survive on shoestring budgets that are renewed, or canceled, by international sponsors on a project-by-project basis.

The offices of the largest NGOs typically contain computers, fax and photocopy machines, telephones and space heaters, and a four-wheel drive vehicle for chauffeuring staff members to project sites. In addition to the professional staff, who are mostly white and university educated, a group of lower-paid employees—"popular educators," who come from urban Aymara backgrounds—maintains the most direct daily involvement with project participants. They, along with the secretary, caretaker, driver, and maid, make up the category of "support staff" [*personal de apoyo*]. NGO salaries reflect one's position in this hierarchy, but they are generally superior to comparable jobs in the state sector and much better than the income of most alteños.

Although clientelism frequently undermines the democratic potential of these urban organizations, and political factionalism often divides them, the churches, neighborhood committees, NGOs, and others, such as civic associations, unions, and folkloric groups, try to uphold a measure of dignity and well-being among urban residents. The abundance of local forms of association in El Alto contrasts markedly with other cities. Consider, for example, Deborah Levenson-Estrada's description of the bleak associational life of Guatemala City's working-class residents:

> For a variety of reasons including political repression and instability of housing and employment, there developed little durable grass roots community organization to shelter the laboring poor from the difficulties of urban life except voluntary fire fighter organizations and Alcoholics Anonymous, groups that depended entirely on their local members. In addition, the city was bereft of private or state-authored systems of relief or improvement because no one with power

was interested in reforming the urban populations' housing, sanitary
conditions, health or morals.   (1994:62)

Similarly, Elizabeth Leeds (1996) describes how drug dealing, state violence, and the absence of state-sponsored social services have disempowered community organizations in low-income neighborhoods of Rio de
Janeiro. She explains that even as procedural democracy expands in Brazil,
poor neighborhoods are growing more violent, and local organizations are
being undermined, because residents must contend with the illegal violence of drug traffickers and the official violence of state security forces.
Leeds observes that

> In a society such as Brazil, where the poorer segments of the popu-
> lation are frequently ignored by the state except in the form of po-
> lice repression, the need to create autonomous local forms of deci-
> sion making and service provision becomes part of survival. When
> these forms are eroded by parallel, authoritarian, and frequently vi-
> olent power structures, then formal democratic structures of the na-
> tional polity become meaningless.
>   The form that drug dealing has taken in the favelas [poor urban
> neighborhoods], due to the state's failure to provide basic services and
> state repression in creating the perception of danger to justify heavy-
> handed police or military action, has permitted the establishment of
> new channels of clientelistic relationships. The drug dealers them-
> selves have in many instances created a forced symbiosis—alternative
> welfare "services" in exchange for protection and anonymity—while
> undermining the authority of legitimately elected local leaders.
>   (1996:77)

Many first-generation rural immigrants also maintain varying degrees
of contact and involvement with their natal communities. Of course, the
quality of these ties varies over time, and some immigrants benefit more directly from them than others, but maintaining connections to rural kinfolk
is a strategy that some immigrants have used successfully to protect themselves from full exposure to the market, the state, and elites during periods
of crisis and unemployment. In this sense they are unlike urban-born industrial proletarians, who may no longer retain these ties and who face
more difficulties weathering the disruptions generated by capitalism because their jobs are their only resources. We should not, however, overstate
the efficacy of urban-rural ties. The extent to which alteños and their rural
kinfolk can continue to partially protect themselves remains an open question, as their survival strategies are placed under more and more pressure.

State policies and the state's resolute refusal to attend to the needs of its citizens are seriously eroding the social relationships upon which people depend for their daily survival. Poor alteños must vie for an increasingly inadequate living, while they are forced to turn to other impoverished residents for some of what they need. The resulting tensions, partially rooted in new and old forms of domination, fuel an array of complex struggles among alteños—young and old, men and women, urban-born and rural immigrants, "Indians" and cholos, employed and underemployed—that simmer beneath the surface of daily life and sometimes erupt into the open.

"Community," insofar as its exists in different places around the city, is an extremely unstable amalgam of social relationships relative to the conflicts and contradictions that generate, sustain, and often dissolve it. Most El Alto neighborhoods are not tightly knit homogeneous places that can be defined by this concept. Indigenous Aymara immigrants live on the same streets with former miners and longtime urban dwellers, and neighborhoods may be little more than reference points for people who must travel far from home in search of jobs, housing, health care, and contact with kinfolk and friends. Because of constant economic insecurity, people are continually forced into a series of contacts with relative strangers. There is considerable movement from one work site to another: from factory work to part-time construction jobs, from domestic service to street vending, from street vending to artisanry, and so forth. Long-term stable employment is virtually unknown. Consequently, putting down roots (*hacer raices*) is not easy, and those who attain a degree of permanency in a particular location do so with great effort.

El Alto's physical development has done little to facilitate the social integration of the city, which has expanded along three major highways and two railway lines. The Viacha and Oruro-Cochabamba highways cut across the city in the south, and the Panamerican Highway transects the city in the north. These thoroughfares have contributed to the growth of El Alto as a dynamic regional entrepôt. They link the city not only to La Paz but also to the rural hinterland, other Bolivian towns and cities, and neighboring Chile. But far from promoting its internal cohesiveness, these highways disarticulate the city's social life. For example, pedestrians trying to cross the Panamerican Highway where it passes the Villa 16 de Julio either risk being crushed by speeding trucks and minibuses, or they walk several blocks to reach an elevated crosswalk. Residents along the other roadways do not even enjoy the benefit of pedestrian crossings, and stop lights are rare.

Similarly, two military bases—both legacies of the cold war—are strategically located at opposite ends of the city, where the military monitors the local population and controls access to La Paz. The air force base in the northern zone dates from the late 1940s, and an army base has controlled the city's southern flank since 1971, when it was established by the regime of General Hugo Banzer Suárez (1971–1978). High walls effectively seal the air force base off from the city, and many residents consider the military's activities behind the walls to belong to a different world. Yet they are well aware of the repressive role that the military often plays in their daily lives.

The army base, for example, is situated on the La Paz–Oruro highway, which connects the capital to the mining districts. Soldiers from this post have frequently disrupted the protests of miners, who have marched on La Paz from the mining centers on numerous occasions, and the army has

Civilians waiting for transportation outside the air force base

more recently put down the demonstrations of striking public school teachers. The bases also provide comfort for those who worry about the intentions of neighboring Chile. Most important, however, is that the military installations ease the anxieties of a small minority of paceño whites, who fear an onslaught of the indigenous masses of El Alto and the surrounding countryside. Such fears are fueled not only by the growing number of poor immigrants that populate the city but also by actual historical events. The encirclement and siege of La Paz in the eighteenth century by indigenous rebels under the leadership of Tupac Katari continues to be a reference point for both whites and indigenous people, who have very different interpretations of its significance.

When I asked residents what defensive purpose the bases served, several responded with sardonic smiles and replied that the military defended La Paz against *la gente* (the people). Yet for many of them, the military's presence in their city passes with little notice or comment most of the time. The military is not actively repressing people, as it does in the coca-producing region of the Chapare. Residents therefore do not perceive of themselves as living in an "occupied city" and at times take the military's presence for granted, because under normal circumstances residents do not perceive the soldiers as threats. Young conscripts on weekend leave flock to the Sunday market in 16 de Julio like hundreds of other people. They may also seek out odd jobs with vendors or local residents to earn money to spend on the various goods and diversions that the market offers. Residents refer affectionately to them as *soldaditos*, or little soldiers. I have frequently heard people express concern for the "poor little soldiers" [*pobres soldaditos*], when exhausted recruits jog in formation back to the air force base at the end of a strenuous day of drills and exercises. The concern of local people is not hard to understand: many of these young men are the sons, brothers, and husbands of El Alto residents.

Living on the Rim

Unlike other Third World cities, such as Singapore, Jakarta, Bangkok, Dhaka, and the free-trade zones on the U.S.-Mexico border, El Alto has not attracted transnational corporations searching for cheap pliable labor. The poor infrastructure and harsh climate may be reasons; another explanation may be the long history of popular mobilization and unionization in Bolivia. Peasant organizations of the altiplano have persistently targeted the state with the demands of rural people, and the Central Obrera Boliviana (COB), the nation's leading trade union organization, has championed workers' rights for decades. Although the COB has suffered major setbacks in recent years, labor militancy is still part of the lived experiences of many alteños. By contrast, immigrants to Thai and Malaysian cities may never have heard of a labor union, a factor that makes these cities highly attractive to globe-trotting corporations.[4]

El Alto remains—for the time being—a backwater of the global economy, a city of immigrants dislocated from their old ways of life. Before the 1950s, most of the five thousand hectares now occupied by El Alto were covered by rural estates and controlled by landlords who lived in La Paz. A rail line connected the region with the port of Guaqui on Lake Titicaca, and most inhabitants of the area lived in the encampment that grew up around the rail terminus. An aviation school, which eventually became the airport, was founded in 1923, and the offices of the Bolivian National Airlines—Lloyd Aéreo Boliviano—were established there in 1925. Some large landlords began to sell off portions of their properties for urban development in the 1940s, but the emergence of El Alto really got underway after the 1952 revolution, which dramatically reorganized the political, social, and economic life of the country (Sandóval and Sostres 1989).

The revolutionary transformation bore directly on the development of El Alto in a number of ways. The government, led by the Movimiento Nacionalista Revolucionario (MNR), abolished unpaid labor. This act freed thousands of Aymara peasants from the control of rural landlords and enabled them to decide where and to whom to sell their labor. In addition, the MNR implemented a sweeping land reform that effectively dismantled the large altiplano haciendas and redistributed the land to former tenants and indigenous communities. After the disappearance of the haciendas and the landlords who controlled them, the beneficiaries of these reforms established new marketing networks that no longer revolved around the estates, and they strove to produce enough food from the newly acquired fields to satisfy the subsistence needs of their households.

Peasants' hopes of subsistence security were short lived, however. The government and foreign-aid organizations directed economic assistance to Bolivia's eastern lowlands, where a new group of agricultural exporters began to emerge on land that had been unaffected by the land reform. Aymara peasants of the altiplano never received the credit, technical assistance, and price supports that enabled lowland commercial agriculture to develop and prosper.[5] Moreover, the subsequent fragmentation of landholdings through inheritance reduced the average size of fields and made subsistence agriculture increasingly difficult. Forced to continue supplementing the returns of agriculture with waged labor, many peasants set their sights on the city of La Paz, and a steady stream of immigrants in the 1950s became a flood by the 1970s and 1980s.

From a few core villas, or neighborhoods, clustered around the area known as La Ceja, El Alto expanded. In 1950 only eleven thousand people lived in the area, but ten years later the number had almost tripled (Sandóval and Sostres 1989). In the 1960s Elvira Canasas was one of the early immigrants to settle in La Ceja, after she and her family left the Caracoles mining camp. More than thirty years later Canasas recalled how quiet and empty the area was, and she remembered the complete absence of water. To obtain it, Canasas, who was a young girl, collected the scalding hot water discharged from the trains after they entered the station. "Everybody wanted that water," she told me, "and I started collecting it when I was ten years old. The other girls and I would wait for the trains from Arica and Guaqui to arrive. Sometimes they came in at one or two o'clock in the morning. We would always be there with our empty cans. The water came out of a pipe by the engines, and sometimes it burned us because it had passed through the motor."

By 1992 the dramatic growth of the city had moved some residents to declare that El Alto was the "Aymara Capital of the World" (Morales 1994), but government bureaucrats saw a city out of control. City officials and paceño elites worried for years that so many new arrivals would disrupt their control of city politics, and they were therefore quite relieved when El Alto became an autonomous city in 1988. Some of their fears were not unfounded. Beginning in the late 1980s alteños, disillusioned with the established political parties, gave overwhelming electoral support to a talk show host named Carlos Palenque and his party, Conciencia de la Patria (CONDEPA). Until his untimely death in 1997, Palenque hosted a popular television and radio program called *La tribuna libre del pueblo,* which addressed the ordinary problems of women and men who lived in the poor neighborhoods of La Paz and El Alto. Individuals brought their difficulties to the show and were supported by "Compadre" Palenque and his female sidekick, the "Comadre" Remedios, an urban Aymara woman, or *cholita.* The couple appeared to listen sympathetically to highly emotional tales of grief and then offered help by denouncing the authorities or intervening with them, appealing to listeners for assistance, or simply expressing their sympathy. Palenque used the program and its popularity to thrust himself onto the national political stage, where mainstream political parties and traditional elites routinely condemned his brand of "cholo populism." Yet CONDEPA captured the mayoralty of El Alto and held it for most of the 1990s, and, with the backing of poor paceños, it won the La Paz mayoralty in 1993.

Although Compadre Palenque never offered more than individualistic solutions to the collective poverty and suffering of people in El Alto and La Paz, he addressed the hopes, fears, and feelings of marginalization of many poor urban Aymaras. While national politicians were waging a determined assault on the lives of the poor, Palenque spoke caringly to them as individuals and appeared to take their suffering seriously. After he died of a heart attack, his image appeared to a La Paz mechanic on a rock, which immediately became the focus of popular devotion and media attention. Many of Palenque's followers refused to believe that he was really dead and declared that he had become "the saint of the poor" [*El santo de los pobres*]. The hopes, fears, frustrations, and dilemmas that he addressed did not diminish with his passing.

El Alto consists of three broadly defined zones and a far-flung perimeter. La Ceja is the heart of El Alto, the seat of municipal government, and the dividing line between the northern and southern regions of the city. La Ceja is the oldest and most commercialized section of the city, and its residents are merchants, teachers, and public employees who are generally more prosperous and have greater access to social services than the occupants of outlying zones. Most popular organizations associated with the city have their headquarters in La Ceja, including the Federación de Juntas de Vecinos de El Alto (FEJUVE); the Central Obrera Regional (COR), an affiliate of the COB; and the Comité Cívico de El Alto, a local civic association.

During the daytime female vendors clog the streets in this part of town. Many come from other parts of the city to sell their wares, and most wear the distinctive dress of urban Aymara women—brightly colored shawls, bowler hats, and full gathered skirts. They are frequently accompanied by small children, who, wrapped securely in a shawl and tied to their mother's back, observe the world as it passes by on the streets. A profusion of minivans competes with the street vendors and pedestrians for space in and along the cobblestoned streets of La Ceja. All public transportation to and from La Paz converges in this area, and the congestion is often overwhelming.

The northern zone is most noted for the heavy concentration of rural Aymara immigrants and a small Aymara petty bourgeoisie based in commerce. One of its villas—the Villa Pacajes—takes its name from the rural province in which so many of the residents were born. In the early morning hours groups of men and women from this region and across the city leave their homes to catch buses for work, and children head off to school. The bleak treeless streets are quiet and eerily deserted in the daytime, when gusts of wind stir up swirling clouds of dust. Those residents who are not working in other parts of the city carry out domestic tasks behind the high walls that enclose their homes. They are typically teenage daughters, who, in their mother's absence, take care of younger siblings, or they are elderly people entrusted with similar tasks. The distant backfiring of a truck occasionally breaks the silence of the streets, or the stillness is disrupted by groups of immigrant women wielding picks and shovels to lay cobblestones and dig drainage ditches under the auspice of the Food for Work Program sponsored by the mayor's office and an NGO. Otherwise, large furry dogs that loll in the sunshine or scavenge for garbage patrol the streets until perceived intruders challenge their territorial claims.

Fiestas periodically brighten the daily round in this part of town. During the days preceding Todos Santos, or the Day of the Dead (All Saints' Day), residents bake large quantities of bread to offer to the spirits of the deceased. They fashion most of the bread into simple loaves, but human bread figures, or *t'anta wawas* (bread babies), are also a common sight in the markets and the homes of alteños during Todos Santos. People take the bread, along with other food and alcohol, to cemeteries around the city, where people visit the graves of deceased loved ones and offer food to wandering souls. Residents produce so much bread on the eve of Todos Santos that purchasing it is virtually impossible for two or three days afterward—demand is so low that bakeries stop production.

Daytime street scene

Family with bread for the Day of the Dead (All Saints' Day)

Children with bread figures, a feature of the Day of the Dead

Neighborhood fiestas that commemorate the founding of various villas also punctuate daily life in El Alto. In the northern zone the largest is the yearly celebration that marks the founding of the Villa 16 de Julio. Dance groups, dressed in elegant costumes, draw throngs of spectators as they parade along the Panamerican Highway and force traffic to detour. This parade—like its more famous counterpart, the Fiesta del Señor del Gran Poder in La Paz—demonstrates the newly acquired wealth and self-confidence of a prosperous group of Aymara merchants.[6] They belong to a relative handful of successful urban entrepreneurs who have the means to craft and assert an extremely visual, expensive, and highly public notion of urban Aymara ethnicity—one that is less available to their more impoverished brethren for whom "Aymaraness" is more commonly associated with rural poverty, backwardness, and being "Indian."

A huge biweekly fair with approximately ten thousand officially recognized vendors also takes place in Villa 16 de Julio. The fair extends over many blocks and vividly displays the extent to which street vending has exploded under neoliberalism. The fair brings merchants and prospective buyers together from all over the country. A heady array of fruits, vegetables, meat, poultry, and dry goods is on display early in the morning, as is a variety of herbs, elixirs, animals, and powders for an assortment of physical ailments. Merchants also peddle used automobiles and trucks, spare parts, stereo equipment, furniture, and small appliances.

Most notable, however, is a vigorous trade in used clothing from the United States. Today more vendors than ever sell secondhand clothing in the 16 de Julio market. Alteños and Bolivians from many walks of life purchase it because their working conditions have stagnated or deteriorated, and they cannot afford the cost of new clothes. One resident, whose street has been taken over by the vendors, observes that now "even the refined people from La Paz come. We see them on the street all the time with their fancy cars and their cellular telephones." These "refined people" are usually sellers who are profiting from trade liberalization, which has created new economic opportunities for local importers and also for U.S.-based textile recycling firms. The latter purchase used clothes from charities in the United States and repackage them in bales for export to the Third World.[7]

While 16 de Julio in particular and the northern zone in general are the most commercially dynamic areas of El Alto, the southern part of the city is the poorest and most underserved. It contains many Aymara immigrants, a large group of former tin miners, and pockets of an impoverished non-Aymara middle class. With the exception of the Ciudad Satélite, where the neat matchbox houses and cobblestone streets resemble a La Paz

Used clothing for sale

Used clothing section of the 16 de Julio Market

suburb, rutted streets, open sewers, and makeshift dwellings fill this region. Angel Pérez, his wife, Maria, and their three children—aged two, three, and twelve—live here, and, like nearly a quarter of all alteños, they are renters. The family occupies a small room with a dirt floor in the Villa Exaltación. The room is divided by a piece of blue plastic. On one side, they have stacked two bunk beds against the wall. The children sleep on top, the parents on the bottom. On the other side is a table, two chairs, and a television, and the family's belongings are piled against the wall. Maria Pérez cooks meals on a small stove in an adjacent space. Although there is electricity, there is no water, and the family must share an outdoor privy with other families. For these accommodations the Pérez family pays $40 a month.

Open sewer in southern El Alto

They would like to own their own home, but when I met the Pérez family in 1995, they had been unable to save much money. They had come to El Alto from La Paz in 1993 to reduce expenses and to be closer to the bi-weekly market in the Villa 16 de Julio, where Angel and Maria Pérez sell quilts and bedspreads. Traveling to work was less expensive and time consuming than from La Paz, and renting a room was more economical as well. Yet fluctuating sales and periodic family emergencies always seemed to eat away any extra earnings that they set aside. Like thousands of other families, they confronted living conditions that consumed their earnings, sapped their energy, extended their work days, and threatened their health in a city that was unable to satisfy their most basic needs.

The Bolivian government's adoption of free-market policies in the mid-1980s substantially aggravated these conditions, and additional reform legislation in the mid-1990s made these policies even tougher. The chapters that follow explore these policies and how they influenced daily life in the city.

3 · Adjusting Poverty

After the Bolivian government's initial embrace of neoliberalism in 1985, subsequent administrations broadened and deepened the process set in motion by Víctor Paz Estenssoro. Some of the most important and far-reaching reforms followed the 1993 election of Gonzalo Sánchez de Lozada to the presidency. Sánchez de Lozada, who designed Bolivia's original neoliberal agenda when he was minister of planning, ran on a platform that emphasized his past success at bringing inflation under control and stabilizing the economy. As president, he headed a coalition of parties that, once in power, passed a series of legal reforms that had two broad objectives: the further reconfiguration of the state apparatus and the continuing transformation of the relationship between the state and Bolivian citizens. Three reform laws were particularly important for El Alto: the Ley de Capitalización (Capitalization Law), the Ley de Participación Popular (Popular Participation Law) and the Ley de Reforma Educativa (Educational Reform Law).

Despite its clever name, the Capitalization Law lays the legal framework for the privatization of state enterprises and the *decapitalization* of the state. It permits the sale of 50 percent of the stock in public entities to private investors, who frequently acquire them at artificially low prices. The government then transfers the remaining stocks to a revamped social security system, which is charged with administering the stocks and distributing an annual pension—the BONOSOL—to individuals aged sixty-five and older. The BONOSOL will supposedly provide elderly Bolivians with a modest income of approximately $250 a year.

Campaign poster of Gonzalo Sánchez de Lozada, 1993

Despite these modest benefits, the law decapitalizes the state in ways that are particularly significant for El Alto. As one local leader notes, the value of Bolivia's oil, natural gas, and mineral reserves and the future income from their sale do not figure into the law. Profits from these resources now flow into the coffers of private corporations, not those of the Bolivian state. The result, he maintains, is that "the state's revenues will be greatly reduced and consist of little more than a nominal tax that the corporations will pay. It is going to be impossible for the state to maintain the salaries of public school teachers and health care workers in the city."

Indeed, the Popular Participation Law and the Educational Reform Law must be understood within this context. The Popular Participation Law aims to decentralize government and to entrust local organizations with greater decision-making power. It proposes to redistribute 20 percent of the state's revenues to municipalities in proportion to their populations. Each municipality in turn is reorganized into Organizaciones Territoriales de Base (OTBs), which in El Alto constitute the neighborhood committees. The OTBs, or juntas de vecinos, are then supposed to use the money for purposes determined by the groups and to elect officials to a Vigilance Committee to oversee expenditures.

This model of local government encounters a number of problems. As state enterprises are privatized and the state itself becomes increasingly decapitalized, it is not at all clear that 20 percent of state revenues will actually mean an improvement for local residents in El Alto. Some people argue that the Popular Participation Law favors El Alto, because the city's dense population will merit a larger share of federal funds than the amount received by smaller cities. Others are much less sanguine. They interpret the new law less as a democratic blueprint for popular political participation than as a new form of domination.

These critics are disturbed by the way that the Popular Participation Law attempts to restructure the very nature of political participation by legitimating and encouraging new forms of political expression while ignoring or marginalizing preexisting ones. In particular, the law emphasizes municipal organizations but ignores the existence and the forms of struggle associated with national and regional entities. Oscar Michel, the president of FEJUVE in El Alto, explains:

> [The Popular Participation Law] goes against the interests of the popular classes. Why? Because we have confederations at the national level. We have federations that are departmental or regional in the case of El Alto. And we have the Central Obrera Boliviana. And the unions and the juntas de vecinos group themselves around these national or departmental institutions. When there is a conflict, it is these national and departmental entities that make pronouncements and organize pressure tactics.
>
> But what happens with the Popular Participation Law? Each neighborhood committee is empowered to make its own arrangements with the state without consulting any overarching organization. The intentions of the government are divide and rule. It intends to debilitate the main organizations by putting local leaders in charge of small areas and [tying them directly to the state]. This guarantees that there are no solid institutions that question the government. It reduces the power of the popular movement.

My conversation with Michel took place in late 1994, a few months after the passage of the Popular Participation Law, amid heated debate and intense political maneuvering generated by the law. CONDEPA, the party that controlled local government, adamantly opposed the new law, and many details about its implementation at the local level remained unclear. Amid the uncertainty that prevailed, political parties jockeyed for position and control over the emergent political structure. Michel, a CONDEPA member, told me that "every party is involved in this [maneuvering] in accord with their interests, projections, and so forth. They are trying to use the law for their own ends. An enormous fight is taking place that lessens the value of civic work."

In light of the political reforms laid out by the Popular Participation Law, the agenda for public education, set forth in the Educational Reform Law, becomes intelligible. The Educational Reform Law transfers much of the responsibility for public education to local municipalities, including the hiring, firing, and supervision of teachers and the upkeep of schools. It abolishes the Education Ministry and no longer guarantees the graduates of teacher-training institutes positions in the public school system. Teachers must approach newly empowered local officials for jobs, but critics say these officials will not receive the money they need to pay teachers' salaries or maintain buildings and classrooms. Most classrooms are barren settings that frequently do not even have enough seats for all the students. Peeling walls, serious overcrowding, and a dearth of materials make learning extremely difficult. Critics claim that the law furthers the de facto privatization of the public school system, forcing teachers to turn to private institutions for employment and obliging those parents who can afford the expense to place their children in private schools (see chapter 5).

A number of fly-by-night private schools have sprouted up to take advantage of the public schools' difficulties. The new religious congregations that now proliferate in the city support some of these private schools. But private schools are not an option that most parents can reasonably consider, and the vast majority of students remain stuck in the deteriorating public system. In addition, although figures for El Alto are not available, the percentage of children in La Paz department aged six to thirteen who do not attend school jumped from 10 percent in 1988 to 17 percent in 1990 (CEDLA/ILDIS 1994). This is because deepening poverty forces children to leave school and find work to help support their families.

As the people of El Alto debated the latest round of neoliberal legislation in the mid-1990s, longtime residents and new immigrants continued to be victims of a process that Lúcio Kowarick terms "urban spoliation"

(1994:32); this form of exploitation arises from the state's unwillingness to provide adequate housing, employment, health care, education, and basic sanitation to residents of peripheral urban neighborhoods. Neoliberalism has not created this situation, as state spending on social services has always been inadequate, but the new neoliberal reforms are likely to aggravate an already acute crisis. Nationwide expenditures on health, housing, educational, and sanitary services fell from 19 percent of the 1987 state budget to 15 percent in 1992 (CEDLA/ILDIS 1994). To make matters worse, the municipal government of La Paz deprives El Alto of important revenues. Airport taxes paid by departing travelers and tolls from the various highways that lead to and from the city never enter local coffers. Similarly, El Alto receives no tax revenues from many local businesses, because the firms either avoid paying taxes altogether, or they pay them in La Paz, where most have their administrative headquarters.

State-sponsored health care is in desperate straits, as symbolized by the 1991 reappearance of cholera—a nineteenth-century scourge that was once thought to have been eliminated. Although the cholera epidemic shocked the sensibilities of congressional representatives, who declared a citywide emergency in El Alto out of fear that the epidemic would spread to La Paz, the resurgence of this dreaded disease should not have surprised anyone. El Alto has two doctors for every thousand residents, and one hospital and twenty-four undersupplied health clinics are the only public facilities available to a half-million people. In contrast, La Paz, which has approximately the same number of residents, has fourteen hospitals, 115 health clinics, and 180 smaller health posts (CEDLA/ILDIS 1994). Public sanitation and deepening unemployment are also worse in El Alto and place people at greater risk of illness.

Those who can afford the expense, or who are driven by sheer desperation, turn to a limited number of private clinics for health care. International development organizations, which have stepped in to ameliorate the worst symptoms of the neoliberal crisis, support some of these clinics. PROSALUD, for example, is an NGO financed by the U.S. Agency for International Development (USAID) that operates six clinics specializing in child and maternal health care. Five are concentrated in one area of the city, where the de facto privatization of the health care system began in the early 1990s. Consultation fees charged by PROSALUD are only nominally higher than those at the public health clinics, and the doctors and nurses receive the same pay as state employees, but PROSALUD requires them to work longer hours, and they enjoy none of the benefits of the state system.

Although the privatization of health care via NGOs has taken place in some neighborhoods abandoned by the state, many parts of the city have neither state- nor NGO-sponsored health care centers to tend to the needs of local people. When a medical crisis strikes residents in these areas, they must rely on their social networks for assistance and activate any ties they may have to influential people. Such was the case in early 1995, when Veronica Mamani, a ten-year-old girl, fell deathly ill with a parasitic infection.

Veronica lived for seven years with her aunt in the Yungas, a series of subtropical mountain valleys on the eastern flank of the Andes. Veronica's mother, Juliana, had sent her daughter there after she remarried and her new husband—Veronica's stepfather—expressed little enthusiasm for the child of his wife's previous relationship. Veronica did not thrive in the Yungas, and when she became extremely weak and sickly, the aunt returned her to Juliana, who lived in El Alto. Juliana, her husband, and their two young children occupied a rented dwelling in a peripheral part of the city. Juliana made a meager income from weaving shawls, and her husband pursued odd jobs around El Alto and La Paz. Health care facilities were completely absent in this part of town, but Juliana participated in a literacy program sponsored by an NGO and turned to the NGO director for assistance with her daughter.

Juliana and a couple of NGO representatives took the child to El Alto's only public hospital at the opposite end of the city. The physician who examined the girl stated that Veronica was severely malnourished and suffered from an acute parasitic infection; indeed, the infestation was so bad that a large lump protruded from her abdomen. After berating Juliana for allowing her daughter to become so sick, he told the group that Veronica had to be hospitalized immediately or she would die. The NGO director then managed to get an ambulance to take the sick child to La Paz, where she was admitted to the Children's Hospital in Miraflores. Shortly thereafter, Veronica underwent surgery to remove the parasitic lump, which was too large and life threatening to be treated with drugs, and for the next two days she seemed on the road to recovery. Then, in the middle of the night she suffered a heart attack and died.

For the next several days the NGO director and Juliana made arrangements for the child's burial. With NGO funds the director purchased a coffin, a plot in the local cemetery, and arranged for a death certificate, even though the child lacked formal identification documents. The director explained that even though these activities and the entire matter of health care lay completely outside the NGO's mandate and realm of expertise, simple compassion required that the organization address the periodic crises that its impoverished constituents faced. Indeed, the entire experience illustrates how the retrenchment of public health care is increasingly forcing residents to turn to NGOs for their basic needs. It also demonstrates how the intensity of El Alto's poverty overwhelms the limited capacity of NGOs while pushing them to take on tasks that have nothing to do with their formal agendas.

The depth of the health care crisis, however, goes far beyond the issue of NGOs, or the relative strengths and weaknesses of public versus private health care, because many alteños harbor deep suspicions about Western medical practitioners. They value the seemingly magical cures that these people can provide with pills and injections, but the race and class prejudices of many health care providers make some alteños—especially recent Aymara immigrants—very uneasy about interacting with them. Florencia Huanca is a sixty-two-year-old Aymara woman who is mortally afraid of hospitals, which she believes are places where people go to die and where their bodies are abused.[1]

When a benign lump developed on her wrist, Huanca's relatives urged her to enter a hospital to have it removed. She described to me her discomfort when hospital personnel made her disrobe and asked her to remove a ring before the operation. She did not understand why she was being asked to remove her clothing and her ring and insisted that she was "not a sick person," but those attending her paid no attention. After the surgery she recalled falling asleep and awakening in an unfamiliar part of the hospital. She did not remember how she got there, but just as she was awakening, someone—a doctor, she thinks—pulled a needle out of her arm. Huanca called out to the person and demanded to know what was happening. The man ignored her and hastily left the room.

Huanca maintained that this individual was really a *kharisiri*, or predatory ghoul, who stole her blood and probably intended to sell it to foreigners for a profit. As proof of this likelihood, she cited the following evidence: although she had quickly bounced back from an earlier, and more serious, gall bladder operation, she was weak and unsteady for several months after the wrist surgery. She added that at the time of the operation, many people in La Paz and El Alto were trafficking in human blood, and because her blood type was rare, she believed she was a logical target for a kharisiri attack.

The murderous activities of marauding ghouls—known variously as kharisiri, *lik'ichiri, pishtaco,* and *ñakaq*—have a long history in the Andes that dates to the sixteenth century. They vividly express the race and class exploitation experienced by indigenous peoples, who, because of persistent unemployment and malnutrition, are intensely insecure about their bodily integrity.[2] The contemporary creatures appear to their prey as cholo intermediaries, doctors, engineers, and "gringo" development workers; in the past, they were more likely to be priests. Traditionally, kharisiris steal their victims' fat, which they then use for a variety of nefarious purposes, such as manufacturing medicines and creams, paying the foreign debt, or lubricating airplanes, but contemporary marauders in poor urban neighborhoods are more likely to covet blood or body parts. In almost every case, however, an outsider or a powerful individual from a superior race, class, or nationality profits from the primitive accumulation of oppressed peoples' vital bodily substances.

The tales graphically depict the feelings of vulnerability among those who are losing control of their lives as well as their bodies. They express the seeming irrationality of poverty and the terror that race and class oppression can assume. Because of these fears, as well as a more general desire to avoid the condescension and racism of Western health care practitioners and the availability of an indigenous non-Western medical tradition, many people turn to a variety of local folk healers for treatment. Others leave health problems untreated or medicate themselves with a variety of drugs from local pharmacies. Most people experiment with a variety of potential solutions until they find relief. Marcelo Mamani, for example, suffered from chronic back pain after being hit by a speeding taxi. When treatment at a local health clinic failed to alleviate his symptoms, Mamani went to a folk healer, who instructed him to purchase several small lizards in the local marketplace, gut them, and apply the still-squirming carcasses to his back under a tight bandage. After two treatments Mamani's back pain disappeared, and he declared that he would never enter a clinic again.

As alteños grapple with a serious health crisis and a crumbling public education system, the lack of state investment in social services devalues the economic worth of the city's growing reserve army of unemployed. This forces people to put in long hours of work to secure at least some of the basic necessities. They travel to work on the minibuses that troll the streets and avenues of the city, and for the thousands of people who work in La Paz, this means sitting in mind-numbing traffic jams that lengthen their workdays and waste their time.

Before the government deregulated urban transportation in the early 1990s, alteños had access to large state-subsidized buses for the daily commute to La Paz, as well as a system of *collectivos* (buses) whose fares were regulated by the state. Although the buses were frequently overcrowded and spewed thick, noxious black smoke into the city's rarified air, they provided relatively cheap transportation for those who had to commute to La Paz every day. After deregulation the government sold its buses, and the large collectivos disappeared from the streets. They were replaced by a plethora of minivans that accommodate a maximum of fifteen passengers. Because of the sheer number of minivans in central La Paz, in the mid-1990s one could literally step outside a building and expect to get a seat immediately, even during rush hour. But it was not so easy for many residents of El Alto. Drivers frequently overcharged on unprofitable routes to distant residential neighborhoods, or they refused to service these areas. Even along El Alto's major thoroughfares, the minibuses traveling down to La Paz filled up quickly during peak times, and this obliged passengers to travel to La Ceja, switch to another minivan, and pay twice, because no system of bus transfers exists. People were also subjected to quixotic fare fluctuations in La Ceja, where the state does not control the fierce competition between drivers.

When alteños are not contending with the transportation debacle and have a moment to relax—usually on a weekend afternoon—they have few public parks and recreational facilities in which to enjoy themselves. To make matters worse, the streets and vacant lots of El Alto function as open sewers, because only a third of the residents have access to some kind of waste disposal system. Even fortunate residents, who live in older neighborhoods endowed with sewer lines, endure the stench produced by ruptured pipes that were never meant to handle the volume of waste flowing through them.

Perhaps more than any other aspect of life in El Alto, housing exemplifies how hard people must work to meet their basic subsistence needs and how state indifference exposes them to hardships. The formal market for land, credit, and housing excludes poor rural immigrants, and although the state once subsidized a limited amount of housing for some public sector employees (e.g., police officers, miners, teachers, and railway workers), the vast majority of rural immigrants has always had to fend for themselves. Nowadays government housing policy, to the extent that one exists at all, turns on the basic principle that the right to a house depends upon individual effort and self-sacrifice. The state tolerates unregulated owner-constructed housing as the political price for accommodating thousands of new immigrants at the lowest cost possible.

Home ownership and the possession of land, even if only a tiny urban lot, appeals to immigrants' seldom-met aspirations for autonomy. A house and the lot on which it stands can be passed on to children, a legacy that provides a material link between the past and the present. Ownership has the potential to liberate immigrants from the demands and exactions of landlords, who are often other immigrants only marginally better off, and it frees them—albeit often momentarily—from the conflicts and pent-up frustrations generated by forced sharing with relatives, other families, and individuals. A home also provides a refuge from the strains of the outside world and a space within which people can exercise greater control over their lives and social relationships.

Irma Escóbar's experiences as a renter and her views on home owner-ship typify those of thousands of other city residents. Escóbar and her fam-ily came to El Alto in the mid-1980s after her husband lost his job as a miner. Although they had purchased a lot through a housing cooperative that was active in the mining community, financial insecurity and unem-ployment prevented the Escóbar family from building its house. The fam-ily rented living quarters for years but in 1994 finally received assistance from an NGO and was able to begin construction. I met Irma Escóbar just two weeks after the family moved into the new domicile, and she summa-rized what renting had entailed for the family: "Being a renter is very dif-ficult [*una vida sarificada*]. The landlords are always watching you. They want to know if you go out a lot, if you use a lot of water, if you are wear-ing out the doors, and if you have the lights turned on until late at night. They even complain about the children and the noise that they make. But now in our little house, we can do whatever we feel like doing."

Yet unemployment, poor health, indebtedness, and a wide range of other factors that make daily life in El Alto so precarious constantly threaten the home as refuge and the relative autonomy that it symbolizes. Also imperiling home owners are state policies that establish the parame-ters within which contending groups—land speculators, recent immi-grants, nouveau-riche resident landlords, and tenants—engage each other in the struggle for access and control over property. These struggles turn on the politics of land development.

Immigrants who wish to own their own home must deal with the in-creasing commodification of urban real estate. High prices for urban lots in central El Alto—a rural area until the mid-1980s—keep many people out of the housing market, and the situation in more peripheral zones with lower land prices is little better. In addition, considerable uncertainty ex-ists about what administrative body is responsible for issuing land titles and legitimizing claims, because continuous urbanization has generated so much administrative chaos that the boundaries between El Alto and the neighboring municipality are not clearly defined. Consequently, who owns what is often unclear, and private real estate developers easily victimize immigrants. These developers, who are often little more than speculators, frequently operate outside the bounds of legality with the complicity of state officials, or they may simply take advantage of the legal confusion to advance their own interests. They are often tied to broader real estate financial networks and work through a variety of local intermediaries.

El Alto has various kinds of speculators, or *loteadores*. One group operates with the appearance of legality. These individuals, organized in small businesses, purchase contiguous land holdings from peasants on the urban periphery, then sell the property to immigrants at inflated prices. Others acquire land through a variety of fraudulent practices, such as falsifying titles to occupied but untitled areas. The loteadores promise immigrant buyers a range of social services, but buyers frequently discover that services are slow to arrive, and the developers, who hold the property titles, start to demand payments far in excess of what the immigrants expected to pay. Desperate to acquire legal title to avoid losing their entire investment, residents try to make the excessive installment payments but become mired in debt. Or they may be forced to leave. In either case, the loteadores continue to profit from appreciating property values.

Still other loteadores promote land invasions by desperate immigrants. These invasions occur on public lands, such as areas that have been set aside for public parks or "green areas," and public authorities with ties to the developers may facilitate the invasions. Squatters can remain on the land as long as they first recognize the loteadores' right to the property by signing a document that grants power of attorney to them. This document then enables the speculators to begin the judicial process of legalizing their theft of public property. Eventually, the loteadores expel the original squatters, subdivide the property, and sell it at a considerable profit. This kind of theft and speculation are not only a way to profit from the desperate housing needs of immigrants but also are means to privatize public lands that they could not otherwise develop.

The Villa Pedro Domingo Murillo in central El Alto emerged from a long and contentious battle between residents and a notorious real estate speculator. Crammed between the airport and the noxious ditch that contains the Río Seco, the villa developed in the early 1980s, when peasants from the northern altiplano, railway workers, and a few ex-miners began to purchase lots from a loteador. Most buyers did not build homes immediately, because they had not consolidated their social and economic ties in the city. Consequently, the lots remained vacant for months and even years in some cases. When settlers did begin to filter into the area, they found that the speculator had sold their plots to multiple owners, and they became mired in disputes with him and the other claimants. To make matters worse, those who had managed to build houses and establish themselves in the villa found that the loteador constantly raised the fees for services, even though they never had received electricity, water, and sewerage. Residents, however, were forced to pay, because the developer constantly found reasons to withhold titles to their properties, even after they had paid for them. Elvira Canasas, a longtime resident, explained:

> We didn't begin to build our house until approximately four years after we got the lot. But after paying for the land, [the developer] did not want to give us the document that showed that we had completed all the payments. He said that we owed more money, because the land was sold very cheaply. But the area was still pure pampa. There were no services. How could he charge us more if there was no water, electricity, or sewer lines?

Represented by local neighborhood committees, residents began to protest the abuses. Some leaders belonged to the political party CONDEPA, and this facilitated their dealings with many local officials. They also benefited from the support of a local church-operated radio station, whose progressive director aired the residents' views. In addition, activist nuns and later a Spanish priest who lived in the villa, intervened with local authorities on behalf of the residents. The priest helped to finance costly legal proceedings and, according to one local leader, "was like an adviser. We [the residents] didn't speak Spanish well enough to deal with the authorities. The authorities didn't understand sufficiently what we tried to express. But Lucho [the priest] walked into their offices and had more influence."

From the mid-1980s until the mid-1990s residents waged court battles, lobbied local politicians, and mounted protest marches through the city. The developer's henchmen threatened the residents' leaders and silenced some residents with bribes. Others participated in the exploitation of fellow residents by actively allying themselves with the developer. Moreover, multiple conflicting land claims pitted residents against each other. Thus the battle with the developer not only created divisions among residents but to a certain extent also defined divisions between emerging sectors of the villa. Andrés Castro, who in 1994 was head of the junta de vecinos in Sector 3, described how alliances had shifted over the years:

> We used to be all part of one sector, but because of the fight [with the developer], we've split into four divisions. Sectors 2 and 3 have always been united and struggling to get the land titles properly reg-

istered, but Sector 4 allied itself with the loteador. Only recently have some of the residents decided to be on our side, but the leaders still refuse to support us because they are controlled by the loteador. Sector 1 is also with us now, even though for awhile it was allied with the loteador.

Although the residents of Villa Pedro Domingo Murillo seemed to be on the verge of victory in 1995, the problems and issues are familiar to many other new El Alto neighborhoods, most of which are not so fortunate.[3] The state's refusal to attend to the critical housing needs of immigrants exposes them to the rapacious activities of real estate speculators and complicit local authorities. In the turmoil that arises from this situation, immigrants must contend not only with the illegal and manipulative practices of land speculators but also with the tensions that conflicting land claims create in the neighborhood.

Building a House, Owning a Home

Immigrants' difficulties do not end after they have successfully established their land claims. They must then make numerous sacrifices to build a house, which is usually a process of several years' duration and turns on the availability of family resources. It requires people with few assets to extend their working days to include holidays and weekends, because they cannot afford to hire wage laborers on a regular basis. Those in the development industry frequently refer to this practice as "self-help," but it is really a form of unpaid overtime, one that weighs increasingly heavily on alteños—especially women—who must use more and more of their "free time" to produce the means of subsistence.

When peasant immigrants begin to build, they usually start with one or two adobe rooms. They may not even occupy the rooms on a regular basis but use them to accommodate visitors from back home on their periodic trips to the city. Once people establish permanent residency and as resources permit, they add additional quarters to accommodate the needs of growing families. They may eventually raze their adobe dwellings and replace them with more durable structures of kiln-fired bricks, but families with fewer resources may simply construct brick facades to partially replace the less fashionable adobe. Building a brick house is expensive, and it invariably obliges families to go into debt, cut expenses, and find additional ways to earn cash. It is possible only when family members are willing and able to collaborate, and in practice this means mobilizing the labor power of women and children.

The experiences of the Choque family are instructive. Pablo Choque and his wife, Felicidad, were born in the 1930s in a rural community on the shores of Lake Titicaca, and they acquired a lot in the Villa 16 de Julio in 1963, when the region was still a windswept pampa. Because Pablo Choque's job as a Baptist preacher kept the family in the neighboring town of Viacha, a caretaker, who was a relative, lived in a small hut on the lot to maintain the Choques' claim. The Choques did not construct an adobe home until the early 1970s, and in the mid-1990s, after living on and off in the city for more than thirty years, they began to construct the house of their dreams.

At this time the Choques did not represent the most impoverished sector of El Alto's Aymara immigrants. Pablo Choque considered himself the epitome of success, and the family had enjoyed considerable upward mobility. It owned two secondhand minibuses; Felicidad Choque managed the buses, which the family operated as urban transport vehicles. Their son, Mario, and daughter, Juana, were high school graduates, and Pablo Choque, who had abandoned his career as a preacher and ascended through the ranks of the public teaching profession, was the director of a local school. Thus the Choques' experience with housing is not typical, but it does illustrate some of the strategies that aspiring home owners adopt in the absence of state and private sector support.

I met Don Pablo, as he likes to be called, in 1994, when he was planning to demolish the adobe house that had been home to his family for several years. In its place he wanted to build two multistory brick houses for an extended family that had grown to include in-laws, four grandsons, and a great-granddaughter. The homes would supply better quarters for the rapidly growing family and provide an inheritance for Mario and Juana; Pablo hoped his children and their families would remain together in the compound. Pablo Choque also wanted the dwellings to serve as an imposing legacy of his hard work and dedication to family. So, at the age of sixty-two, he slowly and sporadically initiated the construction projects, fretting all the while that he would die before they were completed.

Although the Choques were successful and prosperous by local standards, they still did much of the work themselves, including all the interior work (*obra fina*); for example, they brought grasses from the countryside to insulate the roofs, cut down a tree in Pablo Choque's natal community for the floor boards, painted the walls, wired the house, and installed the electrical fixtures. To raise money for construction materials and to pay laborers for specialized tasks, Juana Choque delayed her university education and contributed all her savings from her work as a hairstylist. Felicidad Choque contributed as much as possible from the minibus earnings that Pablo, Mario, and Mario's son Orlando brought into the household.

Yet a constant shortage of cash frequently obliged the Choques to suspend work on the houses for weeks or even months at a time. And occasional emergencies, such as the breakdown of a minibus or a medical problem, diverted funds to other ends. Like similar efforts taking place around the city, the unfinished dwellings often stood with metal support rods protruding from the roofs until the money materialized to add another story, purchase windows, install door frames, and so forth. To raise money Pablo Choque borrowed extensively from an extended network of relatives, friends, political associates, fellow immigrants from his natal community, and fictive kin. But these measures were still not enough.

To make more money the Choques also became landlords. They rented out a series of rudimentary rooms that they had previously constructed around a central courtyard, and from time to time they reorganized their own living arrangements to temporarily accommodate a tenant. Amid the crisis of housing and the lack of viable employment opportunities in the city, mass landlordism represented one way that people could earn a living by taking advantage of the needs of other immigrants. When conducted by arriviste immigrants like the Choques, landlordism exaggerated the fragmentation of El Alto's poor into privileged and oppressed strata. This tendency was particularly pronounced in the Villa 16 de Julio, where, at the time of the 1990 census, renters occupied 87 percent of the dwellings. The many merchants who rented space for their businesses accounted for some of the renters in this villa, but other, less commercially dynamic neighborhoods housed a disproportionate number of people who did not own their dwellings. For example, renters in Villa Pedro Domingo Murillo, who are mainly former peasants, and in Villa Santiago II, who are primarily former miners, represented 68 percent and 80 percent of the residents, respectively (INE 1992).

The Choques had a variety of different arrangements with their tenants, who came from various walks of life. Mateo Mamani, his wife, Miriam, and their two small children occupied three rooms at the back of the lot. Mateo, a welder, used one room for work, and the family lived in the others. Miriam, a washerwoman, laundered clothes in the courtyard. The Mamanis had negotiated a rental agreement with the Choques known as *anticrético,* paying a lump sum of money equal to a year's rent. The Choques, however, were obliged to return the full amount at the end of the stipulated period, when the Mamanis had to either depart or negotiate another payment.

An anticrético arrangement is attractive to tenants because it allows them to live virtually rent free for a period of time, and it appeals to landlords like the Choques who have no access to housing loans from commercial banks. But the arrangement also has drawbacks. Many renters are simply too poor to be able to arrange an anticrético, and the instability of economic conditions in El Alto means they always face the possibility that landlords will not return the money. Indeed, in 1995 both the Choques and the Mamanis worried about the expiration of their anticrético agreement, because it was not clear that the indebted Choques would be able to repay the money.

The Choques also had monthly rental agreements with other tenants. An itinerant merchant rented a single room for his occasional overnight stays in the city. This man lived in the mountain valleys of the Yungas but came periodically to the biweekly market in the villa to buy and sell. Pablo Choque's nephew from the countryside paid a nominal fee for another room, and Doña Casimira, or *la hermana* (the sister), as she was commonly known, occupied yet another. Casimira was an elderly Aymara woman who had been abandoned by her husband and whose only son was an unemployed mine worker. Felicidad Choque had befriended her at a Baptist church meeting. Although Casimira paid little if any rent and did not contribute significantly to the Choques' housing plans, she helped Felicidad and Juana Choque with the domestic tasks, and Felicidad Choque seemed to enjoy her friendship and company.

Perhaps the biggest boon for the Choques came in 1991, when a prominent NGO relocated its headquarters across the street from their home, and a stream of foreigners—including students, an anthropologist, a journalist, and a photographer—began to seek out the NGO for contacts, information, and temporary housing in the villa. The organization arrived in the villa as internationally financed NGOs were proliferating across El Alto, opening a series of new opportunities for local people (see chapters 7 and 8). The Choques, for example, quickly became acquainted with NGO staff members, who purchased cigarettes from the small store that Felicidad Choque operated in front of the house, and these individuals readily referred visiting foreigners to her.

This was how I got to know the Choques. I had been searching for a place to live in El Alto, and because I was interested in the activities of NGOs, living across the street from one seemed like a good idea. The Choques were also particularly interested in renting to me, a gringa, because, as Pablo Choque eventually confided, "We knew that you could pay and that you would eventually leave." Indeed, the ability to pay and the willingness to leave were highly valued qualities that he had not always found in local renters, who were always short of cash and vulnerable to unemployment and illness. In addition, his prior experience with North Americans and Europeans convinced him that they were decent people who made reliable tenants.

He first encountered North Americans in the 1930s, when Baptist missionaries established a school in his natal community and taught him and other children to read and write. The education made both Choques, and especially Felicidad, somewhat unusual among the peasants of their generation; indeed, rural people did not attend school in large numbers until after the 1952 national revolution. Consequently, they both felt a debt of gratitude to the missionaries. Pablo Choque also traveled with the Baptists to the southern United States for a brief visit during the 1960s and was impressed by what he considered to be the superior "progress" of Texas in relation to his own country. He felt that North Americans "know how to do things" and that they could be useful.

He viewed Europeans much the same way; before my arrival two Dutch women and a Belgian photographer referred by the NGO had resided with the family for varying lengths of time. Pablo Choque charged all of us more than the Bolivian tenants, and we paid our rents with coveted inflation-proof U.S. dollars. To a certain extent, we were important status symbols, and our habits, beliefs, and stories made us strangely fascinating and exotic for the family, whose members loved to rank and compare us. A Dutch woman, for example, was the most *alegre* (lively) but gradually fell out of favor after she left, because she stopped writing; the photographer, who stayed only briefly, was notable for his height and his convoluted Spanish, which the grandchildren liked to imitate; I was encouraged to equal, or to outdo, the Thanksgiving meal once prepared by the U.S. missionaries who preceded me. The benefits, the prestige—and the entertainment value—of having foreign tenants came with a price, however: Pablo Choque worried that jealous neighbors would spread rumors that he harbored CIA agents in his home, but these fears did not deter him from asking me to send the family more of my *paisanos* (countrymen).

Aided, then, by an array of renters, the dedicated work of family members, and a series of loans from a range of different people, construction on the houses advanced; by 1997 portions of the buildings were habitable—though not completely finished—and Pablo Choque and his extended family moved in. Sitting in his new brick home—the tallest on the block—

and looking back on his life, Don Pablo could boast that he had come a long way from his natal community on the shores of Lake Titicaca. There his mother—the only parent that he knew—a younger brother, and Pablo had subsisted by catching and marketing fish and, during the pre-1952 era, working occasionally on neighboring haciendas. As he tells the story, hard work, the grace of God, and an ability to seize random events and turn them into personal opportunities helped him realize his goals over the years. "Hay que hacer cosas, hay que hacer cosas" (You have to do things, you have to do things), he frequently reminded his family and anyone else who would listen.

There is no question that daily life in El Alto—even for an established resident like Pablo Choque—demands that people be inventive, as the discipline imposed by neoliberal capitalism compels them to search for novel solutions to an array of problems. Yet Pablo Choque's journey required much more than God's grace and hard work. It depended upon ties to a wide network of different kinds of people and the ways in which broader forces shaped the relationships that he established with them. For example, his early ties to the Baptist Church not only provided him with an education at a time when few peasants of his generation attended school but also opened avenues of social mobility for him through the ministry and, later, in public education. In addition, the coming of the NGO produced a number of well-heeled foreign tenants who helped finance his housing project. The ethos of individualism and hard work to which Don Pablo subscribed was not enough to displace the importance of these relationships and his family's support. His self-serving account of personal accomplishment and social mobility denied the participation of others—many of whom were more vulnerable than he—and it minimized the struggles that shaped his relation to them. More generally, it effaced the tensions between Pablo Choque's desire to claim and assert an image of unqualified social and economic success, on the one hand, and his dependence on, and occasional exploitation of, other people for this success, on the other.

Felicidad Choque played a central—though not always acknowledged—role in the family's upward mobility. Over the years, she attended to all her husband's domestic needs, raised the couple's children, managed the household, ran a small dry-goods store, and traveled regularly to the countryside, where she farmed a plot of land inherited from her parents. She also managed her husband in ways that she could not explicitly acknowledge or openly discuss, because of the challenges that such assertions would pose to their relationship.

For example, Felicidad Choque frequently engaged in creative accounting practices to deter her husband from squandering hard-earned cash on the consumption of alcohol. One Friday evening before they started building the new homes, she, Juana Choque, and I were sitting in the kitchen of the house that was slated for demolition. The kitchen was a focal point of family social life in the early evening, because the warmth of the stove helped stave off the cold outside. As we chatted and cleaned up the dinner dishes, Pablo Choque tottered into the courtyard absolutely pickled in beer. He had been attending a local meeting of the Movimiento Nacionalista Revolucionario (MNR) and announced his arrival by shouting "Viva Bolivia!" and "Viva el MNR!" He then stumbled into the kitchen, where his grandson proceeded to torment him by replying, "Abajo el MNR, Abajo el MNR" (Down with the MNR, Down with the MNR). Livid, and embarrassed by her husband's behavior, Felicidad shooed Pablo outside, returning with a wad of pesos that she shoved into her daughter's hands, ordering the young woman to go immediately and change the bills into U.S. dollars.

After Juana departed, Felicidad Choque explained that the pesos—worth approximately $14—represented the day's earnings from one of the family's minibuses. If her husband saw the money, he would insist that someone buy beer with it and then convince his son or local acquaintances to drink with him. Felicidad Choque, however, intensely resented her husband's drunkenness and the obnoxious and abusive behavior that it often generated. In moments of disgust she referred to him disparagingly as *el borracho* (the drunk). His heavy drinking was also a major reason for his withdrawal from active participation in the Baptist Church, and this further aggravated his relationship with his wife. Felicidad Choque was a devout Baptist and had many friends from the church, but she was able to participate in church activities only when she could negotiate her absence from the household with her husband. Although she enjoyed occasional success, managing his excessive drinking was another matter. Pablo Choque considered the social consumption of alcohol—even in excessive amounts—his right as a man; moreover, certain festive occasions virtually required that he and other participants imbibe heavily. Confronting him about this matter could lead to violent outbursts. By sending her daughter away with the money, Felicidad Choque avoided a direct confrontation, and after her husband fell asleep and Juana returned with the dollars, Felicidad Choque quietly tucked the money away in a safe place.

Such subterfuges and the silences that they entail highlight the tensions between what happens to people and their understandings of these experiences, and what they can discuss, negotiate, and reorganize.[4] Experiences and accompanying silences are crucial to understanding processes of differentiation in the household, as well as in the broader society. The next chapter offers a more complete examination of these processes and their consequences for daily life in El Alto.

4 · Miners and the Politics of Revanchism

The old is dying and the new cannot be born: in this interregnum there arises a great diversity of morbid symptoms.

—Antonio Gramsci, *Sections from the Prison Notebooks*

On a chilly day in July 1996 former miner Leonidas Rojas and I were chatting on his patio, where we had taken refuge from the unheated interior of his home. The searing midday sunshine felt wonderfully hot, but it did little to heat up the thin air of El Alto. Rojas and I were discussing the Bolivian labor movement, a topic that animated him and one that he knew a great deal about. For more than thirty years, Leonidas Rojas had worked in Bolivia's largest and most militant mining complex—Catavi-Siglo XX—where he was active in the mine workers' union. Over the years he had also held various national positions in the Central Obrera Boliviana (COB), which the miners dominated from its inception.

At one point I casually mentioned that in the United States, we celebrate Labor Day in September, not on May 1, as is customary in Bolivia and many other countries. Rojas was incredulous. "What about the martyrs of Chicago?" he asked me. "Don't North Americans know that the police killed the Chicago workers on May First?" I replied that some U.S. citizens were aware of the 1886 police massacre of labor activists in Haymarket Square, but many others were not. "How," he then asked, "has the U.S. government been able to suppress the significance of the occasion for so long?" Rojas found it difficult to believe that U.S. citizens do not understand the significance of their own history, especially because it is a history that holds such importance for working people around the world.

During the labor celebrations associated with May 1, the miners routinely commemorate the "Chicago martyrs," as well as working-class heroes from Bolivia and other parts of the world. Indeed, the way in which Bolivian miners became "workers" entailed the creation of a history that stressed class solidarity and linked miners' struggles to those of working people elsewhere. This history was strongly anti-imperialist, but it also turned on a nationalist vision of the past that emphasized apparent continuities in the struggles of miners against domestic foes, such as the early twentieth-century tin barons and then the Bolivian state. Yet it was silent about the cultural ruptures and social dislocations that created mine "workers" and distinguished them from "Indians" and "peasants." It also had very little to say about the participation of women in the protracted struggles about work and daily life that engulfed the mining communities and sometimes even the entire country.[1]

After the state closed its mines in the 1980s and "relocated" the mining proletariat, the miners' version of their history could not survive the fragmentation of their communities and the debilitation of the union. A much broader struggle for subsistence replaced class struggle, which they had understood in terms of exploitation at the point of production (Nash 1992, 1994b), and confronting El Alto's wretched conditions with the resources that miners had at their disposal was next to impossible. Former miners found themselves subordinated to a new and wider set of competitive relationships with other people whom they increasingly encountered as individuals. They, like Aymara peasant immigrants, were obliged to address the needs and vulnerabilities arising from unemployment and underemployment in El Alto by turning to others like—or almost like—themselves, but these people could not provide everything that was necessary.

Former comrades became competitors for the basic necessities of daily life. Unemployment and forced migration disrupted mutual support networks based in the mining communities and frequently pushed conflicts within households to the breaking point. At the same time, old ways of identifying as workers found little resonance amid the heterogeneous mix of street vendors, petty merchants, and artisans of El Alto. Consequently, forging new alliances to press claims on the state and constructing a vision of the future based on a sense of continuity with the past was extremely problematic.

The experience of Bolivian miners was not unique. In 1973 the repressive military regime of Augusto Pinochet had launched a wave of state terror against the miners of El Teniente, Chile's largest copper mine, while imposing a harsh neoliberal restructuring program designed by economists at the University of Chicago. The military dismantled corporatist welfare programs that had prevailed in Chile since the 1930s and wrought radical changes on the lives of workers. Severe repression and economic policies that cut wages, reduced job security, and abolished benefits for most workers broke up the tightly knit mining community of El Teniente. Miners ceased to believe that collective action could improve their situation, and as individual miners tried to survive in the market economy, consumerism overwhelmed their culture of class solidarity (Klubock 1998).

The fate of miners in Chile and Bolivia is emblematic of the new reserve armies of unemployed or underemployed people that the decline of the Fordist system of labor regulation is creating (e.g., Palmer 1994; Moore 1990; Gilbert 1994). These marginalized individuals and their families draw our attention to relationships among impoverished peoples in areas such as El Alto, where Fordism never took hold and where many of the refugees of capitalist restructuring, with different perspectives and divergent histories, are encountering each other. Miners, once the elite of the Bolivian working class, now confront the task of reconstituting fragmented social relationships and developing new perspectives and institutions to replace old forms of struggle based in the mining communities. Understanding the miners' failed, yet conscious and organized, struggle is crucial to grasping how they confront the desperation and divisions among them and other impoverished alteños.

The experience of defeat and dispersal shapes the ways that miners conceptualize the past, and it informs the ways that they connect with and separate from other people in El Alto. As Steve Striffler (1998) demonstrates in Ecuador, disorganization and defeat—like mobilization and victory—are central aspects of the ongoing process of class formation, and histories of partial or total defeat must be judged together with victories that are almost never absolute. This chapter explores how miners struggle within and against the imposed disorder, as they advance new and old claims within a changing field of power.

Miners and the State

Throughout most of the twentieth century, Bolivian tin miners comprised one of the most militant working classes in Latin America. Their union and the national labor movement, which they led, not only pressed for higher wages and better working conditions in the mines but also advanced a much broader array of political and social demands that shaped national politics for decades. Miners, for example, played a major part in the 1952 revolution that led to the nationalization of major mines and produced important health, education, and welfare benefits for the workers. They were also instrumental in bringing down the first regime of General Hugo Banzer (1971–1978), one of the most repressive military dictatorships in recent Bolivian history.

Isolated in remote encampments high in the Andes, miners developed a strong sense of collective identity and common cause. The unions, organized in the 1920s, and the Federación Sindical de Trabajadores Mineros de Bolivia (FSTMB), formed in 1946, nurtured and expressed this solidarity. The strength of the unions lay not in the number of workers, who were always a small percentage of the Bolivian working class, but in the strategic position that mine workers occupied in the production process and the ways that the unions articulated their experiences. Until the mid-1980s, when cocaine replaced tin as the country's primary export commodity, mineral sales accounted for the majority of Bolivia's foreign exchange earnings, and union-led strikes therefore had repercussions well beyond the mining communities. Indeed, the strength of the miners' class-based solidarity and the strategic position that mine workers occupied in the export economy explain the victories that workers occasionally enjoyed and their ability to have things their way at least some of the time.[2]

In assessing the long history of collective action in Bolivia's tin mines, it is perhaps easy to accept the miners' official version of their past and to attribute to workers' struggles a unity of goals and purpose that never completely existed. Class solidarity developed not only in opposition to the state but also out of conflicts and divisions among working people themselves. Over time, worker solidarity varied according to a number of factors, such as the quality and honesty of leaders, internal skill hierarchies, and the effectiveness of state repression. Similarly, as rural people were drawn into, or expelled from, the mining economy, the continual creation and transformation of cultural categories affected worker unity and the ways that people identified themselves and their relationships to each other.

Throughout the twentieth century, for example, "miners" and "Indians" were unequal and opposed categories, despite the considerable similarities that characterized the individuals so defined. Workers born in the largest mining complex of Catavi-Siglo XX referred derogatorily to peasant immigrants as "Indians," who were ostensibly less civilized than themselves. Such distinctions were most sharply drawn in the major mining camps, which paradoxically were the centers of greatest worker militancy.[3] By the midtwentieth century, many workers in these camps had few, if any, ties to rural peasant communities, and their fathers had often been mine workers before them. They also belonged to an urbanized culture that they shared with merchants and so-called *vecinos de pueblo,* or town dwellers, who exploited peasants and were routinely despised by them. Many miners of Catavi-Siglo XX spoke Quechua and Spanish and associated Aymara, another indigenous language, with the backward countryside. Peasants, for their part, commonly lumped these workers and merchants together and called them cholos, a pejorative.

Thus the largest mining camps, especially Catavi-Siglo XX, produced a major share of prominent labor leaders who ascended to high-level positions in the national labor movement. They tended to be relatively well educated, because, after the 1952 revolution, the public schools in the mining districts were the best in the country, and most miners had little firsthand experience of life in the countryside, where schooling rarely extended beyond the third grade. Although these men consistently advocated worker-peasant solidarity in their public pronouncements, peasants frequently experienced miners' entreaties as condescending and paternalistic. A peasant leader commented in the 1970s that "the miners talk a lot about helping us and about [our] common struggle; but after they take to the streets, [miners] call a peasant to carry their bundles and pay them with a little piece of bread" (Harris and Albó 1984:109).

Worker solidarity, then, represented the victory of certain perspectives among miners that carried more resonance and had a stronger institutional base than others. It emerged, at least in part, from struggles among working people about the best way to engage the political and economic power of capitalism in the mining centers; as historian Steven Volk says, the union movement, not political parties, gave form and meaning to this solidarity (1975). The state constantly sought to undermine it and to foment armed conflicts between miners and peasants but never completely achieved these objectives. Then, in the mid-1980s, the relative inefficiency and diminishing reserves of the state-operated mines made them a focus of neoliberal restructuring.[4]

The first major blow to workers came in 1985 when the state curtailed subsidized food allotments. The state had long subsidized four basic items—meat, bread, sugar, and rice—through company stores, or *pulperías*. The withdrawal of the subsidy, which could amount to as much as half of a worker's income, would have been a major setback for miners even under relatively stable economic conditions, but skyrocketing prices on the free market and wage freezes in the aftermath of Supreme Decree 21060 demolished household budgets. The consumer price index rose 174 percent between August 1985 and August 1986, as prices adjusted to their "real levels." Meanwhile, the average miner's wage was set at $60 per month in August 1985 and had diminished to $43 per month a year later (Latin America Bureau 1987:14–15).

Miners were quick to respond to the unfolding disaster. They understood the New Economic Policy as an assault on the working class and particularly the miners' union. More generally, they saw it as an attempt to privatize the economy and role back the gains that workers had won in the 1952 revolution. Through a long series of meetings, marches, and demonstrations, they fought to defend their jobs and protect their way of life.

In 1986, delegates to the Twenty-first Congress of the FSTMB approved the "Catavi Thesis," which outlined a union-directed plan for the reactivation of COMIBOL, the state mining corporation, that would not reduce the number of workers. The plan, according to one worker, stated that "we had to go and produce despite all of our problems. The miners agreed to sacrifice themselves even more, in spite of the government's insensitivity, because the most fundamental thing was to maintain a source of jobs." Later the same year five thousand miners and their supporters set out from Oruro on the celebrated "March for Life and Peace" to La Paz, but the army stopped them before they reached their final destination, and police arrested about two hundred people (Nash 1992).

The COB responded by calling an ineffective one-day general strike. It was then forced to suspend the march and sit down with government representatives at the negotiating table, where COB leaders signed an agreement that provided for the retention of only half of COMIBOL's employees. The rank-and-file subsequently rejected the agreement, because it did not contain sufficient financial compensation for those miners who were being forced to quit. This precipitated a major split within the miners' union, as workers became divided about the best way to proceed: some argued that they had to defend jobs at all costs, whereas others sought to better negotiate the conditions of job surrender.

The latter group had lost faith in any possibility of reactivating COMIBOL and desperately wanted to secure some financial compensation from the company before it went bankrupt and left them with nothing to show for their years of service. Their fear was understandable. All miners had seen their salaries reduced to almost nothing, and the company no longer paid even these pittances on time. COMIBOL not only curtailed basic food subsidies to the pulperías but also stopped providing spare parts for machinery. Medicines were no longer available in the company hospitals, and COMIBOL-operated schools lacked supplies. The government had already forced workers older than sixty into early retirement while encouraging those aged fifty to fifty-five to take "voluntary retirement."

The government's assault on the miners highlighted the latter's almost complete dependence on the state for the minimal necessities of life. Moreover, as cocaine replaced tin as the country's primary export commodity, the miners' union lost the leverage that it had once used to advance political and economic claims with the state, and it became deeply divided. The strike became ineffective as a weapon for resistance, and work stoppages only expedited the decline of the industry by releasing COMIBOL from the obligation to pay wages.

A sense of panic pervaded the mining centers in late 1985 and 1986, as people weighed their need to keep working against the government's pressures to quit. Ex-miner Romulo Mercado described the rising feeling of hysteria that pervaded Catavi-Siglo XX:

> There were rumors that they were going to close the mine. [Workers feared that they] were going to be without jobs and that longtime miners, like me and my father, would lose our benefits. Where was the company going to get the money to pay us? This psychosis made people desperate, and they began to present letters of voluntary resignation. In the middle of December 1985, four hundred workers over fifty-five quit. For all their years of work, they only received a maximum of fifteen hundred dollars, and to receive this they had to give up their homes. They picked up the money at the door of the administration building, where a truck loaded with all their possessions waited to take them away.

The dispersal of the mining workforce did not happen all at once. It was slow and sporadic until 1986, the year thousands of miners departed, and then diminished once again, as periodic mine closures and reorganizations further depleted the number of workers for the next several years. A new term—*los relocalizados* (the relocated ones)—emerged to describe displaced workers. It arose from the government's initial promise to provide ex-miners with new jobs and to relocate them to other parts of the country, but the label proved to be misleading. The government rarely provided alternative employment.

Throughout the late 1980s and 1990s the government bought workers off with wildly different settlements. For example, the first group of workers to leave the mines received $1,500 as compensation, but a second contingent that departed in late 1986 obtained $3,000. In 1987 the government dangled a "three-for-one" offer before the remaining hold outs—it would make payments at three times the standard rate to those who quit voluntarily. The state further sweetened the deal in 1990—a $1,000 bonus for each year of work—in a bid to dislodge a relatively small number of stalwarts. Not surprisingly, a major demand that emerged from the ranks of the relocalizados was that the government equalize its payments to everyone.[5]

Miners adopted a variety of survival strategies as they departed from the mines. The majority went to large urban centers, such as El Alto and Cochabamba, where they hoped job opportunities were greatest. Those with the most years of service in the mines had acquired small lots and houses through a cooperative housing program; the less fortunate counted on the assistance of urban relatives. Another group organized themselves into mining cooperatives and continued working those parts of the mines that the government was not selling off to foreign corporations. These individuals had little, if any, capital for exploration, tools, and repairs, and their social benefits no longer existed. A small group of miners returned to their communities of origin, where they still retained access to land. Others migrated to lowland frontier zones. They hoped to claim or purchase unsettled land, particularly in the mountain valleys of the Chapare where coca leaf cultivation was attracting many immigrants. Finally, some unemployed saw no future in Bolivia and left for the major cities of neighboring countries, such as Chile, Brazil, and Argentina.[6]

Those miners who settled in El Alto joined a heterogeneous labor force that was considerably more diversified than the mining communities, and few found new jobs. The factory positions in El Alto's nascent industrial sector were rapidly disappearing in the 1980s, and employers were slow to hire ex-miners because of their well-deserved reputation as labor militants. Unemployed miners often had no choice but to participate in the poorly paid and insecure work that engaged the vast majority of El Alto's residents. They entered a variety of different labor processes, and the economic distinctions between them and peasant immigrants were often blurred.

Yet even as alteños increasingly shared a more generalized poverty, a new relationship between domination and subordination emerged that turned on their increasing autonomy as individuals. This was particularly the case with former miners. In the aftermath of the disruption of their communities, the virtual destruction of the union, and ex-miners' immersion in a highly commodified economy, where the basic necessities of daily life were no longer subsidized, the ties that had once bound them to each other and the state were severed. Former miners could not make effective claims on the state as individuals; moreover, with the exception of its repressive apparatus, the state's presence in El Alto was diminishing. Compared to the mining communities, where the omnipresence of COMIBOL overshadowed work and daily life, in El Alto the state was much more removed from the daily round.

Displaced miners quickly learned that the terms for engaging the dominant society were different than in the past. And the lessons of the past did not always apply to the present. Yet because of the way that economic restructuring had ruptured their own social relations, developing strategies and approaches for confronting domination proved to be extremely difficult in the depressed economic situation of the city.

Security, Subsistence, and Struggle

Establishing themselves in El Alto was not an easy process for most miners and their families. Although some people had acquired homes in El Alto through a state-sponsored cooperative program, most had not. Families had to rent rooms or move in with relatives; some even lived in tent encampments for a time. Those who eventually built their own homes did so by using their redundancy payments to purchase urban lots.

One of the most brutal consequences for many families was the dissolution of the delicate balance between cooperation and conflict that had characterized gender relations in households. The relocation of the mining proletariat not only reterritorialized the working class; it also redivided this segment of the labor force. It pushed more women into the labor force as their male companions lost work and were unable to obtain comparable positions. Although their earnings were meager, women's contribution to domestic income did grow in proportion to men's. This challenged men's already besieged sense of themselves as providers and prompted confrontations about work and domestic labor arrangements within households. As one man explained:

> A lot of people started drinking and marriages broke up. Women out of desperation went with other men [who were not their companions] because the men had some sort of job. It was everybody for themselves. There were many compañeros who were skilled workers—electricians, mechanics, drillers—but they could not find work so they started to drink. In the mines, there was always solidarity: you knew if your compañero was sick and then went to help him, and you complained to management when the company didn't provide food to the pulperías. Here, no. If you die, you die.

The disruptions entailed by forced migration were also stressful for children, who learned hard lessons about social position and exclusion. Many left school, because the desperate financial straits of their families obliged them to find work. Others could not immediately find places in overcrowded public schools, which were unable to accommodate late-term arrivals. All experienced the pain, loss, and anxiety that relocation entailed.

As children became helplessly enmeshed in the changing dynamics of class, they found themselves in the impossible position of being both loved and resented by their parents, who had to contend with debilitating economic circumstances that made children a burden. Children also witnessed the rupture of the domestic and social power of their fathers and the conflicts that frequently ensued between fathers and mothers. Fathers had once claimed considerable authority in households because of their ability to provide for families. Although what they offered was often very meager, and their livelihoods were always threatened by poor health, accidents in the mines, and the vagaries of the mining economy, life as a miner was preferable to unemployment and its daily humiliations in El Alto. In fact, if one had to be a poor Bolivian, being a miner was better than a lot of other occupations, because of the benefits—schools, health care, pensions, and subsidized housing and food—that the miners had extracted from the state. Being a miner could also be *classy,* at least as they were regarded by Left-leaning urban intellectuals who admired the miners' political tenacity.[7] But as the position that miners occupied in Bolivian society changed, so too did the meaning that miners held for their children.

Children were poorly equipped to make sense of the changing life circumstances of their families. Before settling in El Alto, most already knew that they could not always have what they wanted, but this message was driven home even more forcefully in the city. The large marketplaces of El Alto and La Paz tantalized children with an array of expensive consumer goods. Yet the goods were completely beyond the reach of impoverished mining families and reinforced a painful lesson about class exclusion that children were already learning far too well. Aggravating the children's longings was the influx of expensive commodities that neoliberal policies encouraged. These longings were not simply a manifestation of greed or a nascent consumerism propelled by increased globalization. They were, rather, an appropriate expression of the unfulfilled desires created by a society that allowed some people to possess the things that these children were denied.[8]

The strains of imposed poverty in an unfamiliar environment were particularly difficult for sixteen-year-old Juana Revollo. She came to El Alto in 1986 with her parents, Ema and Jaime Revollo, four brothers, and a sister after her father lost his job in the Colquiri mine. The family was fortunate to own a modest house, which her parents had originally envisioned as a retirement home, and her father initially hoped to subsidize the family's expenses by placing his $2,000 severance payment in a high-interest investment scheme that would supposedly produce a monthly yield of $200. Shady individuals were promoting a number of similar investment plans among the relocalizados. Juana's father heeded the investment advice of a *compadre* (a godparent to one of the Revollo children), who claimed that he had been reaping generous returns on his capital for two years. Yet the very month that Juana's father invested his money, the scheme collapsed, and like many other former miners he lost all his money.[9]

The family's situation became more precarious. Ema and Jaime Revollo sought out a series of part-time jobs. Jaime Revollo manufactured adobe bricks for a time and then found short-term employment on a road construction project that was financed by the World Bank in the aftermath of its structural adjustment agreement with the Bolivian government. Ema Revollo sold baked goods on the street. Both parents left home early in the morning and did not return until late in the evening, and the four oldest siblings, who had completed high school before leaving Colquiri, searched for jobs as well. When the family was together, mounting tensions and anxieties about the economic difficulties strained relationships between family members. Jaime Revollo, for example, was utterly despondent about the loss of his entire severance payment and started drinking heavily. This, in turn, prompted more frequent fights with his wife; to make matters worse, neither parent seemed to have much time for Juana.

Juana Revollo grew depressed. She could no longer tolerate life with her family and decided to leave home. She did so to escape the emotional stress and to earn money for herself that she could not request from her parents. With a friend, she went to Cochabamba, where she found a job as a domestic servant. But the work did not go well. The employer refused to pay her a wage and provided only a food ration in exchange for hours of hard, demeaning work. After seven months, Juana Revollo had had enough and returned to El Alto without a cent to her name. She eventually married and moved to another part of the city.

Reflecting on the situation in 1994, several years after their daughter's return, Jaime and Ema Revollo blamed themselves. Jaime Revollo explained that "the children were very disoriented [by the move to El Alto], but we, as parents, were unable to orient them, because we didn't know what to do, either. Leaving the mine, we were like children in diapers." Jaime Revollo blamed his naïveté on the miners' union, which he believed had failed to adequately prepare people for life in El Alto. "They [the leaders] knew about the low price of tin, and they should have at least told us that decree 21060 was going to bring certain consequences. They should have oriented us: this is going to happen, that is going to happen. It's the leadership's obligation to orient us. But the problems came, and they simply put us aside."

As former miners grappled with the difficulties of life as relocalizados and set about the task of finding employment, intense competition among individuals rapidly replaced the collective solidarity of the tin mines. The miners frequently expressed this competition in ethnic stereotypes: some relocalizados claimed that the Aymaras were "closed" and socially inaccessible; many Aymara immigrants, for their part, viewed the relocalizados from the mines as arrogant and overbearing. Sometimes animosities boiled over in soccer matches.

Jaime and Ema Revollo, for example, lived in a neighborhood where former miners and Aymara immigrants lived side by side, and soccer matches among the young men of the neighborhood frequently erupted into fights. Ema Revollo explained that "the miners' children are better prepared and usually win the matches, but the Aymaras are very jealous and want to win too. There are always fights." Her husband added that "there are even fights among the fathers who come to watch, because the play is very hard. And the Aymaras criticize us [*nos echan palo*]. They call us crazy miners in Aymara. They don't participate well."

Nowhere, however, was the competition more intense than in the realm of street vending, where women vendors sit side by side on sheets of blue plastic or woven shawls for hours, selling identical products and earning very little by the end of day. They voice a common complaint that "there are more sellers than buyers" [*Hay más vendedores que compradores*]. Genoveva Villarroel, the leader of an organization representing street vendors in one part of the city, explained that her job primarily involves the mediation of disputes between women. These fights, she said, "are usually about jealousy, because one person sells more than the other."

The experience of Fermina Díaz, a relocalizada from the Corocoro mine, is typical of many others'. When twenty-year-old Díaz, her parents, and her seven siblings moved to El Alto, the family was obliged to scrape together an income from a variety of sources. The father and eldest brothers worked sporadically on construction projects, while Díaz and her mother prepared food and sold it on the street in a distant, more commercialized part of the city. Because they were too poor to pay for transportation, the two women carried their wares and walked.

The sale of food initially provided a modicum of income for the family, but as competition from other vendors in the area increased, the women lost more money than they earned and finally ceased selling altogether.[10] Commenting on the other vendors, Díaz stated that they were "really bad. People here are very egotistical, and they don't know how to cooperate. If you ask them something, they'll give you the wrong answer or say that they don't know, and they always answer in Aymara. I don't understand Aymara, only a few words." She then went on to negatively compare this experience with the more cooperative atmosphere of the mining region, where neighbors knew each other and collaborated. For Fermina Díaz the past had acquired an idyllic quality that distinguished it from the contentious divided present. Indeed, constructing new cooperative networks with others whom they encountered as competitors was extremely problematic. The sense of collective oppression that emerged from a way of life and work so directly controlled by the mining company was absent in the individualized ways that these women found themselves situated in the labor process. Identifying as "workers," which had always been a designation more closely associated with men, lost any meaning that it might still have retained for these women, and this posed new problems for developing a path to the future that retained some continuity with past experience and struggles.[11]

Leonidas Rojas's situation is a good example. He came to El Alto with a well-formulated sense of himself as a worker, developed through years of union activism, work in the mine, and confrontations with the state-owned mining corporation and the Bolivian armed forces. The many versions of Marxism that shaped political debate among the miners also shaped his view of himself as a worker. In one of our conversations he explained what being a worker meant to him. We were talking on a bench, surrounded by female street vendors, in one of El Alto's many open-air markets. "A worker," he said, "lives from the sale of his labor power and cannot exploit others because he does not own or control the means of production." I gestured toward the street vendors and asked about them. The women were not workers by his definition, because they did not sell their labor power, but they did not own means of production, either. Rojas insisted that despite the common poverty of these women, which they shared with many former miners, the vendors were not really workers because of their "petty bourgeois mentality" and their "constant preoccupation with social mobility."

Yet when his health permitted, Rojas himself was engaged in commercial activities similar to those of the women he described as "petty bourgeois." After leaving Siglo XX, he had refused to invest his redundancy payment in a secondhand minibus and become an urban transporter, because, like many working people, he viewed the transporters as exploiters. He disliked banks for the same reason and, in any case, did not trust them with his money. But Rojas eventually decided to "put his money to work" by traveling to Chile, purchasing merchandise in the commercial port of Iquique, and reselling the goods to consumers in El Alto and La Paz at higher prices. Did this not make him petty bourgeois and an exploiter? "No," he explained, because he "still had his formation as a worker" [*formación obrera*].

Clearly, Rojas's sense of class pride, developed in the mining center, continued to be an important source of personal dignity and respect for him. Yet neoliberal restructuring had forced him to interact and compete with others who were much like him and had undermined the social relationships that constituted the very foundation of worker solidarity. Indeed, when he told me that he "still had his formation as a worker," Rojas was explicitly referring to an orientation that he had acquired in the past, not something that emerged from his present social relationships. By defining himself in opposition to the Aymara vendors who surrounded us in the marketplace, Rojas was clearly distancing himself from these less educated, ethnically distinct women, who were, like him, engaging in a form of work that was not entirely of their choosing.

Even as reestablishing worker solidarity proved illusive, dealing with the negative stereotypes associated with being relocalizados grew more burdensome and difficult to overcome. Functionaries of the emergent neoliberal state increasingly defined miners and their unemployed brethren as parasites (Nash 1994a:12), and public sympathy for the relocalizados, which had initially been strong, began to decline as well. In 1992 a La Paz daily declared that the conflict between the government and the relocalizados was over.[12] The erosion of sympathetic support among city dwellers came in the context of an economic crisis that threatened many people's jobs and identities, and support for the relocalizados became an indulgence that fewer people would allow themselves. The public and the government increasingly ignored public protests by former miners and their families. This situation moved relocalizados to adopt desperate and futile tactics to call attention to their situation: some crucified their bodies on fences and flagpoles in highly public places, while others dangled from upper-story windows, threatening to jump. These tactics initially shocked public consciousness but inflicted little or no damage on those most responsible for the miners' plight. Meanwhile, an organization formed to represent their interests vis-à-vis the government grew moribund and ineffectual.

For Romulo Mercado the denigration of the relocalizados and the conflicts that erupted among miners in the aftermath of Supreme Decree 21060 recast the meaning of the lessons that he had learned from work and life in the mining centers. Union activism ceased to be a reference point for collective action, and he chose to distance himself from the pain and humiliation of the past and the present as he became immersed in new social relationships in El Alto. "To put it concretely," he told me, "I was a dedicated union activist. I grabbed hold of Siglo XX and said that I would die there with my companions" [*compañeros*]. Because of this political commitment Mercado refused to leave with the first contingent of relocalizados, vowing instead to fight for the retention of jobs and the revitalization of the mine. Such determination and militancy were nothing new for him. His union activities had led to periods of exile during the years of military rule, when he had worked underground in La Paz to help persecuted workers leave the country. Yet in the mid-1980s Mercado gradually came to the realization that the battle was lost.

He and his family left the mine with a $3,000 severance payment. Although he was fortunate to possess a small urban lot, the family used the bulk of the severance pay to construct a home. Mercado, however, did not have a job and all his attempts to secure one were futile. Relatives, acquaintances, and the union were either unwilling or unable to help him, and, perhaps most painful of all, his former workmates were divided and fighting among themselves.

Mercado became depressed; he had lost not only the ability to support his family but his dignity as a worker. He passed through a period of excessive drinking but eventually pulled himself together and entered teacher-training school. For two and a half years he studied, while his family scrapped by on the money that he and his wife earned from part-time employment. Then, in 1988 he acquired his first teaching position and subsequently acquired the seniority necessary to move up in the system and fight the same battles all over again.

When I met Mercado in 1996, he had been teaching for eight years, and he told me that he does not publicly refer to himself as a relocalizado.

> It's not because I am ashamed. The problem is that society thinks that I'm something that does damage to people. There is incredible denigration of the relocalizado. Why is this? It's because relocalizados are manipulated by politicians; their leaders rob them; the government fools them; people blockade roads in the name of the relocalizados, and [nongovernmental organizations] get money from abroad in the name of the relocalizados and then do nothing. Everything is the fault of the relocalizado. They have become a sickness in this country. You can't go into an office and say that you are a relocalizado—anything but that. They treat you very badly.

As Mercado joined the ranks of El Alto teachers, he became part of a profession that, despite the proletarian salaries, conferred a higher social status than that of market vendor or day laborer. By representing himself as a teacher, rather than a worker or a relocalizado, he distanced himself from domination and the demeaning ways that the larger society portrayed relocalizados. He also separated himself from a long history of collective struggle that came to appear increasingly futile and pointless in the context of a present where competition and individual opportunism, rather than cooperation, increasingly structured relations among and between old workmates and their Aymara neighbors.

His success in separating himself from these struggles was by no means complete, however. In the aftermath of Supreme Decree 21060 and the reorganization of mineral production, state bureaucrats and the World Bank turned to reforming the public education system and scrutinizing the jobs of thousands of teachers, whose occupational security had been eroding for years. The 1994 Educational Reform Law, which emerged from their deliberations, sought to undermine the teachers' union and make it more difficult for teachers to retain their positions (see chapter 5). The teachers did not react passively to these threats; indeed, after the defeat of the tin miners, they moved to the forefront of popular resistance to the privatization of the public sector, and the similarities between the plight of the miners and the situation of teachers were not lost on Mercado. "The essence of [the Educational Reform Law] is to privatize public education," he said. "And if education is privatized, a lot of teachers are going to be 'relocated,' so to speak, just like the miners." Yet Mercado was reticent about taking a more active part in the teachers' union, despite pressure from his colleagues to do so. "I was a tremendous fanatic," he told me. "At this stage of my life, I just have to say no. What for?"

Shaping the Present

The lives of Romulo Mercado, Fermina Díaz, and Leonidas Rojas illustrate how the dislocations occasioned by the reorganization of mineral production gave rise to new tensions surrounding social reproduction and subsistence. Clearly, these are tensions that people cannot completely resolve through their social relations, and their past experience provides little guidance to the future. The economy has brutalized former miners because of the ways it forces them to engage each other in order to survive; this brutalization creates a collective bad faith, as it undermines trust and the ability to collectively organize. Former miners and other impoverished immigrants now face a crucial strategic question: how can they construct a form of solidarity in El Alto from an ethnically diverse social constituency characterized by widely different individual histories, a mosaic of work relations, and intense internal competitiveness? In the absence of strong representative organizations, former miners and other poor alteños have a difficult time formulating demands and advancing them with the state and international organizations.

Any form of independent grassroots organization must contend with a handful of political parties, which represent the interests of dominant groups, and a number of nongovernmental organizations (NGOs), which often maintain ties to the parties but are more directly accountable to a variety of different international organizations. The parties and the NGOs control some of the essentials of subsistence in the city—jobs, credit, access to social services, and even, in some instances, food, which they distribute through a variety of local organizations. They contend with each other for control of these organizations—neighborhood associations, mothers' clubs, and the like—and at times the NGOs may even create local organizations.

"Affiliating" with a party or an NGO is one way that former miners and other poor residents address the daily problems of subsistence. Many ex-miners occupy leadership positions in a variety of parties, NGOs, and popular organizations. As one former miner explains: "Many relocalizados have become leaders [in El Alto], because the mines were revolutionary universities, especially Catavi and Siglo XX. They have a long history of producing important leaders. And when the miners rose up, there were revolutions and coup d'états." Several immigrant Aymaras with whom I met also recognize the leadership skills of the miners and acknowledge that they "talk well" [*hablan bien*], but their status—as former miners and others affiliated with the parties and NGOs—frequently robs them of their autonomy. The social fragmentation that forces them to engage these institutions in order to meet their basic needs multiplies as they become clients of these organizations, a relationship that deprives them of any political initiative, individual or collective. Factional cleavages come to characterize the struggle for resources. These cleavages are not based on horizontal class alliances but turn on ties of patronage and dependence that people use to forge shifting alliances tinged with partisan politics or imbued with the discourse of NGOs.

Fermina Díaz, for example, was no innocent to the workings of political parties and signed up with several on the eve of the 1993 elections in the hope of extracting a few benefits. As she explained:

> Militants from all the parties came to [my neighborhood] to rent space prior to the elections. The MNR [Movimiento Nacionalista Revolucionaria] was in the plaza; a little beyond was CONDEPA

[Conciencia de la Patria]; and over their was the UCS [Unión Cívica Solidaridad]. That's how it was. They all set up tables where people could register. I signed up with them all and got t-shirts from everyone. You've got to take advantage of them just like they take advantage of us.

To emphasize her point, Díaz took off the sweater she was wearing and displayed a tattered t-shirt. It bore the image of ex-dictator Hugo Banzer Suárez and the logo of his political party.

Despite his personal dislike of the mainstream parties, Romulo Mercado had also affiliated briefly with one of them at election time. As he explained: "I, the longtime enemy of the MNR and a leader in Siglo XX, went to a couple of MNR meetings. Why? Because they told us that they would help if they got elected. I thought maybe they would. They took us to their proclamations so that it would seem like they had a mass of people behind them. But when they got into power, nothing happened."

As his comments indicate, party patronage networks emerge most intensively at election time, when the parties need votes and at least the appearance of massive popular support. Yet for both strategic and financial reasons, a party's willingness and ability to maintain a vast system of clients on a regular basis is much more problematic; more important, the mainstream parties are not speaking to the needs of people like Romulo Mercado, Fermina Díaz, and Leonidas Rojas.

One major consequence of neoliberalism for ex-miners has been the debilitation of class-based organizations through which they had built up a sense of shared struggle, expressed in the language of class and class solidarity. Consequently, exploitation has become much more rooted in the fabric of local social relationships. As miners and their families confront the difficulties posed by daily life in an impoverished city, they must develop new approaches and affiliations. The past is of only limited use in this endeavor. At the neighborhood level, however, some former miners have reestablished affective ties with people they knew in the mining communities, and these bonds continue to have meaning. At the funeral of an ex-miner in the Ciudad Satélite neighborhood, for example, most people in attendance were other former miners and their family members from Catavi-Siglo XX. And Romulo Mercado allowed that although the past is gone forever, people who worked together for years still seek each other out in El Alto. "The friendship was very deep," he said. "Maybe with the passage of time, it will disappear, but the ties are very strong. . . . I would like my daughter to marry someone from my town."

After the government dismantled the mining communities and rendered the miners' union toothless, public school teachers moved to center stage in the popular struggle against neoliberalism. Public school teachers still have a combative union that has staked out its members' objections to the neoliberal attempts to reform teachers and public education. The next chapter explores teachers' confrontations with the state and the divisions between them and parents, which the 1994 Educational Reform Law has aggravated.

5 · School Discipline

The sound of exploding tear gas was unmistakable—pah! pah! pah! It rose above the din of traffic and punctuated the quotidian noises of midmorning social life in El Alto. White smoke curled upward, wafting around buildings in the distance and dissipating in the blue sky overhead. "Be careful if you go outside," warned my landlady, Felicidad Choque, as we stood in the courtyard of her home. "It's the police and the teachers again." I did not need to be reminded.

It was late March 1995, and several days earlier thousands of striking public school teachers from the surrounding countryside had arrived in El Alto. They had marched for days along the dusty roads of the Bolivian high plateau to join their urban colleagues to protest a law that mandated sweeping reforms to the system of public education. Soldiers and police sprayed the teachers with rubber bullets and tear gas to preempt their attempt to enter La Paz and hold a demonstration. In the days that followed, small bands of angry teachers, frustrated by continued police repression, staged "lightning blockades" that barricaded roads and interrupted traffic until police moved in to disperse the protesters. What Choque and I heard was the teargasing of one such blockade.

Bolivia was not the only place where public education came under fire in the early months of 1995. George Pataki, the Republican governor of New York, had pushed through the legislature deep cuts in his state's education budget, prompting protests by students and faculty in New York City. Nicaraguan teachers staged a forty-two-day strike to secure wage increases, and their counterparts in Haiti and Colombia mounted similar protests. These were just the latest in a growing number of demonstrations that expressed the discontent of public school teachers, and public sector employees generally, throughout the hemisphere. By limiting financial support for public education, governments can more easily balance their budgets, and, in the case of Third World countries, proceed with the spending cuts that the World Bank and the International Monetary Fund demand.

Bolivian teachers have been vigorous opponents of neoliberal attempts to transform the ways that ordinary people relate to and participate in institutionalized political orders. They have steadfastly challenged the 1994 Educational Reform Law, which emphasizes primary schooling and conceptualizes public education as less the responsibility of the federal government than of local authorities, parents, and the teachers that they select. Although it demonstrates the power of government elites to impose their vision of education, many alteños have not fully accepted this vision because of the teachers' strong resistance to it. Nevertheless, the law now provides the framework within which alteños—especially teachers and parents—are addressing their considerable differences about the future of public education in the city. As it closes opportunities for some, it appears to create possibilities for others.

This chapter explores the eight-week national teachers' strike against the 1994 Educational Reform Law and the tensions from which it emerged. The teachers in El Alto and La Paz were at the center of the protest, because opposition to the reform was strongest in these cities. At stake for the teachers were job security, wages, and the right to continue practicing their profession amid an eroding public education system. The government, for its part, was concerned about whose vision of education would prevail at a time when international pressure made "reform" virtually mandatory. The ferment put enormous pressure on teachers. On the one hand, they had to contend with a concerted effort by the state to undermine their job security. On the other hand, they had to confront parents for whom they are contradictory figures. Parents frequently believe that teachers do not care about children and improving the quality of education but simply look out for their own selfish interests. Disgruntled parents were heartened by a provision in the Educational Reform Law that transfers more power over what happens in school to them and to local municipalities. But most parents also understand that teachers—like most parents—earn paltry salaries that are inadequate for supporting a family.

These cleavages, as well as bonds of solidarity, emerged during the strike. To fully understand them, we must first briefly consider the nature of public education and explore the plight in which public school teachers have found themselves.

Public Education in El Alto

After the 1952 Bolivian national revolution, the Movimiento Nacionalista Revolucionario (MNR) supported the development of a public education system that aspired to reach thousands of Quechua- and Aymara-speaking peasants. Free public education, MNR leaders believed, was not only a way to consolidate power and respond to the demands of newly enfranchised indigenous peoples but was also an instrument for forging a national identity and overcoming deep ethnic and regional differences. At the same time, a number of state-sponsored teacher-training schools emerged to prepare women and men for positions in the new schools. These training institutes, called normal schools, opened new channels of upward mobility for peasants and members of the lower class who aspired to professional careers and wanted to continue their education beyond high school. The state guaranteed jobs to graduates in a system that expanded during the 1950s. But, beginning in the 1970s, government neglect, economic crisis, and the free-market reforms that began in 1985 combined to undermine public education, which had always been underfunded.

According to the 1990 census, 35 percent of Bolivia's six million inhabitants are functionally illiterate. In El Alto the situation is worse: 71 percent of the men and 77 percent of the women aged fifteen and older have never completed elementary school (INE 1992), and many high school graduates still have great difficulty reading and writing. The reasons for this situation are rooted in the city's dire poverty and the failure of the state to support public education more systematically. Rapidly expanding immigrant neighborhoods lack schools, and students from these areas are forced to travel to other districts, where underfunded schools, inadequate and outdated instructional materials, and overcrowded classrooms of fifty to seventy students make learning nearly impossible. To make matters worse, school instruction takes place in Spanish, yet Aymara and to a lesser extent Quechua are the first languages of many children, who speak Spanish imperfectly, if at all. The exigencies of life in an impoverished city also contribute to high dropout rates. The demands of the agricultural cycle oblige children to leave school and assist rural kinfolk or parents who continue to hold small plots in the countryside. Many children also work as shoe shiners, domestic servants, and fare collectors on city buses to provide an income to their cash-strapped families.

Under these circumstances El Alto's 18,196 public school teachers are hard pressed to deliver a quality education. I discovered some of the problems that teachers and students face when, late in the morning on a chilly, sunny day, I visited an elementary school in El Alto's northern zone. The one-story white-washed building reflected the glare of the sun and surrounded a dusty, sun-baked courtyard. The principal, whom I met on an earlier visit, was a stocky man in his forties. He greeted me and escorted me to a fourth-grade classroom, where I took a seat on a back bench. No posters, class projects, or student artwork decorated the walls, only peeling paint and a cracked blackboard. About sixty students sat in pairs behind old wooden desks. A few giggled and cast curious glances at me as they waited for the class to begin. The teacher was a young woman in her twenties. She wore a pink sweater, a skirt, and black pumps and tied her hair in a long ponytail. Quieting the boisterous children was not easy for her, but she eventually began a lesson on health and nutrition that was part of a pilot program sponsored by the government and an NGO. After reviewing the basic food groups and giving examples from each, she elicited students' participation in constructing a balanced diet for their families. As I listened to the responses, I wondered how many children actually came from families with the means to provide them with balanced nutritious diets. Two little boys seated near me had tuned out entirely. They squirmed in their seats as they pinched and poked each other. The teacher told them to pay attention. In an attempt to maintain discipline and keep the other students focused, she walked up and down the rows of desks, posing questions more directly to the children as she proceeded. From time to time, she added emphasis to certain points by writing on the blackboard at the front of the class. Yet by misspelling certain words by confusing "c" and "s," the teacher undermined this pedagogical technique.

Of course, the teachers too are products of this deficient system and impoverished environment, and their salaries, which range from $98 to $170 a month, make satisfying the economic necessities of their own households a constant struggle.[1] Transportation to and from work can easily cost $10 a month; considering expenses for food, rent, clothing, and electricity, it is not hard to understand the economic difficulties that teachers face. During a discussion of the problems of Bolivian education and the learning problems of malnourished children, Ruben Zambrano, a young teacher with a beginning salary, pointed out that teachers are also poorly nourished. "It's also a question of food," he said. "If we are not well fed, it's hard [to think about] the lessons. One falls asleep."

Because of the low salaries, teaching is widely viewed as a second-rate profession; it is not the career of choice for those with the means and the opportunities to study law, medicine, engineering, and other, more lucrative professions.[2] Fifty-four percent (2,224) of El Alto teachers are women, although in the countryside, where women rarely study beyond the third grade, men dominate teaching. Nearly a quarter (24.4 percent) of all El Alto teachers do not have a degree from a teaching institute and are congregated at the bottom of the pay scale, where they are classified as "interim teachers" [*maestros interinos*] (UNAS 1994). Because of low salaries women cannot support their households on the income from their jobs. Those who are single parents often live with relatives who help defray some of their expenses. It is also common for teachers—men and women—to hold down two teaching jobs or to engage in other activities, such as petty commerce, to support themselves. But attrition from burnout is routine; almost half of El Alto's teachers have held their jobs for nine years or less (UNAS 1994).

Clearly, the public education system is in dire need of reform, and El Alto residents, other Bolivians, and many teachers have long recognized this. To understand the controversy surrounding educational reform, however, and especially the 1994 Educational Reform Law, we must place public education and the reform legislation within the broader context of global economic restructuring.

Reform and Resistance

The impetus to reform Bolivia's educational system came during the 1992 National Congress of Education, which brought together delegates from a number of popular, church, and state organizations to discuss the problems of Bolivian education. The Consejo Nacional de Educación (CONED) emerged from this meeting and drew up a series of recommendations for a far-reaching education reform program. CONED produced a document backed by a broad consensus of labor and popular organizations that became known as the Ley Marco de la Reforma Educativa. Although a number of its suggestions—such as bilingual education, updated teaching methodologies, and a greater sensitivity to gender—appeared in the Educational Reform Law of 1994, the law itself lacked the popular support of the Ley Marco. The Bolivian Congress—which took a dim view of the social groups aligned behind the Ley Marco and under pressure from the World Bank to approve the law—enacted it hurriedly. Indeed, the Educational Reform Law, passed on July 7, 1994, bore the heavy imprint of the Equipo Técnico de Apoya a la Reforma Educativa (ETARE), a World Bank–sponsored technical advisory group that submitted to the government its own recommendations for transforming public education (Codina 1994).

The Bolivian Educational Reform Law is designed to extend the free-market policies that Víctor Paz Estenssoro initiated in 1985. Like the Popular Participation Law to which it is closely linked, the new education law advocates multiculturalism by acknowledging the importance of bilingual education, but it aggravates the growing class differences that are reshaping Bolivian society. Under the new law the state no longer guarantees jobs to the graduates of teacher-training institutes, and it redefines teachers, once considered professionals, as "superior technicians" [*técnicos superiores*]. Then, under the pretext of improving the quality of instruction, the original version of the law required teachers to pass a competency examination within five years to retain their positions and to be considered for promotion.

In principle, teachers are not opposed to higher professional standards, and those whom I met wanted to further their development by taking university courses. Yet, they argued, the state was not committed to helping them meet new goals, and the exams would become a tool for thinning their ranks, because they would be unable to preform well. In 1995 some teachers saw the reform as a cynical attempt to reduce the public payroll—97 percent of the educational budget was earmarked for salaries. Sonia Vidaurre began her career as a teacher in the mining complex of Catavi-Siglo XX but was "relocated" to El Alto in 1986 after the mining cutbacks began. According to Vidaurre, whom I interviewed during the strike:

> When we have to start taking the exams, the government will start firing teachers little by little. What will happen to our retirement [benefits]? They will automatically disappear. This is a relocation where [the state] wants to rid itself [of the responsibility] for its citizens. The miners were the first group, and they were the largest and the strongest. Now they want to do the same thing to the teachers. Soon we will have to do exactly as they say.

In contrast, Noel Aguirre fully supported the idea of an educational reform but could not afford the time off to take the university courses that he needed to pass the competency exam. Aguirre, thirty-three, was an elementary school teacher who had taught in an El Alto primary school for eleven years. To supplement his salary and support his three children, he also worked afternoons in a private school where his wife taught. His exhausting schedule left him little time to study. Aguirre's day began at 8:30 A.M. and ended late in the afternoon. His classes typically contained fifty to seventy-five children. "I leave school totally exhausted," he said. "I don't have energy for anything. And my wife feels the same way. So she's tired; I'm tired; and both of us have little interest in the children. The kids make noise, and we get mad because we have absolutely no more energy. After a little dinner and some coffee we fall into bed so we can get up the next day and start the same routine all over again."

In addition, Aguirre lived in a new settlement on the outer perimeter of El Alto, and traveling to the university in central La Paz for evening classes took an hour to an hour and a half in each direction. "Give me time," he said emphatically, "but the government will not do this for us."

Although the threatened exams placed new pressures on already over-worked and underpaid teachers, the most ominous aspect of the new law was the decentralization of the entire educational system. The Educational Reform Law permits the state to pass off responsibility for public education to cash-strapped municipalities, and it gives local bodies greater power in the hiring, retention, and promotion of teachers. According to Article No. 47, municipal treasuries "will finance the construction, maintenance and replacement of [school buildings], equipment and didactic material." Yet the state does not provide municipalities with enough money to maintain schools, much less build new ones to accommodate the needs of a rapidly expanding population. The shifting financial responsibility means that educational costs are passed along to parents in the form of maintenance expenses, exam fees, and charges for supplies, and this makes public education less accessible to many poor children.

Another effect of decentralization, claim teachers, is the de facto privatization of public education. As one man explained to me: "Teachers are necessarily going to be obliged to seek work in private institutions and that will seal the death of public education in Bolivia. Education will be converted into a luxury."

The government is indeed forcing alteños to live off a previous generation's educational investment, which will make the potential effects of greater local control over education much harder to recognize. A two-tiered educational system is already emerging in the city. New private schools have sprung up, overwhelmingly staffed by moonlighting teachers from the public system. In these institutions, however, teachers are not paid better than in the public system, and they receive no benefits and are not unionized.[3] Yet the schools attract parents who can afford them, because the strikes that plague the public system do not disrupt classes.

The law's attempt to undermine the union only deepened teachers' suspicions of the intentions of the government. The original version of the law made it more difficult for the union to raise money—it eliminated a 1 percent payroll deduction that supported union activities. This represented an effort by neoliberal reformers to make union membership voluntary and not mandatory, as had long been the case.[4] Teacher Alex Morales—the director of education and culture for El Alto's Central Obrera Regional—believed that the government wanted to bust the union, which was a constant thorn in its side. The government's behavior "is not gratuitous," he said. "The fewer unions that [the government] has before it, the easier it will be to implement neoliberal policy. A union without financial support cannot survive, because nothing is free." El Alto teacher Antonio Sánchez concurred. "The government wants to disappear the union," he asserted. Indeed, the decentralization of public education dilutes the power of the union, because it no longer negotiates with a central authority. Victor Prado, executive secretary of the Urban Teachers' Confederation, summarized the changes as "an administrative reform and not [a reform] of education in general" ("Ruidosa marcha de cacerolas" 1995:4).

National opposition to the reform law began to build immediately after its passage in July 1994. A one-day strike on February 10, 1995, only ten days after the initiation of the school year, was a harbinger of deeper strife. Many Bolivians saw this conflict as the opening gambit in what they thought was the regular annual series of protests, strikes, and negotiations between teachers and the state. But 1995 was not like past years. In addition to the usual demands for wage increases, teachers insisted that the government repeal the Educational Reform Law and thereby challenged a key element of the government's neoliberal doctrine.

Teachers' resolve to resist the law mounted throughout February and March. After two additional one-day strikes in February, the union declared on March 13 an indefinite national strike to force the government to repeal the reform and attend to their wage demands. They were supported by the Central Obrera Boliviana (COB), which on March 22 announced an indefinite general strike; the COB's negotiations with the government over a series of issues, including the educational reform, minimum wage increases, and coca cultivation in the Chapare region, had deadlocked. Although support for the general strike was weak, teachers in La Paz and El Alto, as well as those in the surrounding countryside, were

Teachers in La Paz demonstrate against the Educational Reform Law in 1995.

generally supportive of it, and all three hundred public schools in El Alto remained closed.

Over the next weeks the government used various tactics to pressure teachers back to work. It threatened to hire replacement workers, refused to pay wages, and disseminated disinformation about the strength of the strike, exaggerating the extent to which teachers were working and ignoring the call to strike. And whenever they had a chance, government functionaries tried to isolate and discredit union leaders by branding them "Trotskyist extremists" and "dictatorial." When none of these tactics worked, the government reverted to overt repression.

On March 22 rural teachers converged on El Alto. The city awoke that morning to police and military occupation. Soldiers wielding batons and shooting tear gas and rubber bullets broke up the march and arrested leaders. A week later eighty thousand residents of El Alto, responding to a call by the COB, marched through the city, demanding that the government attend to the COB's demands for wage increases, as well as peasants' demands to be permitted to grow coca leaf, and repeal of the Educational Reform Law.[5] Unwilling to negotiate, but threatened by the teachers' challenge and its ongoing conflicts with the coca growers, which multiplied in 1995 after the U.S. government intensified pressure on the Bolivian government to eradicate coca fields, the national government declared a state of siege on April 18. Police rounded up more than three hundred peasant and labor leaders and shipped them off to isolated prisons in the lowland jungles and frontier regions. The government prohibited meetings of more than three people, required citizens to request formal permission to travel—as well as to hold social gatherings such as weddings, birthdays, and so forth—and suspended civil rights. It also imposed a curfew from midnight to 6 A.M.

Unlike previous states of siege declared by military dictators, however, the draconian measures of 1995 barely disrupted the lives of many residents of La Paz, because they were selectively enforced. City streets did not become deserted after dark. Newspapers continued to publish, and radio stations remained on the air. Well-heeled paceños whose children attended private schools experienced very little change in their daily schedule. Indeed, for many people, social life did not deviate from its normal course. Teachers, however, confronted considerable difficulty coordinating the strike under martial law. The government had outlawed union meetings, and all the major leaders were either in prison or in hiding.[6] Rank-and-file teachers were also uncertain about how far the government would carry its campaign against them, and many were feeling the financial crunch of a strike that had already lasted five weeks. On the morning after the imposition of the state of siege, however, teachers began meeting clandestinely in their schools with local union delegates to assess the situation and plot a strategy for the days ahead. One such meeting occurred at a primary school, the Colegio San Salvador.

Forging Solidarity in the Colegio San Salvador

The Colegio San Salvador is located in La Paz's northern zone, below the rim of the canyon that separates El Alto from La Paz. It is an area of steep cobblestoned streets that until recently housed light manufacturing industries and an urban working class. Much of the industry is now gone and residents must make their living in the ubiquitous informal sector. About 540 children attend the school, which is not far from the headquarters of an elite army battalion. In 1995 the school had a faculty of twenty-nine, only three of whom were men. Most of these female teachers were urban-born, longtime residents of La Paz. Teaching was less an avenue of social mobility for them—as it is for rural men and new immigrants—than a vocation, and it was the most accessible profession for working-class women in the city.

Eleven of these women gathered nervously in the school's courtyard on the morning of April 19. The day was chilly and overcast. As they awaited the arrival of others, the teachers huddled together, clenching shawls and sweaters tightly around their bodies and speculating about who would and would not appear. Their representative was to have attended a citywide meeting of union delegates that morning to vote on continuing the strike, but the declaration of the state of siege and the police occupation of the union hall precluded any major assembly. Although the San Salvador staff had met regularly in the school since the beginning of the strike, this time was clearly different. Individuals cast uneasy glances every time someone knocked on the school's heavy wooden door; they were afraid the police would break in and arrest them. One woman counseled others to tell the police, if they should appear, that the teachers were simply waiting for students to arrive. Indeed, on imposing the state of siege the night before, the government had ordered the teachers back to work and threatened to fire them and hire replacement workers if they did not obey.

Because of the uncertainty created by the state of siege, some teachers did not risk coming to school that day, but others were simply treating the strike "like a vacation," according to several of the teachers present. The absentees, who supplemented their paltry wages with petty commerce, were using the strike to dedicate themselves to their commercial activities. Those present, however, did not have other jobs and were borrowing money and relying on the support of spouses and relatives to see them through the strike. They wanted to discuss the implications of the state of siege, allay each other's fears, and, more than anything, decide whether to continue the strike in light of the latest government actions.

Berta Choque, an articulate heavy-set woman who wore blue jeans and dangly earrings, directed the meeting. In recent days Choque, a single mother in her late twenties, had been raising money to feed her child by selling a powdered milk allotment that the state provided to needy mothers. She was also the school's de facto union delegate. She had been the official representative for eight years but resigned after the birth of her child. The faculty subsequently delegated union responsibility to Etna Romero, an unlikely candidate because, as one teacher complained, "she is too influenced by the officialist views of her husband." Romero also had a reputation for acting against group decisions in the past. By imposing the job on her, teachers had hoped to develop Romero's sense of responsibility and involvement and limit her disruptive behavior. The success of this tactic, however, was not evident on April 19. Romero did not attend the meeting, and Berta Choque assumed her old responsibilities, which she had never entirely abandoned.

The first person to speak was Maria del Carmen Moscoso, a diminutive forty-year-old woman with twenty-two years of teaching experience. Like other teachers in her position, Moscoso resented being forced to take a competency examination after years on the job, but she expressed doubts about continuing the strike. "We have to analyze how far we are willing to go," she said. "After all, we depend on our work and don't want to go to such extremes as to get fired en masse and replaced by high school graduates." Other women expressed similar reservations, but Inés Velasco, a fifty-year-old widow, counseled caution and a wait-and-see attitude. Given the peripheral location of the Colegio San Salvador, she did not think that its teachers would be the first fired if the government actually carried through with its threat. She urged those present to continue evaluating the situation every day and not to be intimidated. After more discussion the women agreed to continue the strike but resolved to meet again in three days to re-assess their position. Choque and Vilma Peralta, the school's director, stressed the importance of frequent meetings, despite the restrictions imposed by the state of siege, so that teachers would not feel isolated and become susceptible to government propaganda.

On Friday, April 21, the teachers met again. This time a majority was present, and anxieties ran high. Although the government had not fired anyone, a government minister continued to make threats. He announced that pay vouchers would be distributed the following Monday only to those teachers who showed up for work and that salaries would be discounted for every day of the strike. At the same time radio stations sympathetic to the strikers broadcast statements from union leaders in jail or in hiding that urged teachers to maintain the strike. The Colegio San Salvador teachers once again found themselves at a crossroad, where they had to make a decision that could affect their jobs and their futures. And again they were divided over the best course of action.

One young woman pointed out that other schools were slowly returning to work and that the Colegio San Salvador should do the same. Another woman, Nancí, the school secretary and a widow from El Alto, declared that she would show up at 8:30 A.M. on Monday morning so that nobody could fire her, and a woman seated next to her quickly asserted that she would do the same. Etna Romero, present for the first time since the state of siege began, also felt that teachers should return to work.

Nevertheless, the more radical teachers again counseled patience and caution. As she had done before, Inés Velasco advised people to come on Monday to evaluate the situation and make a decision based on developments in the rest of the city. By being present, she argued, they would be able to defend their jobs, but that did not mean that they had to teach, which she felt should not happen until the entire rank-and-file voted to end the strike and jailed leaders were released. Berta Choque and Vilma Peralta supported this position. In a subtle rebuke to those threatening to act on their own, Choque suggested that everyone arrive together on Monday at 8:30 to maintain unity. Solidarity, she stressed, was crucial. Why, she asked, should they return to work if the government discounted their paychecks? Given the length of the strike to date, they still would be left with virtually nothing. She further argued that nobody would be fired on the first day of a supposed return to work; only after a majority of schools had gone back, she claimed, would this really happen. Choque concluded by urging people to take government claims about schools' ending the strike with a grain of salt. The Colegio San Salvador, she pointed out, was on a list of schools that a TV station had reported as having started classes.

As teachers argued back and forth, several women present remained silent. Elia Ormachea was deeply conflicted about the strike and her participation in it. As the mother of three, Ormachea was having difficulty keeping food on the table. She was already in debt, and supplies that she had stockpiled after the last strike were running out. Ormachea was also a devout Seventh-day Adventist and was acting against her religious beliefs by participating in a strike. "We [the Adventists] are supposed to support God and the authorities," she had told me earlier. "Therefore when I participate in a demonstration, I can't shout insults because we respect the authorities. More than anything, I go to avoid the fine that the union levies against those who do not participate." Yet why, I wanted to know, would she risk imprisonment by attending an illegal meeting? "I have to support my compañeros," she said. "I obey whatever they decide so as not to divide us. It's a little conflictive for me." Given these contradictions in her own position, Ormachea did not venture any opinions, one way or the other, during the meeting. Other women, less torn by their religious beliefs but insecure about expressing themselves in the debate, also remained on the sidelines.

Once again the teachers decided to continue the strike, persuaded in large measure by the arguments of Choque and Velasco. And again they resolved to continue meeting periodically. But their next meeting never occurred. As the teachers assembled a week later, an anonymous phone caller tipped them off about an imminent police raid. Alarmed by the call, people quickly dispersed, except Choque and director Peralta, who eventually determined that the call was a hoax, perpetrated by an irate parent angered by the teachers' continued refusal to end the strike.

Parents and Teachers

Parents in the poor and working-class neighborhoods of El Alto and La Paz are deeply committed to the education of their children. Education, they believe, is a road out of poverty and a way to ensure a more secure future. Parents therefore frequently make great sacrifices for education. Those who can afford the expense send their children to private schools, although parents say the quality of education is often no better, and sometimes worse, than in the public schools. But the constant strikes that plague the public system never disrupt classes at the private schools, which subject teachers to rigid administrative discipline. The vast majority of parents, however, cannot furnish their children with the luxury of a private school education. They must make do with the public system, where labor unrest disrupts the educational process and, according to many parents, teachers are poorly prepared to exercise their profession. Thus parents' feelings about the strike were decidedly mixed.

Those parents who backed the teachers appreciated that they earned low salaries, and some parents, who had experienced cutbacks in other areas of the public sector, supported teachers, because they feared that the reform would privatize public education and throw teachers out of work. For these reasons, they backed the teachers' demands and were highly critical of the reform and the government's heavy-handed tactics, such as the use of tear gas in residential neighborhoods to disperse demonstrators. Women like Francisca Mendoza, whose six children attended public school and whose eldest son taught in a public school, supported the strikers because her son's wages were important to the survival of her household. "He has to strike because his wages are not enough," she explained. Taxi driver Fermin Ortega, whose two children attended public school, also backed the strike. "The government isn't interested in solving anything," he said. "[Everything it does] is with bullets and gas."

Other parents in El Alto, however, deeply resented teachers and felt that their children were the primary victims of the strike. Like all parents, they wanted their children educated by well-trained professionals, but they were not satisfied with teachers' professional behavior or their qualifications. The irregular attendance record of teachers was a constant complaint of parents.

Teachers, they said, typically extended school vacations by failing to appear on the days preceding and following official holidays. Weekends also generated high Monday morning attrition, and when teachers did show up, they were invariably late. Male teachers often arrived drunk. This, said angry parents, was unprofessional conduct that the state should penalize.

A particularly low point in the strike came in early April, when rural teachers, who attempted to stage a march in central La Paz, clashed with parents from the Association of Household Heads of Bolivia, who carried out a parallel demonstration. Teachers, according to the official press, started the violence with taunts of "officialists" and "sellouts" and then burned a placard of the opposing group. But it was clear that the police supported the Association of Household Heads and may even have encouraged the violence. Police officers not only failed to disperse the parents' march, as they had the teachers', but allowed the groups to encounter each other.

Part of the animosity between parents and teachers springs from the ambivalent position that many teachers occupy, somewhere between white-collar professional and day laborer or peasant. Indeed, public education has long been linked to the civilizing mission of the Bolivian state, which views education as a vehicle for incorporating the Indian masses into a homogeneous national culture. Yet this process of incorporation is never complete, and teachers are both products and practitioners of public education. Many parents, who have experienced no social mobility, charge teachers with discrimination against their own people. They claim that teachers denigrate the Aymara culture and are abusive and authoritarian in the classroom. For these parents, teachers appear less as the exploited victims of an unjust state policy than as domineering social climbers.

For these parents the strike was not about improving education for their children; it reflected the intransigence and self-serving attitudes of teachers and their union. The elderly grandmother of five students at the Colegio San Salvador was disturbed by the teachers' refusal to return to work. "My grandchildren are tired of playing," she fumed. "They want to go back to school." This woman, who sold sweets in front of the school, was also distressed because business at her small stand had dropped off dramatically with the suspension of classes. Another angry mother complained: "A year never passes with normal classes. There are always strikes and that is why public education is viewed so poorly. The teachers never agree with anything that the government says. They're really not so badly paid given the number of hours that they work and they get two long vacations a year. Any other public employee has to work all day long." She further criticized the low professional qualifications of public school teachers. "They call themselves professionals," she said, "but many have not gone to the normal school."

Teachers also alienated some parents with questionable protest tactics that did little to disrupt the state but upset many ordinary citizens. One Sunday evening, for example, my husband and I were returning to the city from a small town in the mountain valleys of La Paz department. We were traveling on a bus that was crowded with peasants and working people, most of whom were the parents and grandparents of school-aged children. As the bus approached the altiplano town of Batallas over a rough gravel highway, it overtook a group of perhaps fifty teachers who were walking along the side of the road. They had not thrown up barricades, a common protest technique, but it soon became evident that we had come upon a demonstration and that the teachers did not want the bus to pass. As the driver slowed to go around the group, a shower of stones and rocks fell on the bus. One rock broke a rear window and injured a female passenger. Some protesters then climbed onto the luggage rack and began hurling bags to the ground. The terrified driver veered off onto a side road, plunged the bus through a shallow river after discovering that the bridge over it was blocked by another group of protesters, and began a long circuitous detour to the city. When we finally arrived, many tired passengers were not feeling particularly sympathetic to the teachers and their demands.

Parents' divided opinions about the strike were reflected in the Federation of Parents of El Alto, an organization that represents a majority of the parents of public school children. The federation, which is dominated by members of CONDEPA and belongs to the COB, supported the teachers insofar as their demands for higher wages were concerned, but it refused to call for the repeal of the educational reform legislation. The federation backed the Educational Reform Law, because it believed that the law would compel teachers to improve. It was also sympathetic to the notion that parents should have more control over the education of their children. As one federation leader explained: "We must realize that there are teachers who are not even high school graduates. These people have encrusted themselves onto the current struggle as a way of blocking changes to the system. They are never going to agree with the reform, because they are the ones who will never pass the test. . . . They entered the profession through political favoritism, . . . or family connections." Moreover, desperate parents in several local affiliates of the federation raised money to pay teachers to work during the strike, but this usually did not work because of union vigilance.

What disgruntled parents could not accomplish, however, the government's intransigence and repression finally achieved. The COB called off the nationwide general strike on April 30, when three leaders, operating clandestinely and without consulting the rank-and-file, signed an agreement with the government. Without the COB's support the teachers had little choice but to follow suit. They could not hold out indefinitely without a strike fund, and the eight-week strike had already exacted a high price from teachers and their families. It was a crushing defeat: not only did the Educational Reform Law remain intact but teachers were not even sure that their lost wages would be paid. Teachers' union leaders—the most radical in the Bolivian labor movement—were irate and accused COB leaders of selling out the movement. Rank-and-file teachers also felt disillusioned that their long weeks of sacrifice had seemingly brought nothing.

The defeat of the strikers did not end the controversy surrounding public education, and more strikes and demonstrations followed in subsequent years. The teachers managed to force the government to modify the Educational Reform Law in some respects. A new clause states that no teacher in service before 1994 can be removed because of changes introduced by the law. And all teachers continued to be represented by the union and paid union dues.

The teachers' strike demonstrates that, despite the defeats and setbacks suffered by the Bolivian labor movement, class-based organizations continue to be a vital organizational form that is crucial to resisting the imposition of corrosive neoliberal policies. The teachers' strike galvanized a level of popular support in El Alto and the poor neighborhoods of La Paz that had not been seen in the recent past. Genaro Flores, former executive secretary of the COB and a peasant leader, found reason for hope in the popular response:

> [The strike] was not a total defeat. In the past, it was the miners who fought for the poor and the working class. Now it is the teachers, and the population supported them and understood that it is not just a wage problem. The strike was a way for people to reorganize themselves and become [more] conscious of the problems with education in Bolivia. The reform came very quickly without anyone really understanding what it was about, because it's a project of the International Monetary Fund and the World Bank.

Implicit in what Flores said is that class-based struggles and organizations in Bolivia have an enduring history, and they remain key to progressive social transformations.

Contrary to one sector of public opinion in La Paz, teachers did not oppose the law because they were against reforming education in Bolivia. Rather, they wanted to protect the few shreds of job security that remained after more than a decade of neoliberal reforms in Bolivia and to preserve their dignity as teachers. Yet this objective was jeopardized by the cleavages that divide parents and teachers and that were, at least in part, aggravated by the Educational Reform Law.

The law tantalized local people with the possibility of greater power over public education. It nurtured the hope that, after decades of inept central management, corruption, and discrimination against indigenous and poor urban children, schools could actually respond more effectively to their educational needs. Yet the power to effectively shape public education never really lay with local people, despite the rhetoric of the reform law. And to have any claim on the limited possibilities offered by the law, alteños were asked to accept the gradual erosion of teachers' limited job security. Thus many people found themselves in an impossible position, compelled to choose between teachers and children.

Parents see their children's futures increasingly frustrated by a crumbling public education system and teachers whom they perceive as lazy and incompetent. Teachers, for these parents, have benefited to a limited degree from the system but are unable, and sometimes unwilling, to educate children in ways that respect their cultural integrity and adequately prepare them. Yet teachers, despite their best efforts, cannot always deliver the instructional quality that parents expect from them. Their job security is rapidly disappearing, and they cannot support their own families on the wages that they earn. Moreover, El Alto's pervasive poverty affects public education in myriad ways: poverty, for example, forces children to leave school at an early age, and it leaves children hungry and malnourished and thus unable to learn well.

Perhaps the strike's most hopeful legacy is that it intensified the debate about racism and teacher accountability in the public school system, and, as Genaro Flores suggested, heightened public debate and awareness of neoliberalism. Building solidarity among alteños in the future will depend upon the ability of teachers, parents, and students to engage in discussions about educational quality, professional responsibility, and cultural integrity, as well as the broader issues of political and economic inequality that shape public education. Teachers need to convince skeptics that they are genuinely concerned about educating children, who also bear the brunt of the public education system's numerous inadequacies, and that teachers are indeed the champions of a public education system that is threatened by the reformist zeal of neoliberal planners in distant foreign capitals.

6 · The Military and Daily Life

War is the extension of politics by other means.

—Carl von Clausewitz

As neoliberal reforms reduce the economic autonomy of public school teachers and other alteños, the state must find ways to control people for both security and development reasons. The growing immiseration of city dwellers threatens the fragile stability of social life, and the state—using the police and the military—must deal with the confusion and unruliness its policies have created. Militant schoolteachers pose the most direct challenge to the established order in El Alto, but many different public sector workers across the country also demonstrated against cutbacks and privatization during the 1990s. Indeed, a week hardly passed in the mid-1990s without some organized protest in El Alto or La Paz. Similarly, despite repeated clashes with state security forces charged with fighting the U.S.-backed "War on Drugs," peasant producers of the Chapare region have consistently confronted the state about the right to cultivate coca. Their numbers have grown because ex-miners and ruined cultivators from the highland valleys are resettling in the Chapare and turning to coca leaf cultivation in the absence of viable economic alternatives.

Order and disorder are recurrent issues for the Bolivian military, which has always harbored concerns about internal "subversion." Not surprisingly, the Bolivian armed forces and those of other Latin American countries have more successfully defended their budgets against cutbacks than those state agencies charged with social welfare responsibilities (Franko 1994). The military and the police force are increasingly the only viable entities through which the state exercises its power in El Alto. Yet the armed forces are themselves confronting new pressures and demands. The end of the cold war has obliged the high command to identify new enemies. So-called narcotraffickers, who lead the U.S. enemies list, are an obvious choice, but fighting the illegal drug traffic has not been easy. The military's own involvement in cocaine trafficking has compromised the armed forces in the eyes of the United States, the Bolivian military's longtime patron. In addition, the notion of militarizing the drug controversy has little civilian support, and the economic crisis has hampered the military's capacity to develop an external defense mission. Military bases around the country are bereft of supplies, the officer corps is demoralized, and to meet their basic needs conscripts often work illegally for civilians. The armed forces must also confront civilian demands that it respect democratic processes and play a constructive part in national affairs.

The military's search for a new mission and the neoliberal restructuring of the state are generating a significant shift in the relationship between the armed forces and poor men and women in El Alto. Moreover, this shift is permitting the military to extend its influence and control deeper into people's daily lives through the practice of compulsory military service. The state has long used military service for two main purposes: to recruit troops for an ongoing battle against alleged subversives and "communists," and to create particular kinds of "civilized" male citizens by using instruction in military beliefs and practices to instill a sense of belonging and obedience to the nation-state. Nowadays, however, creating nations and citizens has ceased to be a major concern of the Bolivian state, and economic crisis and neoliberal reforms have shifted the burden of troop maintenance from the state to impoverished recruits and their families. Nevertheless, the benefits and entitlements that military service purportedly offer remain extremely important to poor people as state social service agencies wither and viable employment options fail to materialize.

Because they must increasingly turn to the military to deal with their own poverty, poor peasants and urban dwellers are not demanding a radical transformation of the armed forces. Rather, most of them want the military to provide more opportunities, and compulsory military service enjoys a remarkable degree of popular support. This support emerges from the contradictory ways that poor men and women must engage the armed forces to ensure their own daily survival in a society that routinely excludes them. The efficacy of compulsory military service is, however, eroding, as economic restructuring and shifting geopolitics threaten to undermine an unusually effective system of incorporation, co-optation, and political control. The armed forces must therefore find ways to burnish their image.

One strategy, launched in the 1990s, is to use soldiers to implement a variety of development schemes, such as health education programs, agricultural extension projects, and environmental protection initiatives. Military development programs show the public that the armed forces are not needlessly consuming scarce national resources and that they are teaching recruits skills that are useful in a democratic society. They also imply that the military's participation in resolving social and economic problems is legitimate, and they blur the boundaries between civilian and military arenas. Poverty thus becomes the entry point for reinforcing and expanding the repressive apparatus of the neoliberal state. This chapter explores the consequences of this low-intensity version of militarized democracy for the evolving relationship between the armed forces and ordinary people in El Alto.[1]

Masculinity, Military Service, and Citizenship

Thousands of young men from around the country are inducted into the Bolivian armed forces every year. They come from the most powerless sectors of society: Quechua, Aymara, and Guarani peasant communities and poor urban neighborhoods such as El Alto. Two times a year—once in January and again in June—these men must respond to the military's calls for recruits, because one year of military service is a legal obligation for all ablebodied men. Conscripts on El Alto bases come from the city and rural Aymara communities. At induction time they arrive at the army and air force bases with a few personal possessions in distinctive wooden suitcases and line up to be processed. All recruits must undergo a medical exam to determine whether they are fit for service. The military then issues uniforms to the physically fit and shaves their heads. Urban-born young men with high school educations are likely to perform their duty in El Alto, but many others—especially illiterate peasants—are assigned to a variety of other bases around the country.

Although compulsory military service has grown more controversial in recent years, the vast majority of Bolivian men still fulfill their obligations to the armed forces, and they often do so with considerable enthusiasm. Most young men look forward to a stint in the army, where most serve, and family members and friends have generally supported and encouraged the young men to enlist. Why is this the case?

This question has no simple answer; the reasons are both straightforward and complex. On the one hand, military service is a legal requirement, understood as a prerequisite for many forms of urban employment, both public and private. Perhaps more important, young men may have acquiesced to military service in the 1980s and 1990s because Bolivia, unlike Peru and various Central American countries, was not mired in bloody warfare, nor was it ruled by repressive military dictators. On the other hand, compulsory military service facilitates more ambivalent processes: even as the state uses it to create particular kinds of male citizens, conscripts lay claim to militarized conceptions of masculinity tied to beliefs about bravery, competence, and patriotic duty. They do so to earn respect from women (mothers, wives, sisters, and girlfriends) and male peers, both as defenders of the nation and, more broadly, as strong responsible male citizens who can make decisions and lead others.

Military service is one of the most important prerequisites for the development of successful subaltern manhood, because it signifies rights to power and citizenship and supposedly instills the courage that a man needs to confront life's daily challenges. Through the experience of military service, men assert a dignified sense of masculinity that serves as a counterpoint to the degradation experienced from more dominant males and an economic system that assigns them to the least desirable occupations. Military service has enabled them to challenge their exclusion from full participation in Bolivian society and to contest more genteel notions of masculinity associated with upper-class males who avoid military service altogether.

Yet self-affirmation and the legitimate desire for respect are also intricately tied to ongoing patterns of collusion with hegemonic uses and representations of poor men, and these are bound to evolving relationships of inequality among the subjugated peoples of El Alto. Conscripts collude with hyperaggressive notions of masculinity that demean women, "weaker" men, and civilians in general and that conjoin maleness with citizenship. They further assert an imposed falsehood: soldiers defend the interests of *all* Bolivians from an array of internal and external threats. By so doing, they aggravate the estrangement between men and women and deepen their alienation from their class peers and the history of indigenous peoples in Bolivia. Material constraints and beliefs about gender lead poor men to participate in a state institution that contributes to the oppression of dominated peoples.

Military service is a central arena in which the state struggles to enforce certain forms of identification while discrediting or marginalizing others. This process is very uneven, because it silences and empowers poor men and women in different and contradictory ways. Consequently, cultural claims are formulated against those who exploit and emerge from the historic divisions and animosities that structure social relations within oppressed groups (Sider 1993, 1996). In El Alto these divisions pit men against women, the urban born against immigrants, and the relatively well-to-do against the desperately poor, and so forth. Thus beliefs and practices forged in the context of domination, and at least partially oppositional, may also serve as instruments of oppression or obfuscation. The construction of masculinity within the Bolivian armed forces illustrates this process; indeed, the military is the premier state institution charged with the legitimate use of force in society, and after years of structural adjustment reforms, the urban poor and peasants have an ambivalent relationship to it.

The state has used the institution of the armed forces to conjoin key concepts of masculinity and beliefs about citizenship that the poor claim as they simultaneously accommodate domination and assert their own interests vis-à-vis each other and the dominant society. Other notions of masculinity and, of course, all notions of femininity are ignored, ridiculed, or marginalized. Conscripts thus become "men" and "citizens" in ambiguous ways, as the young men are used and represented in different ways by the military. Military service both differentiates conscripts from elite white males and incorporates conscripts into society. The process also differentiates military conscripts from their female peers and men who have not done military service. The resulting ruptures that emerge among the poor from these patterns of differentiation and incorporation undermine attempts to shape understandings of masculinity, femininity, and citizenship that can be used to fundamentally transform relations of domination, rather than simply contest some of them.

To appreciate the evolving nature of the relationship between the state and impoverished peoples, and how it is developing in the context of economic restructuring, we must first consider how militarism, masculinity, and citizenship became conjoined. This requires a consideration of two separate but related processes: the U.S.-financed expansion of the armed forces during the cold war, and the Bolivian state's long-term civilizing agenda for indigenous peoples that was abetted by the populist nationalism of the 1952 revolution. The large-scale militarization of masculinity initially occurred on the anvil of anticommunism and nationalism. The discussion then turns to a consideration of the growing financial burden of military service for poor families and a consideration of how the armed forces are harnessing military service to "development" objectives, which threaten to further embed military practices and understandings in the very fabric of society and reinforce the repressive power of the state.

The Military and Bolivian Society

Since 1904 military service has been mandatory for all Bolivian males, but for the first half of the twentieth century, indigenous peoples, who were not persuaded by appeals to patriotic duty and did not possess a well-developed sense of national identity, shunned the military. Indigenous men not only avoided service during peacetime but engaged in large-scale draft evasion during the Chaco War (1932–1935), a costly and bloody dispute with Paraguay over the arid lands of the Gran Chaco. Draft evasion was so common that the military regularly resorted to violence to conscript a fighting force. The educator Elizardo Pérez, writing about the experiences of one community on the shores of Lake Titicaca, reported that "one day, at four o'clock in the morning, soldiers from the Achacachi base broke into the huts of the Indians and dragged them off to the base without paying any attention to their ages or what they said [and] . . . in less than 24 hours, the poor Indians left Achacachi for the trenches without even being allowed to say good-bye to their loved ones" (1992:167).

Such tactics reflected the army's desperate need for able-bodied men on the Paraguayan front, where enormous casualties were exacting a heavy toll from the Bolivian army. Yet rural landowners and the army high command felt a profound ambivalence about arming Indians. Landlords in the department of Sucre argued that "the army is the most pernicious [place] for the Indian because in addition to completely changing his customs, it deprives agriculture of robust arms and transforms Indians into armed dangers" (quoted in Arze Aguirre 1987:55). Similarly, the prefect of Potosí department claimed that Indians only joined the army in order to use military training in "their struggles against white landowners." He went on to ask, "Will the militarization of the Indian be a new national danger? This is the question that merits thought by statesmen" (quoted in Arze Aguirre 1987:55). Because of these fears the high command stressed that rural indigenous men would not fight on the front lines and sent them to labor in the rear guard, clearing land and building roads. Yet wartime demands for able-bodied men quickly made this policy collapse, and it was never strictly applied.

Social tensions did not ease at war's end. Participation in the army and the experience of the war itself created a new sense of national identity among Indian war veterans. In addition, the enormous loss of life, Bolivia's crushing defeat, and the corruption and incompetence of the white officers provoked a crisis within the armed forces and generated challenges to the entire political system. These tensions erupted in the 1952 national revolution, which brought to power the Movimiento Nacionalista Revolucionario (MNR).

In a move to consolidate power the MNR neutralized the army by reducing the budget, eliminating disloyal officers, and cutting the number of military personnel from twenty thousand to five thousand (Hudson and Hanratty 1991). It then moved quickly to arm the civilian population, which was overwhelmingly loyal to it. Armed civilian militias composed of peasants, tin miners, and factory workers essentially replaced the army for a number of years, until the MNR grew uneasy with these increasingly militant organizations and decided to rebuild the armed forces.

The United States assisted the MNR's efforts to reconstitute the armed forces in the mid-1950s. Caught up in a rising wave of cold war hysteria, the U.S. government increased military expenditures for technical assistance for Bolivia's armed forces. It also began training Bolivian officers, who returned to Bolivia after several months on a U.S. base. Imbued with the teachings of their U.S. counterparts, the Bolivian officers instructed local troops in the skills of soldiering. The MNR, for its part, hoped to keep the armed forces loyal to the civilian government by appointing officers with known MNR sympathies to important command positions and permitting poor mestizos to enter officer-training programs. Its political rhetoric downplayed the deep class and ethnic differences that continued to divide Bolivia and promoted a nationalist discourse that figured Bolivians as equal members of a homogeneous nation. The enfranchisement of indigenous peoples was the first and most dramatic way in which the party created a broad new category of citizen, and military service was another arena in which the state carried out its civilizing project.

The creation of "citizen-soldiers" was possible because U.S. military aid rose from a mere $100,000 in 1958 to $3.2 million in 1964, when the army overthrew the MNR and ruled almost without interruption for the next eighteen years (Hudson and Hanratty 1991). With the continuous influx of U.S. military aid, both before and after the overthrow of the MNR, the Bolivian military could incorporate large numbers of indigenous peoples and poor urban dwellers into the armed forces. Suppressing "internal enemies," who were called communists, became a central goal of the Bolivian military, and it was also the touchstone of U.S. policy, especially in the aftermath of the 1959 Cuban Revolution.

Throughout the 1960s and 1970s the Bolivian military encountered little difficulty recruiting the men that it needed. Former soldiers recalled—and news photos from the period show—the long lines of recruits that invariably formed outside the bases in El Alto during the Banzer regime. Substantial U.S. financial support facilitated operations, and living conditions on army bases were better than they would become in the 1980s. More important, the military ruled the country with an iron grip, and draft dodgers were likely to bear heavy consequences for their actions. The university, which became an attractive alternative to military service for some men after the return of civilian rule, was also closed for much of the 1970s.

At this point, we might ask how the military has confronted the task of making men out of boys and forging "citizens" out of the male masses. How too do claims about class, ethnicity, and regional affiliation exist in tense dialogue with this totalizing project?

Alliances and Defiances

The efforts of militaries to instill civic consciousness among persons marginalized by their states is a persistent theme in the experiences of many countries (Weber 1976; Enloe 1980; Segal 1989; Glatthaar 1990). In Bolivia a key aspect of basic training and the formation of male citizens is that recruits experience the military as omnipotent and omniscient. The military incorporates the young inductees, controlling and regimenting every aspect of their lives and cutting off or severely restricting their ties to the broader society. To become a man and a soldier requires that recruits be separated from home, especially the care and influence of their mothers, and be controlled by older unrelated males. The military then strives to subordinate the inductees' individuality to the identity of the male group and instill rigid conformity and compliance to military values.[2]

This is a gendered process of moral regulation in which the armed forces define the parameters of appropriate male behavior and link masculinity and citizenship to the successful completion of military service; indeed, commanders link military obligations as closely to civic duty as to the actual practice of warfare. The imposition of acceptable forms of masculinity that prize aggressiveness, male camaraderie, discipline, autonomy, and obedience to authority creates militarized male Bolivians. As certain forms of individual and collective identification receive the official seal of approval, the state denies legitimate expression to others. This is a process that depends on the acceptance of young men and is reinforced by their simultaneous brutalization, an aspect of the "civilizing" experience that is central to military training and much anticipated by prospective recruits. It must overcome deep regional and ethnic cleavages.

Until very recently the military has tried to mix men from different parts of the country in the same barracks in order to break down strong regional sentiments. In addition to the more abstract purpose of creating male citizens who identify as "Bolivian," rather than as Aymaras, lowlanders, and so forth, this policy also has a direct practical rationale: military leaders believe that conscripts are more likely to shoot "subversives" if they do not come from the same regional or ethnic background. Financial constraints have limited this policy in recent years, but the Bolivian military still sends large numbers of highland conscripts to the lowlands, because of a constant dearth of lowland recruits.[3]

The first three months of military service are dedicated to basic training in which new recruits engage in endless drills and marching. Conscripts also learn how to use weapons and prepare to fight. During this period troops suffer the abuse of commanding officers and the dominance of a more experienced group of conscripts known as the *antiguos,* or old-timers, who entered the service six months earlier. Officers verbally and even physically castigate the newcomers for violations of military discipline, misunderstanding commands, and not carrying out required exercises. Superiors refer to the recruits as *sarna,* or mange, and shape militarized masculinity in these contexts through the symbolic debasement of women and homosexuals. They also call recruits whores (*putas*), faggots (*maricones*), little ladies (*señoritas*), and other gendered insults. Punishment for an infraction of the rules may entail dressing as a woman and parading around the base or, as one ex-conscript described, sleeping naked with another man in a physical embrace.

Closely tied to this rigid hierarchy is an ideology of male equality and bonding. This ideology pervades basic training and conflates combat preparedness with beliefs about masculinity: troops share the same food and living accommodations, wear the same uniforms, display identical shaved heads, conform to the same rigid codes of behavior, and train for war, the ultimate test of their manhood. They are taught to rely only on themselves and each other and to distrust civilians, who are considered weak, incompetent, and lacking the discipline and responsibility of a uniformed soldier. As one ex-recruit described the experience to me: "You learn how to survive in the barracks, because there is no help from your family. You only get help from yourself and those who live with you. It's a really beautiful experience, because you are isolated with others [men] who become even more than your brothers because they share everything with you. The guy who is beside you is more important than your own family." Indeed, the strong self-reliant man who works with other men is the desired product of this training.[4]

Encountering "the enemy" in actual confrontations or, what is more likely, in mock skirmishes and exercises, heightens male bonding and camaraderie among recruits. The identity of the enemy varies with time and place; for example, troops who served near the Peruvian border during the 1980s learned about the Shining Path guerrilla insurgency; the cold war turned domestic critics into foes; drug traffickers in the 1980s and 1990s posed the most direct hazard for conscripts in Cochabamba and Santa Cruz departments; and those serving near the Chilean border always perceived Chile and its armed forces as the preeminent danger. Opposition to these groups, which are portrayed as threats to Bolivia, creates among conscripts a heightened sense of national identity and nationalism, and military commanders encourage conscripts to see themselves as the nation's most valued defenders.

Yet recruits reproduce in the barracks their class, regional, and ethnic divisions, which threaten to undermine the military's totalizing project, even as conscripts encounter "enemies," bond with each other, and experience overwhelming pressure to conform to military values. Though the military mixes together recruits from diverse regional backgrounds, informants consistently recount that high school graduates, who are more likely to be urban born and fluent Spanish speakers, stand a better chance of remaining on urban bases, whereas authorities send peasants to much more onerous rural and frontier postings. Moreover, peasants often experience greater difficulty in understanding orders and lessons, which are conducted entirely in Spanish, and they must therefore endure more abuse from commanding officers and the old-timers. Authorities are also less likely to choose peasants for advanced instruction after basic training; their destiny frequently is to labor on arduous civic action programs, such as clearing ditches and making roads.

Intense regional sentiments further complicate these class and ethnic divisions. Ricardo Salinas, an urban-born paceño who served in Cochabamba department in 1994, was intimidated by all the *cochabambinos* (residents of Cochabamba department) in his barracks. "The old-timers really scared me," he said. "There were more cochabambinos than paceños. When we [the newcomers] arrived, they asked us who were the paceños and told us to raise our hands. Then they said, 'Sarnas, you are going to die.'" Thus even as the military seeks to undermine class, ethnic, and regional divisions in an effort to enforce a putative nationalism, military training reinforces such divisions.

Some men in fact find military service intolerable and may even go to the extreme of deserting, which undermines the military's omnipotent self-representation and is viewed as treasonous. Félix Chuquimia recounted to me how his commanding officers on a lowland base in the 1980s obliged him and other highland conscripts to beat a paceño deserter who had been captured and returned. In another instance, according to Chuquimia, commanding officers forced two deserters to dress as women: "The officials forced them to trot around the base carrying their [unloaded] guns, bricks, and old tires. They had to shout, 'I'm a woman, not a man.' One of them even fainted a couple of times, and we [the troops] were ordered to throw water on them. If we did not obey, the officials would punish us. This is what happens to people for deserting. You just have to endure." In this instance, commanding officers identified traitors with women. By involving highland conscripts in the deserters' punishment, these lowland-born officers not only made the conscripts accomplices but also reinforced a militarized male identity closely linked to patriotic duty and separated from specific regional and ethnic identifications.

We have seen that a concerted effort by the armed forces to forge such connections among the lower classes dates only to the 1952 revolution. The populist nationalism of the MNR and, most important, the financial support of the U.S. government were necessary for incorporating large numbers of men into the armed services. Yet because of the inherent difficulty—indeed, the impossibility—of completely incorporating a dominated people into an allegedly homogeneous national community, contemporary examples of peasants, miners, and slum dwellers' actively opposing the armed forces and the state are numerous (Barrios de Chungara 1978; Nash 1979; Justicia y Paz 1975). This opposition has also been passive.

The return of civilian rule in 1982 tempered the military's domination of society, and the armed forces experienced more difficulty filling their troop quotas in the 1980s, when the numbers of young men who responded to recruitment calls declined. After public threats to draft dodgers failed to produce the desired effects, the armed forces on several occasions resorted to kidnapping and conscription sweeps of poor neighborhoods. In the highland city of Oruro, for example, military personnel dressed in civilian clothing infiltrated a soccer game and seized several men who could not prove that they had completed military service ("Religiosos denuncian abusos" 1987). A year later parents and school directors in La Paz denounced the military police for apprehending male students as they left school ("Se denuncia persecución" 1988). Similarly, peasant leaders of the Confederación Sindical Única de Trabajadores Campesinos de Bolivia (CSUTCB), a national peasant confederation, annoyed the military high command in 1990 with a resolution that urged parents and their sons to ignore the military's calls for recruits. Leaders argued that young men should not lend themselves to the repression of their own people and the further militarization of the coca-producing regions.[5]

By the 1980s young men—particularly those from urban areas—became less willing to dedicate a year of their lives to military service for a number of reasons. Some felt that military service obstructed their pursuit of higher education and taught them nothing that was useful in civilian life. Those with the means to pursue a public university education in La Paz were most likely to express this view. For others, the revelations of widespread military corruption, fiscal mismanagement, and human rights abuses that became public in the aftermath of military rule diminished the appeal of the armed forces, and conditions on military bases grew steadily worse during the economic crisis. Despite their discontent, however, most of these men were generally not protesting military service per se; rather, they were unhappy with the military's inability to offer them better prospects for the future.

Press accounts reported steep cutbacks of 46 to 56 percent of the annual military budget during 1986.[6] The advent of neoliberalism led to the privatization of fourteen military-operated enterprises, caused supply shortages on several bases, undermined the practice of compulsory military service, and produced a crisis among officers, who complained that their salaries were insufficient to maintain lifestyles commensurate with their rank.[7] The latter claimed that they had to moonlight in other occupations and that their wives had to take jobs. The vision of wives toiling for wages was, they asserted, the most powerful symbol of their collective denigration by the state, and it diminished the prestige of the armed forces.

Nowadays troops often find themselves forced to work illegally for civilians to supplement the inadequate food rations that the army provides. In 1992, for example, the state allocated a paltry 25 cents per day to feed and clothe each soldier. Born in an indigenous highland community, Felix Amaya performed his military service in the 1980s, when he was sent to an army base in the eastern lowlands. The food, according to Amaya, "was really dramatic. There was a time when it was basically just water. We'd get five beans and a piece of bone swimming in water. Just soup." To deal with the situation Amaya and other troops like him sought clandestine work with civilians so that they could purchase food from merchants, even though their activities violated strict army rules. Amaya explained:

> Generally, we went to a small town on Sundays to work for the merchants. They gave us food and a few little things for the week, but it was very dangerous to work there. A few guys were caught and punished by the army, who told them that they had made the institution look bad. From then on, I went to the countryside, where I got to know some people who became almost like family to me. I helped

them clear their fields and plant corn and yucca. They would feed me on Sundays and give me as much food as I could hide in my knapsack and carry back to the base.

Similarly, Daniel Saval, who served near the Chilean border in the 1980s, commented that "the food was really terrible. Very few provisions reached the frontier [bases]. We ate soup in which a few little noodles danced around. That is why you had to bring your own provisions from home."

The military increasingly obliges families of army conscripts to subsidize its budget with their own meager resources. The armed forces do not publicly acknowledge the burden that poor families are assuming, but one army official, whom I interviewed in 1995, is highly critical of what he privately refers to as an unofficial "enrollment tax" [*tasa de inscripción*]. He describes how the poorest families pay a disproportionate share of this "tax," because their children are commonly posted on remote, poorly equipped bases. Relatives—especially mothers—must travel long distances to take food, bedding, and medicines to their sons, and they incur substantial transportation and lodging expenses in the process.

A female street vendor in El Alto provided more details. When her son entered the army, she had to purchase the requisite boots for him, because the military did not have the money to provide them. Moreover, when the military sent the boy to a cold remote post on the Chilean frontier, she made the long journey to the base every two weeks to take food and other provisions to him. The journeys not only consumed the meager income that she—a single mother—earned as a street vendor but she also had to spend money on what she described as *un hotel de mala muerte* (a bad death hotel), because she could not stay on the base. To make matters worse, the military has stranded some recruits who have completed their patriotic duty, forcing them to pay for transportation to return home. This not only created problems for the young men but also considerable worry and hardship for their family members. On at least one occasion exasperated parents protested the treatment of their sons in front of El Alto's bases.

Hundreds of parents from the peasant communities surrounding El Alto denounced military commanders in 1992 and threatened to go on a hunger strike, because the army had abandoned their sons in the eastern lowlands. The young men had enlisted at the army and air force bases in El Alto and were then shipped out to posts in the departments of El Beni and Pando. Upon completing their tour of duty, however, the military did not return the soldiers to El Alto. Parents, who had been in El Alto awaiting the arrival of their sons for almost a month, complained that they were being compelled to spend money unnecessarily in the city. They also claimed that the army was no longer supporting their children, who were working for local farmers in order to maintain themselves until the military sent them back.[8]

Despite their unhappiness, however, these parents were not protesting military service; they were simply demanding that the military take better care of its charges. Most Aymara peasant families and urban immigrants continue to support compulsory male military service. Popular ideas about how a boy becomes a man and a citizen in highland communities and El Alto exist in tense interaction with the increasing physical and financial burden that the armed forces place on poor men and their families. Such ideas not only aid the state's conscription efforts but threaten the masculinities of young men who do not serve in the military. Popular notions of masculinity emerge in part from the efforts of male peasants and poor urban dwellers to engage dominant institutions, such as the military, in order to prove their worth, find personal dignity, and establish claims to membership in the nation. But in so doing the oppressed may simultaneously become collusive with their very domination by participating in the creation of beliefs about masculinity, femininity, and citizenship that are destructive within their communities and households.

Sissies and "New Citizens": Suffering for Manhood

A complex array of pressures and motivations prompts young Bolivian men from La Paz, El Alto, and the surrounding hinterland to enlist in the armed forces every year. For some young men the military offers the possibility of adventure and an opportunity to visit other parts of the country. According to the military itself, service provides recruits with opportunities to learn electrical, mechanical, and carpentry skills, yet only one of the men I interviewed mentioned the acquisition of skills useful in civilian life as a reason for serving. Although the reasons have varied over time, two primary explanations for responding to the military's biannual calls for men stand out among former soldiers: the importance of the *libreta militar* (military booklet—essentially an honorable discharge), which documents the successful completion of military duty and is required for key transactions with the state and for obtaining work in urban factories and businesses, and the desire to validate themselves as men in the eyes of families, peers, and communities. Establishing themselves as men requires the competence necessary to support themselves and a family amid considerable economic adversity and to participate in community positions of authority.

Obtaining the military booklet is not a concern for middle- and upper-class young men who wish to avoid military service. Once past the age of twenty-three, when an individual is no longer eligible for service, a man may pay a fee to obtain equivalent documentation. The cost in recent years has varied from $200 to $500, which is prohibitive for men from poor peasant and urban backgrounds, because they typically earn only a few dollars for an entire day's labor.[9]

For poor men military service is the only practical means of acquiring the military booklet, which is quite literally a prerequisite for citizenship. Only with this document can a man register with the state and acquire a national identity card. The libreta is also indispensable for other key relationships with the state, such as obtaining a passport or a degree from the state university. Similarly, military documentation is essential for obtaining employment in many businesses and factories of urban La Paz, where employers use it to guarantee a disciplined Spanish-speaking labor force.

The military booklet is thus part of the civilizing process that symbolically incorporates young men into the nation and the capitalist discipline of the labor process. Furthermore, with the collusion of their commanding officers, recruits may use the booklet as a way to change their Indian surnames to Spanish ones. But while it symbolically creates citizens, the booklet also facilitates the converse: the categorization of "aliens" within the boundaries of the state, a designation that is all too close to the lived experiences of poor men.

The experiences of former tin miner Raul Gutiérrez illustrate the subtle and overt forms of violence associated with processes of exclusion and incorporation. When I interviewed him, Gutiérrez recognized the importance of the military booklet for the professional aspirations of his son, whom he had sent off to boot camp even though the senior Gutiérrez hates the army and is frightened by the sight of soldiers. Gutiérrez survived a horrific army massacre in the Caracoles tin mine after the 1980 military coup d'état of General Luís García Meza, and intolerable working conditions subsequently forced Gutiérrez and his family to move to El Alto to search for other work. According to Gutiérrez:

> The military entered the mine and went on a rampage. We thought the soldiers were drugged, because they were foaming at the mouth. They beat everybody that they caught and killed innocent people. They raped women and even put dynamite in the mouths of some

people and blew it up. People had to crawl like dogs to find hiding places, where they were forced to remain for the three days that the army occupied the mine. . . . To this day I hate and fear the army. Soldiers think that they can take advantage of people because they wear a uniform.

Gutiérrez, however, recognizes the importance of military documentation. "It's an indispensable document," he said. "My sons are going to be professionals some day, and they will be asked for their military booklets." Indeed, the military's continuing regulation of society and Gutiérrez's hopes of a professional future for his sons virtually require a passive stance toward the military repression that he has experienced in the past. The military domination of Bolivian society has in this way reshaped aspects of social life.

For many young men the importance of establishing their manhood is also a central reason for military service. They believe that service is indispensable to becoming responsible disciplined men who are capable of making decisions, heading a family, and commanding others. As Felix Mamani, a rural immigrant who resides in El Alto, told me, "In the countryside, people think that you are a coward if you don't go to the barracks; that is, they think you're like a woman. The community pushes young men toward military service, and [we] have to go in order not to be faggots. It's a question of manliness." Residents of highland Aymara communities refer to returning peasant recruits as *machaq ciudadano*, or literally, new citizen, and, if domestic resources permit, celebrate them with eating, drinking, and dancing. Rolando Cusicanqui, a twenty-six-year-old immigrant from the Lake Titicaca region, understood machaq ciudadano as someone who is "able to be fully involved in society and participate with adults. Someone who is considered to be a responsible person and who can fully take part in a series of events, meetings, and so forth." Similarly, when Fernando Huanca falsified his birth certificate in 1974 to enter the military when he was still too young to enlist legally, he did so because he had heard about the "new citizens" and wanted to be one. According to Huanca:

I was born in Igachi and grew up an orphan. When I was fifteen or sixteen years old, the other boys always acted like they were better than me. Seeing the way that they behaved, I thought, I'm also a man. I'm also someone [*gente*]. What difference is there between someone who goes to the barracks and one who does not? I wanted to understand this. I'd heard about new citizens, and for the pride [of being a new citizen], I enlisted.

In the immigrant neighborhoods of El Alto and La Paz the connections between manhood and citizenship are equally evident, if somewhat more diffuse. Military service is not so directly linked to the assumption of community positions of authority, but young men still hope to earn the respect of families and peers by participating in a rite of passage that is understood as a prerequisite for full male adulthood and a duty of every good Bolivian man. They also hope to obtain the documentation necessary for permanent positions in a factory, business, or state agency and thus escape from the poverty and insecurity of the informal economy.

One day, for example, I was chatting with Orlando Huañapaco, twenty-one, and his fiancée, Alicia Quispe, about their upcoming wedding. When I asked if they were nervous about getting married, Quispe confessed to some premarital jitters, but Huañapaco denied any such unmanly emotions. "How could I be nervous," he asked rhetorically, "when I have done my military service?" He then went on to describe his recent experiences in the army. According to Huañapaco, his commanding officer had forced him to stand naked in front of a large number of troops, and he maintained that the experience had forced him to develop nerves of steel. His account was clearly intended to impress his fiancée and me and to demonstrate that he was a mature adult, capable of assuming the responsibilities of a married man. Yet unbeknown to his fiancée, Huañapaco had never completed military service, because he injured his back in a fight with another recruit and had to seek a medical discharge. Struggling against chronic back pain, Huañapaco, with the help of his grandfather, was quietly saving money to buy his way out of any further military service, and he was clearly worried that others would perceive him as inadequate for doing so.

His anxieties were similar to those of Francisco Pérez. Pérez recalled the mockery of his high school peers, who claimed he was not man enough to bear the rigors of military life. Pérez, a self-described loner, says that these taunts stimulated a flood of self-doubt and that this was among the reasons he enlisted in the late 1980s. He remembered that after completing the obligatory year in the military, his father, who had always encouraged him to enlist, began to treat him very differently. "'You've been to the barracks,'" Pérez said his father told him. "'Now you are a man and can do what you want with your life. You can marry or do anything that you please.'" Like Pérez, other informants recounted how their families prohibited them from consuming alcoholic beverages before they did their military service and how their families invariably lifted this prohibition after their return home.

Key to the transformation of these young men is the experience of suffering. Suffering is not only something that they anticipate before enlisting but also an experience that, when safely in the past, they constantly embellish and reinvent, as ex-soldiers represent themselves to others and assert claims within evolving social relationships. Given the myriad ways in which these young men and their families suffer every day of their lives with poor health, low wages, bad harvests, and racism, it is shocking to listen to them boast of their transformative experiences of hardship, which must be understood as part of a desperate and painful search for dignity and self-worth.[10]

Rufino Amaya, for example, dreamed of and eventually received a posting to a distant frontier base in the tropical lowlands, where living conditions were particularly harsh. The isolation of the base meant that during weekend leaves he could not visit friends and family members, and he frequently did not have enough to eat because commanding officers were selling troop rations for personal profit. The food shortages prompted him to work as an agricultural laborer during leaves so that he could buy bread and other basic necessities, even though working for civilians was a punishable offense. Yet, as Amaya told me, "The person who goes to the barracks, especially from the highlands, suffers a lot during the year, but those who do not serve never experience what corporal punishment is like and are more or less semi-men. [People in my community] criticize the ones who serve nearby. They say that they've just been to the kitchen."

Amaya went on to describe how highland men like himself were better suited for the rigorous tests of military manhood. "[In my group] we were one hundred sixty-one paceños and eighty *orientales* [residents of the eastern lowlands]. The orientales were very weak . . . and when things got rough, they started deserting. But the *colla* [highlander] man—as they call us—deserts very little, because he is able to endure any kind of hard work." Many other informants related similar accounts. One individual even likened the Aymaras' propensity for military service and allegedly superior soldiering abilities to their history as a "warlike people."[11]

We can recognize a number of self-destructive beliefs in these assertions: suffering is a prerequisite for manhood; people like themselves can tolerate suffering more than others; and Aymaras have special abilities for warfare. To make these claims is to participate in the making of a dominant fiction. It creates a virtue from suffering, a condition imposed on the Aymaras by both the military and, more generally, the form that class and ethnic domination takes in Bolivia. It also links extreme suffering in the military with an exalted form of manhood and thereby denies the very real daily suffering of women and other men who cannot or will not participate in the rituals of militarized masculinity. Finally, it misconstrues Aymara history, in which warfare was integral to the process of Incan and particularly European domination but has little to do with any essential Aymara characteristics.

At this point we must explore in greater depth the way that militarism and men's experiences in the military shape ongoing social relationships in their home communities and neighborhoods. How specifically do militarized notions of masculinity inform the relationships between male peers, between men and women, and between subaltern men and male members of the white middle and upper classes? And how too are these beliefs sustained in the context of inequality?

Contending with Militarism in Daily Life

Recruits never do become true citizens after completing military service and returning to civilian life. This happens despite the civilizing mission of the armed forces, the concerted efforts to produce "real men," and the considerable extent to which young men claim and assert destructive imposed beliefs about themselves in their search for respect. The realization of their continuing marginalization leaves many men feeling disillusioned, and they question the point of dedicating a year of their lives to the armed forces. In most cases, they are no better prepared for a job than before they entered the military, and the few decent jobs that remain in La Paz after years of economic crisis, restructuring, and state retrenchment cannot possibly accommodate everyone. Young men typically return to their impoverished villages or seek a livelihood as gardeners, chauffeurs, part-time construction workers, and vendors in the urban informal economy and in low-paid positions, such as police officer, in the state bureaucracy. Thus excluded from the economic rewards of the dominant society, they remain ineluctably "Indian" in its eyes, and some, not surprisingly, conclude that the entire experience was an enormous waste of time.

Of course, men's military experience varies, as does their understanding of militarism. The experience of military service, once safely in the past, assumes different meanings for them in the context of changing social relationships in the present. Felix Amaya, for his part, understood the military very differently as a university student and former Socialist Party member than he did thirteen years earlier as a teenage army recruit fresh from the countryside. "Look," he told me, "peasants in civilian life understand who the army defends. I went to the barracks with a lot of expectations. I thought that afterward I would easily get a job [in the city], and I thought that people in the city would respect me. But it wasn't that way. . . . Everything was false. It was then that I realized that the army just protects the bourgeoisie, but that was only after I got out."

In failing to meet the expectations of Amaya and other recruits like him, the military has trained a potential source of opposition. Yet the nature of the opposition is ambiguous. Military service, as mentioned earlier, is key to acquiring certain kinds of urban jobs that provide a modicum of economic security. It is also important for participating in the male world of formal community politics, taking part in discussions and decisions, establishing a family, and being perceived by others as a leader. These men do not easily cast aside the suffering, male camaraderie, and discipline that supposedly made them male citizens in the first place, because these factors help to ratify male empowerment by excluding women and those subaltern men who have not passed through the armed forces. These forms of male entitlement constitute an affirmation of male citizenship, albeit of a subordinate form within the broader context of Bolivian society.

Military experience also provides ammunition for the construction of masculinity and the assertion of male power in other settings. It is typically part of the repartee of all-male social gatherings, such as weekend drinking parties, which closely combine male solidarity and competition. Exaggerated tales of suffering, hyperbolic anecdotes of bravery in the face of fear, and inflated accounts of cleverness when confronted by abusive superiors shape the male bonding that occurs amid the music blaring from cassette players, commentaries on daily life, and invitations to drink.[12] Yet this bantering and one-upmanship can easily move from friendly jousting to violent competition and thus become a form of domination and ranking among men.[13]

Whatever the outcome, though, stories of military life—which, as Broyles (1990:33) notes, are usually false in important details—are always about buttressing the power of certain kinds of men. These stories link a particular concept of masculinity to military performance. Some men use military tales to enhance the importance of their militarized identities and to exclude from key arenas of male sociality both young men and those who have not passed through the armed forces. They also, of course, exclude women, who usually hover in the background during these gatherings and await a summons to bring the next round of beer.

Former conscripts also use the competence and citizenship equated with postmilitary manhood to assert their dignity and claim respect from more powerful middle- and upper-class males. The latter view military service as a waste of time they can more usefully spend studying, and they fear the prospect of serving with Indian and lower-class men in a context in which military hierarchies theoretically take precedence over class and ethnic ones. Some even view the soldiers' claims to manhood as presumptuous. One individual, for example, criticized the peasant practice of requiring military service for male marriage partners because it was, he claimed, based on mistaken beliefs about how men acquire a sense of responsibility. Ex-soldiers are highly critical of these men, whom they view as unpatriotic sissies. One scoffed:

> They're mamas' boys. They come from a different social class than we do, and their form of thinking and reasoning is so distinct that they forget about their patriotic duty. They are much more individualistic [than we are]; they forget about the nation so that they can be totally independent. The upper class only thinks about its future and its social position and generally not about the country and what could happen one day.

This man and others like him were particularly critical when, in early 1995, a public scandal enveloped a high-ranking government official who had falsified his military booklet to avoid service.[14] Sixty-year-old Rufino Tejar, for example, was absolutely disgusted. He sneered:

> These parliamentarians say that they are the fathers of the country, but they are the first ones to avoid the barracks. These little gentlemen wouldn't know where to shoot. They always come from privileged families. They're mamas' boys. They can fix anything with money, but then they fill these government positions and demand that everyone else obey the law. They should be removed from their jobs and obliged to serve in the military at their age.

Tejar's remarks that these men claim to be "the fathers of the country" suggest something of the paternalism and the denigration that shapes the reality of actual encounters between men of different classes. It is as waiters, gardeners, chauffeurs, shoe shiners, handymen, and janitors that indigenous and poor urban men typically meet white males of the upper class. These structurally subordinate positions require them to display deference, subordination, and humility. They are not only demeaning but also place men in relationships to more powerful males that are analogous to those of women in male-female relationships. Because lower-class men cannot command the labor power of others and they possess none of the wealth necessary to embellish an elegant lifestyle and control, provide for, and protect women, these men and those from subordinate ethnic groups experience greater difficulty backing up their claims of personal power and sexual potency than their class and ethnic superiors. Moreover, the class privileges of the latter enable them to develop a well-mannered, dignified, and controlled masculinity, one that is contrasted with the behavior of poor men. Depending on the context, poor men may be labeled weak and ineffectual by elite whites *or* condemned for impulsive and irrational outbursts of violence.

Thus in certain contexts many poor urban and peasant men have considerable difficulty cultivating and defending a positive image of themselves as men vis-à-vis more dominant males. Surviving the trials and tribulations of military service is one way in which they can affirm their masculine power and rights to citizenship. In the absence of recruits from the upper echelons of Bolivian society, poor urban and indigenous men can claim the experience of compulsory military service as strictly their own and use it as a weapon in their ongoing struggles for respect and dignity in a society that routinely denies them both.

We should, however, view their assertions with caution. It is important to bear in mind that subordinate and dominant notions of masculinity degrade women and are premised in large part on the ability of men to control and dominate women. Given this, we might expect to find women in highland Aymara communities and the villas of El Alto considerably less enthusiastic about military service than their male family members. Some evidence does exist to support such a view. Mothers commonly recall the tears and deep sadness with which they dispatched their sons to the barracks; they also remember the fears that their sons would be abused in the armed forces and return permanently disabled. Yet these women hope that completing military service and obtaining the requisite documentation will ensure a more prosperous future for their sons. Indeed, a mother struggling too hard to withhold her son from the military might be seen as depriving him of the chance to attain full male adulthood.[15]

Those women whose sons have no prospects of upward mobility provide the most enthusiastic support for compulsory military service. Many of these women, like men, believe that military training and discipline will produce responsible, mature adult males, and they have ample reasons to want this to occur. Men who are unable or unwilling to support their families; who spend hard-earned cash on drink, cigarettes, and other women; and who are physically abusive frequently disappoint poor women. Military service, the women hope, will develop men into reliable, serious adults and serve as a guarantee to women and their male relatives that a prospective husband will fulfill his social and economic responsibilities to the domestic unit.

These women are suspicious of men who have not done military service. A street vendor in El Alto, for example, described disparagingly a forty-year-old male acquaintance who never served. "He gets occasional jobs that don't pay well, but he can't go to work in a factory [because he doesn't have his military booklet]," she explained. "This is where irresponsibility comes from. The military booklet structures one's future and encourages responsibility." She went on to discuss how women who get stuck with such men have to work more outside the home to support their families.

Men may in fact become more responsible—in other words, dedicated to family and home—after military service. Rufino Pérez, for example, told me that he "saw things more seriously" after returning from the barracks in the 1990s. "I wasn't the same prankster that I had been before," he said. "My friends noted this and so did my family. In my community, when one arrives from the barracks, people give you more responsibilities because you are now one among adults. I was no longer juvenile and assumed these responsibilities myself. I was another member of society."

Yet men's relationships to militarism do not always bring positive benefits for the women whom they encounter in civilian life. The experiences of Arminda Mamani illustrate how the expectations of women are frequently unfulfilled. Arminda Mamani, forty-five, is a divorcee with two sons. Born into a family of artisans in a small provincial town, she moved to La Paz in 1970 and was working as a secretary when we met. Mamani's two sons lived without a father in the home for most of their lives, and she always encouraged them to pursue respect and economic security through higher education instead of going into the military. She viewed the military as a waste of time and did not want her sons to associate with "Indians" in the barracks. However, her ex-husband, his female relatives, and his six brothers strongly opposed her views. This side of the family maintained a strong tradition of male military service and constantly chided Mamani's elder son, Sergio, for failing to enlist. Sergio, for his part, was content with his decision not to serve. He had not only his mother's full support but a newfound sense of dignity as the first member of his family to attend university.

Despite her success with Sergio, Mamani was frustrated with her younger son. This boy, Pancho, became a juvenile delinquent in high school; he constantly skipped classes, stole household items and sold them on the street, and argued incessantly with his mother. "Every year that he was in school," Mamani said, "I told him that if he didn't study and behave better, I was going to send him to the barracks." She finally carried out the threat and successfully appealed to an acquaintance with military connections to have the boy sent as far away as possible. She was backed up by her sisters, who, like Mamani, viewed the barracks as a reform school for problem boys. Pancho spent a year in the army on the lowland frontier but, according to Mamani, returned worse than he had departed.

> When he returned, I realized that it had not done him any good, and he was not reformed. The only thing that he acquired was his military booklet, but he was even more obnoxious than before. He thought that he had more rights, because now he was a man, an adult, and could therefore do whatever he felt like. Just because he had his military booklet, he thought he could arrive home at whatever time he pleased and get drunk whenever he wished. He told me that I wasn't a good mother because I didn't give a party when he returned, like all the others [families].

The disappointment that Arminda Mamani felt about her son's sojourn in the military is not uncommon. Indeed, the high level of domestic violence in El Alto suggests that many men are not living up to women's expectations. In 1993, 53 percent of the reported incidences of violence in El Alto involved cases of violence against women, and of these cases the overwhelming majority (87 percent) entailed abuse by spouses or male companions (Subsecretaría 1994). Although domestic violence is far too complex a phenomenon to be reduced to the effects of militarization on men, such abuse does reflect the strains that poverty and another decade of "lost development" are placing on men and women, as well as the misogyny inherent in military training.

Women are not the only people who are disappointed by male military service. As previously mentioned, many veterans are critical of military service because it provided them with little preparation or training for meaningful jobs in civilian life. These complaints, and the complete avoidance of military service by those with access to a university education, pose a growing challenge to the armed forces. How can they sustain the legitimacy of male military service when the "communist" threat has subsided and the military itself is increasingly unable to live up to popular expectations?

The armed forces must increasingly address this question, and a broad sector of the civilian population is pressing them to do so, because these citizens believe that the military should play a more constructive role in a democracy. The armed forces are experimenting with a variety of solutions. Under considerable popular pressure, they implemented a "premilitary" program in 1996 for high school students that enables them to complete military service on weekends and holidays. The program does not disrupt their studies and enables graduates to pursue work or higher education without sacrificing a year to the army. Some sectors of the armed forces are also seeking to harness military service to social and economic "development" schemes in Aymara communities of the altiplano and in the poor neighborhoods of El Alto. Their halting turn to development is not entirely new. Indeed, a concern for "security and development" preoccupied the armed forces during the cold war and prompted several development and civic action initiatives at the time. The renewed interest emerges from growing concern about the future of the Bolivian armed forces, particularly the direction and continued legitimacy of male military service. The outcome has profound implications for the changing relationship between the armed forces and impoverished peoples.

Hearts and Minds

The growing immiseration of Bolivian society and changing geopolitics have prompted calls for the armed forces to play a more constructive role in ameliorating the economic hardships, one that breaks with the authoritarian and repressive practices associated with the era of military rule. And, although the armed forces would like to play a bigger part in the U.S.-sponsored war on drugs, the involvement of high-ranking officers in the illegal cocaine traffic has limited its ability to do so. The U.S. government is highly suspicious of the willingness and ability of the armed forces to combat cocaine smuggling, and it has partially bypassed the traditional armed forces by training and financing UMOPAR (Unidad Móvil de Patrullaje Rural), a militarized police force also known as the "Leopardos," to fight the drug war. Although UMOPAR has ties to the armed forces, it works closely with the U.S. Drug Enforcement Administration, and career advancement is subject to the approval of the U.S. embassy in La Paz. The traditional armed forces' involvement in the drug war is technically limited to a few key activities: three air force units support counternarcotics operations; the navy assists UMOPAR river patrols for drugs; and the army provides transportation for certain operations (Human Rights Watch/Americas 1996).

Also, militant unions assert the right of peasants to grow coca, and many civilians from various walks of life believe that the cultivation of coca leaves is less destabilizing than the harsh measures that the United States imposes to suppress it. In addition, the U.S. war against drug dealers and coca growers provokes strong nationalist sentiments among many Bolivians, who believe that the United States should first address the drug problem at home. Most important, however, is that Bolivians understand that laundered drug money sustains the national economy in numerous ways at a time when traditional sources of foreign exchange, such as tin, have collapsed (Léons and Sanabria 1997). For these reasons, then, an expanded military role in the drug war has little support.

With little domestic enthusiasm for fighting a war declared by the United States, and circumvented by UMOPAR, the armed forces must craft a new mission even as structural adjustment reforms have reduced their state-allocated budget. Certain segments of the military elite have begun to stake out new territory by advocating military-inspired social and economic development initiatives. Such initiatives, they claim, demonstrate the willingness of the armed forces to address Bolivia's dire poverty and to participate in a democratic society, and they use this argument to approach international development organizations for the financing to implement these programs.

In 1986, for example, Luis Fernando Valle, then the minister of defense, responded to cuts in his ministry by claiming that "the armed forces are not necessarily charged with military tasks but also teach twenty-five thousand peasant conscripts to read and write every year . . . [and this] benefits the entire nation."[16] Five years later the Defense Ministry acquired financial support from the United Nations to provide literacy training to conscripts.[17] It also obtained financial support from Germany to use army recruits to implement a reforestation scheme, and another internationally financed military project—Campaña de Acción Comunitaria Multiple (CADACOM)—promoted health and infrastructure endeavors in highland communities.

The Centinelas de la Salud program also emerged in the context of the military's civic-mindedness. Initiated in 1992 with funding from the Pan American Health Organization, the World Bank, and other prominent international development agencies, Centinelas de la Salud is in effect on all the nation's military bases. Over a ten-year period its annual goal is to teach basic health concepts and disease prevention procedures to thirty to forty thousand male conscripts. The program takes several weeks; conscripts attend after they finish their three months of basic training, and drill sergeants and low-level officers, who are mestizos, carry out the instruction.

Young men learn about the microorganic causes of disease and the importance of vaccinations for disease prevention. The teaching also focuses on hygiene, diet, and sanitation as cornerstones of good health, and it pays considerable attention to maternal health, child development, family planning, and sexually transmitted diseases. The objectives are twofold: to educate future male household heads about primary health care and disease prevention, and to use veterans to disseminate this information in poor rural communities and urban neighborhoods after they complete their military service (MDH/SNS 1994).

Instructors use military terminology instead of medical terms to educate young recruits. Thus the program depicts pathogenic microorganisms as enemy invaders, the human body as the Bolivian nation, and the skin as the national border, which is subject to "penetration" by the enemy. Infections become battles between good defenders and bad enemies that are fought with armaments such as pills, or prevented with vaccinations, which carry instructions to the defenders. Instructors then extend these analogies to explain particular diseases. For example, they describe tuberculosis as the work of delinquent subversives, otherwise known as guerrillas, who silently entrench themselves in the lungs. To combat these tenacious enemies, the body's defenders need abundant arms (i.e., medications) and many months to confront and ultimately annihilate the tubercular threat. Soldiers also learn that "enemy invasions" can cause postpartum health complications. Problems arise when women give birth in unsanitary conditions, which permit enemy invaders to penetrate the womb's "unprotected frontiers" and wreak havoc on the female body.[18]

Janette Vidaurre, the national coordinator of Centinelas de la Salud, claims that the program has been a huge success. It boasts eighty thousand trained recruits since its inception, and project supporters eagerly point to the multiplier effect that these individuals, and those still to be trained, will have on society. Vidaurre also defends the use of military language and instructors. She maintains that military terminology is the easiest language for troops to understand after three months of basic training and asserts that military officials make good instructors because of their brutality. She explains that "they teach them with the whip" [*les enseñan con huasca*]. Vidaurre can also produce test results from before and after the program that document conscripts' expanded knowledge, and she has many glowing program evaluations from the soldiers themselves. Yet closer analysis reveals reasons for skepticism about both Vidaurre's claims and the fundamental goal of the project.

The program continues a long tradition of racist paternalism toward peasants and indigenous peoples, whereby the goal of military service is to incorporate Indians into an ostensibly homogeneous nation. Describing what she perceives to be one of the program's major contributions, Vidaurre states that children cared for by program veterans are "of particularly clean appearance and had some good habits not commonly seen in the ethnic groups to which they belonged" (Vidaurre 1994:345). Similarly, two colonels found the assimilationist possibilities of the Centinelas de la Salud program encouraging. One told me that the health program "teaches troops how to brush their teeth with toothpaste, which they normally don't know how to do, and then go home and demonstrate the same skills to people in their communities."

The paternalism and the condescension of these officials is overshadowed, however, by far more serious problems. For the military, household heads are male by definition, and the program seeks to strengthen men's positions within households, rural communities, and poor urban neighborhoods. The instruction infuses health care and disease prevention with highly gendered, militaristic beliefs about the body. This militarized medical knowledge empowers men and then encourages them to take control of women's bodies in the context of their homes. Centinelas de la Salud thus aggravates preexisting gender inequalities, and it blurs civilian and military spheres by further embedding military beliefs and values in Bolivian society.

The merging of civilian and military arenas extends well beyond the household. Centinelas de la Salud also seeks to develop ties between public health care workers, ex-soldiers, and the military. Conscripts who graduate from Centinelas de la Salud are encouraged by military officials to register with public health clinics, and to act as unpaid health care extension workers when they return to civilian life. Their volunteer work might include reporting outbreaks of contagious diseases, participating in campaigns to eliminate garbage dumps, constructing latrines and distributing vaccinations, or organizing "community talks" about preventative medicine (MDM/SNS 1994). Public health clinics are also supposed to give preferential treatment to the veterans and the people they refer for treatment. The program thus seeks to provide the armed forces with a role in public health care at a time when civilian social service agencies, particularly those charged with health care, are withering.

Although it is still too early to judge the success of Centinelas de la Salud, the program represents the "soft" side of the military's continuing efforts to control poor Bolivians, who have always been at the center of the armed forces' concerns about order and disorder. "Development" and security concerns are not only issues for the Bolivian military but also a growing consideration of the militaries of the United States and other Latin American countries. For example, the U.S. Defense Department's budget for civic action programs in Bolivia expanded by 650 percent between 1996 and 1998 (Latin America Working Group 1998). The U.S. military carries out civic action initiatives during army exercises and training operations that take place primarily in the Chapare and lowland regions, where the United States considers drug trafficking a problem. Civic action in these areas consists of road construction, vaccination campaigns, and well digging, and both Bolivian civilian and military personnel frequently participate.[19]

By appearing to address pressing social issues, the U.S. and Bolivian militaries hope to strengthen their legitimacy in a nominally democratic Bolivian society. The Bolivian military also hopes to capture additional funding from leading international aid agencies, as its longtime patron, the United States, channels funding exclusively to combat the lowland drug traffic. Development funding can help to sustain compulsory military service in Bolivia and bolster the military's pretensions of addressing the country's dire poverty. Yet shoring up patriarchy, militarizing the delivery of health care, and relying on unpaid soldiers to sustain an underfunded health care system are hardly solutions. Such practices could contribute to simmering discontent with the status quo and tempt the Bolivian military to abandon its current willingness to tolerate some forms of political democracy and return to the more oppressive forms of rule that characterized the past. These practices could also continue to incorporate increasing numbers of poor Bolivians and deepen the militarization of everyday life.

The military remains the most important, and increasingly the only, state institution with which poor alteños must contend. As it seeks to define a new mission in the post–cold war era, the armed forces are faced with the growing impoverishment of Bolivian society and the resulting tensions and conflicts. Even if the military manages to respond to the requests of the poor for more skills and opportunities, the life circumstances of impoverished people are unlikely to improve. Young conscripts are even more likely to turn against the world of poor and indigenous people—the very world to which they belong.

Part 2

•

Reconfigurations

7 · Power Lines

On International Women's Day, March 8, 1995, several thousand women and men marched through central La Paz, demanding that the government of Gonzalo Sánchez de Lozada grant wage increases, honor the eight-hour workday, and respect peasants' right to grow coca. Billed as the "March of the Empty Pots," the demonstration was organized by the COB, and it was only one of several that took place in different Bolivian cities. The speeches and rhetoric that preceded the La Paz march condemned the neoliberal policies of the government, which protesters blamed for the increasing impoverishment of the working class. COB leader Cristina Márquez, for example, asserted, "Women will not be on their knees. . . . We have to unite, then men and women together will smash the neoliberal model."[1]

As Márquez spoke these words, about sixty Bolivian professionals were meeting in the upper-middle-class residential neighborhood of Sopocachi, where they formed part of the First Departmental Congress of Nongovernmental Organizations (NGOs). These men and women represented NGOs and NGO networks based in La Paz, and they were meeting at the request of the La Paz department's prefect, who urged them to coordinate NGO activities in order to better represent the needs of civil society to the state and international lending organizations. The NGOs claimed expertise in grassroots development and portrayed themselves as closely allied with "civil society," but none of those present spelled out what this frequently asserted alliance meant. Thus while some working-class Bolivians represented themselves in the boisterous street demonstration, NGO representatives could remain comfortably on the sidelines, where they refrained from making any public statements in support of the marchers' demands.

The NGO representatives gathered in Sopocachi saw themselves at an important crossroad. Following the passage of the 1994 Popular Participation Law, which mandated the decentralization of certain government functions, the state began to embrace NGOs in an unprecedented fashion. It invited NGOs to place their expertise in local development at the service of the state and to collaborate with municipal officials on specific projects. The government representative to the NGO congress, Jorge Inofuentes, argued that by supporting the new law, NGOs could help broaden the reach of the state and make its presence felt in every corner of the country while supporting greater local involvement in participatory development. Considering this request and clarifying their relationship with the state was thus a major priority of the NGO delegates gathered in Sopocachi.

The choice before them appeared fairly clear cut, and it was laid out by an NGO director who gave the keynote address. "The state," he said, "is obliging us to become involved with it. Are we going to continue to be antistate, or are we going to play a functional role within the state?" The apparent urgency of these questions belied the ties that already existed between NGOs and state agencies and that in some cases had been developing for years. Some well-informed NGOs, for example, anticipated the Popular Participation Law long before it became a reality and were already collaborating with municipal officials on development projects. They had understood that decentralization could mean more business for them. Other NGOs maintained close ties with the Ministry of Human Development, which was created by Sánchez de Lozada in 1993, and contributed personnel to the various subsecretariats that comprised it. And for several years most NGOs had developed and managed projects that remained within the general parameters of state-supported neoliberalism.

Some scholars claim that NGOs represent new forms of social organization independent of state tutelage and that they strengthen the ability of poor people to determine their own future (e.g., Cernea 1989; *World Development* 1987; Ritchey-Vance 1990; Edwards and Hulme 1996; and Carroll 1992). They also argue that more effective engagement between NGOs and the state can improve the design and delivery of development programs. Their analyses, however, frequently overlook the ways in which NGOs and states may already be intimately related (e.g., Bebbington and Thiele 1993). These authors, who in some cases are also employed by international development agencies, champion NGOs because of their purported democratic tendencies and their capacity to provide services that enable people to compete in a market economy. Yet, as Fisher (1997) points out, the connections between democracy and development are not always spelled out in their analyses, and they generally accept neoliberalism, rather than critically engage it.

Others scholars are more critical of NGOs and the entire development industry. Escobar, for example, completely rejects the notion of development because of its association with a disabling Western discourse that caricatures subaltern peoples through demeaning stereotypes. He looks to local people, especially social movements, for "alternatives to development" (1995). Although discourses about development are certainly associated with Third World poverty, Escobar's postmodernist approach glosses over the ways in which local people seize on dominant discourses, infuse them with new meaning, and use them in their struggles to create better living conditions. Escobar also completely ignores the nondiscursive material relationships of power that shape broader processes of accumulation and patterns of income distribution, as well as the encounters between local people, NGOs, and the state (Edelman 1999; Little and Painter 1995).

Studies by Edelman (1991), Rivera Cusicanqui (1990), and Arellano-López and Petras (1994) are more attentive to these processes. They question the manner in which greater direct local dependence on international funding by means of NGOs influences the ability of people to determine their future. Edelman (1991), for example, documents how the availability of development aid led a Costa Rican peasant movement to become dependent on foreign "cooperation," creating frictions that contributed to its demise. Similarly, Rivera Cusicanqui (1992) demonstrates that development NGOs that posit the individual as the basic unit of economic development and political democracy undermine indigenous forms of collective organization. And Arellano-López and Petras (1994) argue that NGOs aggravate the isolation of grassroots organizations by enabling the state to ignore them. Through historically situated accounts, these authors explore how peasants and middle-class intellectuals, respectively, maneuver for access to international funding within a changing political and economic context. In their accounts NGOs are less apolitical actors separate from the state than an important arena in which to explore the struggles of contending social groups in local, national, and international contexts.

This chapter examines the context in which diverse development NGOs emerged in Bolivia, particularly in El Alto. It explores the conflicts and the shifting alliances that shaped their relationships to each other and the Bolivian state and that reorganized the relationship between the state and local people. Bolivia experienced a veritable explosion of development NGOs in the 1980s, as state social service agencies retrenched, international organizations sought to palliate the economic crisis, and Bolivians from different walks of life contended with what the United Nations called a "lost decade of development." The NGOs began to assume some social welfare services formerly assigned to the state.

A handful of NGOs had emerged from political struggles in the 1970s. For the most part they were affiliated with progressive European funding agencies and tied to Left-leaning Bolivian political parties. As the neoliberal juggernaut swept Bolivia, however, their agendas not only shifted but they were forced to compete with a new group of "neoliberal" NGOs, linked especially to the U.S. Agency for International Development (USAID). Some of the latter NGOs spearheaded the restructuring of urban inequality by pioneering new forms of surplus extraction and ways to discipline the population through microcredit schemes and food handouts that targeted poor women. These initiatives relied on indebtedness and unwaged female labor to encourage entrepreneurialism, individualism, and competition—key attributes of the kind of capitalist society that they strove to create.

From Opposition to Accommodation: NGOs and the State

During the eighteen years of nearly uninterrupted military rule that preceded Bolivia's redemocratization, a handful of organizations that would subsequently be called NGOs maintained an antagonistic relationship with the Bolivian state. They sought the restitution of democracy, and in some cases the creation of a socialist society, by supporting various popular organizations struggling to establish a foothold under the repressive conditions of dictatorship. In the wake of redemocratization, however, their relationship with the state began to change, and their numbers burgeoned. Conservative figures showed that more than four hundred NGOs emerged in Bolivia during the twelve years between 1980 and 1992, but only one hundred such institutions initiated operations from 1960 to 1980 (Sandóval 1992).

Three sets of events gave rise to "development" or "intermediary" NGOs in Bolivia: the Alliance for Progress (1961), the Second Vatican Council (1965) and the Medellín Congress (1968), and the Banzer coup of 1971. The Alliance for Progress, succeeded in the 1970s by the New Directions mandate for USAID, earmarked funding for local institutions, such as cooperatives, to improve the incomes of the poor. This initiative grew out of a perceived communist threat to the Third World after the Cuban Revolution, and most of the funding was channeled to rural areas, where the communist menace was believed to be greatest. One consequence was the creation of a relatively better-off group of peasants who would presumably not support radical political movements (Gill 1985).

Other Bolivian NGOs arose from religious congregations, especially the Catholic Church. The changes set in motion by the Second Vatican Council and the Medellín Congress, in which the church defined its "preferential option for the poor," moved progressive religious to dedicate more effort to improving the material conditions of the poorest sectors of society and to supporting local forms of democratic organization. Committed individuals founded institutions to work toward this end and dedicated more of their efforts and resources to rural areas.

Finally, and most important, the repressive social and political conditions brought on by the long reign of Hugo Banzer (1971–1978) inspired the growth of a number of secular NGOs dedicated to the struggle for democracy. Although all NGOs did not conceptualize democracy in the same way, they were united in their opposition to the dictatorship. They were typically linked to the Movimiento de Izquierda Revolucionaria (MIR), which was itself connected to the international social democratic movement from which it received financial support. MIR militants founded NGOs with financial support from foreign solidarity groups and development organizations that was channeled through the party. During the dictatorship the MIR Party, more than other parties on the Left, developed NGOs for two reasons: NGOs enabled them to experiment with alternative social programs and to gain experience in running them, and they gave the MIR an opportunity to influence and protect a political base when open debate was impossible. Some MIRistas, like activists from other progressive parties, also acquired jobs with NGOs and used them as a base for their political activities. Although this practice frequently created problems within the institutions, some NGO directors were known to simply look the other way (*hacer la vista gorda*).

A certain mystique enshrouded those NGOs that vied with the Banzer regime and supported local forms of democratic organization in the 1970s and early 1980s, when it was dangerous to do so. These NGOs and the church-affiliated organizations shared many of the same objectives. Their programs focused on popular education and consciousness raising, and personnel commonly circulated between them. As a result, the military harassed both secular and religious NGOs and labeled them "subversive."

With the return of civilian rule, however, NGOs that were once the determined adversaries of the state began to cooperate with it, even as new tensions emerged. At the same time, newer "neoliberal" NGOs appeared that
had never shared the social and political visions of older, more established
organizations. Rivalries developed among and between old and new
NGOs, as they competed with each other for access to an increasing flow
of international development dollars channeled to Bolivia.

The outlines of these relationships began to emerge in 1982, when democratically elected Hernán Siles Suazo was inaugurated as president. Siles
headed the Unidad Democrática Popular (UDP), a coalition that included
the MIR and other centrist and Left-leaning political parties that had opposed the military. The resumption of democratic rule gave NGOs more
space in which to operate. It allowed some NGOs to emerge from the shadows and permitted the founding of a series of new ones.[2] At the same time
the relationships between NGOs and political parties in many cases became
less direct. The parties no longer needed the NGOs for political cover, even
though they continued to covet international funding and the grassroots
constituencies attracted by the NGOs. According to a longtime NGO director, political parties preferred "to control seven municipalities rather than
one NGO."[3] At the same time, many NGOs declared their "autonomy"
from the political parties as a reaction to past "manipulation" by them.

By the late 1980s a new relationship between NGOs and the state had
begun, prompted in part by the worldwide shift to neoliberal policies and
the dissolution of the Left's basic schema for conceptualizing alternative social and economic policies; this framework gave the state a primary role in
providing subsidies to the poor, protecting national industries from foreign
competition through import-substitution policies, and managing key national industries, such as mining, oil, and telecommunications.[4] The approach was discredited in Bolivia by the Left's association with the UDP's
economic policies, which were so disastrous that Siles was forced to leave
office one year before his term expired. The parliamentary Left subsequently became weak and ineffective. Alliances shifted and new factions
emerged. The MIR moved sharply to the Right, and its left wing split off
in 1985 to form the Movimiento Bolivia Libre (MBL), taking most of the
MIR-affiliated NGOs with it.

The structural adjustment reforms of the mid-1980s facilitated a more
conciliatory relationship between NGOs and the state. These reforms
stimulated a flood of international support for nominally private NGOs.
The World Bank and other international organizations supported some
NGOs on the ground that the private sector and unimpeded market forces

could most effectively palliate Bolivia's intractable poverty—especially the heavy social and economic burden that structural adjustment placed on the poor. These international organizations believed that NGOs were more bureaucratically agile, technically proficient, and in touch with the poor than the graft-riddled and inefficient agencies of the state, and large multilateral agencies began to experiment with them. They channeled enormous amounts of resources to NGOs through the Social Emergency Fund, a short-term development initiative that was established in 1985 to palliate the social effects of Paz Estenssoro's economic restructuring program.[5] Between 1985 and 1990 the fund made more than $200 million available for short-term employment and the provision of key social services that the state was increasingly unable to dispense, such as preventative health care and infrastructural development.

Although many NGOs initially refused to work with the Social Emergency Fund, 51 percent of the 551 organizations that received funding from it were NGOs (Sandóval et al. 1989). More foreign aid poured into Bolivia in the late 1980s. In 1988, for example, Bolivia received $392 million in development assistance, and this figure increased to $738.2 million in 1990 (Van Niekerk 1992). NGOs benefited from a portion of these funds, which broke down their initial resistance to structural adjustment and collaboration with the World Bank and the state, and they gradually accepted greater responsibility for fighting poverty within a neoliberal policy context (Graham 1992; Arellano-López and Petras 1994).

Massive government corruption also prompted greater domestic support for NGOs and neoliberal policies. High-ranking officials in the MIR-led administration of Jaime Paz Zamora (1989–1993) were implicated in a series of scandals on a scale that shocked even Bolivians long accustomed to government misconduct. These scandals, accompanied by the simultaneous collapse of Eastern European and Soviet socialism, contributed to a growing public perception among the middle and upper classes that free-market policies and total reliance on the private sector constituted the only viable remedy for the country's dire poverty.[6] NGOs flourished in this environment flush with international funds and support for the private sector. Their numbers grew rapidly, and a new group of neoliberal NGOs began to appear that had no connections to the Bolivian Left, popular movements, or the progressive wing of the Catholic Church. They were heavily supported by USAID and embodied the free-market ideology that was sweeping Bolivia.

The sole purpose of the neoliberal NGOs was to implement the social policies mandated for Bolivia by powerful international organizations. To this end these organizations, which were not limited to Bolivia, operated as private sector alternatives, or replacements, for public sector service delivery and offered "targeted" programs especially designed for certain sectors of the population, such as poor mothers and young children.[7] They questioned the model of universal free social services and promoted targeting as a more efficient means to channel scarce resources to the neediest people in the growing informal urban economy. Their programs in El Alto initially focused on stopgap measures, such as food-for-work schemes that involved poor women, but as the Bolivian economy gradually stabilized, technical training and small business development through the provision of high-interest "microcredit" became the central activity of these NGOs. Program directors tended to see neoliberal policy reforms as an opportunity for the poor rather than as an assault on them. This was, in part, because a high proportion of NGO program directors had earned business degrees or received technical training, and they contrasted with the priests, sociologists, and educators who had staffed Left-leaning NGOs in the 1970s and early 1980s. Yet neoliberal poverty reduction programs did not translate into a significant reduction of poverty in El Alto. This was because "targeting," as Vilas points out, could not answer a basic question: "What does the notion of target groups mean when 60 to 80 percent of the population lives below the poverty line, either because of the impact of structural reform or for pre-existing or other reasons?" (Vilas 1997:24).

A closer look at a food-for-work scheme and microcredit lending reveals how they are creating new inequalities and changing the relationship between local people and the state. Poor women are the linchpin in this process.

Feminizing Poverty and Extracting Surplus: Microcredit and Food-for-Work Programs

Women participate in NGO programs more than men, a phenomenon consistent with the higher levels of female participation in most organizations of civil society. The NGOs of El Alto are especially interested in women: approximately one-third of the city's NGOs deal only with the female residents of the city, and the primary beneficiaries of at least 50 percent of all El Alto NGOs are women. "Gender" (read women) is a fashionable topic among NGOs, and several NGOs perceive women's unpaid labor as a means to combat some of the negative consequences of the economic crisis. Ironically, however, the intensification of unwaged female labor *is* an effect of the crisis. For example, the responsibility for dealing with the deterioration of health care, the problems caused by the absence of water in many villas, and those associated with a dearth of day care centers fall disproportionately on women, who must intensify their working days to satisfy these and other basic necessities. And, because women suffer from persistent gender discrimination and are assigned the task of child care, they are less mobile than men, who enjoy greater flexibility in the search for paid employment.

The Food-for-Work program takes advantage of women's vulnerabilities and targets their unpaid labor to construct public works in El Alto. Unwaged labor, the NGOs assert, is a resource for community development, not a direct casualty of the neoliberal class war against the rights and interests of ordinary Bolivians, especially women. The program offers food handouts in exchange for backbreaking labor on a variety of community-sponsored "self-help" public works projects. Although a program based on unpaid labor and subsidized food might appear incongruous in an era of free-market triumphalism, unwaged female labor and food handouts are important mechanisms for managing political stability in a period of economic austerity, and they provide an important subsidy to the cash-strapped municipality. Yet Food-for-Work places a burden on the shoulders of very poor women who are already forced to carry a heavy load. The initiative perpetuates the idea that unpaid labor for other people is "women's work," and it does not address the key feature of women's subordination—the difficulty most women have in mobilizing sufficient resources independently of men.

"Food-for-Work," or Acción Communal, as it is locally known, puts alteños to work cobblestoning streets, constructing plazas and sewers, landscaping hillsides, and digging drainage ditches. It is tied to the mayor's office, administered locally by a church-based NGO—the Adventist Development Relief Agency (ADRA)—and financed with surplus agricultural produce through a U.S. program funded under Public Law 480 that is channeled through USAID. Four to seven thousand people, overwhelmingly women (90 percent), work for food in El Alto every year, and participants represent the poorest, most marginalized households of the city.[8]

The program operates as follows: Neighborhood residents provide the labor for local projects that the mayor's office and ADRA have approved. The residents typically form work gangs of ten to thirty-five people, who may work a maximum of seventy-two hours per month and must supply their own shovels and picks. Although women are supposed to remain in their own neighborhoods, projects are not always available locally, and many women walk long distances to sites far from their homes. They hear of openings through word of mouth, or they may simply approach group leaders and ask to be incorporated in an ongoing activity. ADRA technicians supervise the women and remunerate them at the end of every month with a 55-kilogram package of food from ADRA's huge warehouse on the outskirts of the city. The package invariably contains wheat flour and two or three other items, such as cooking oil, corn flour, lentils, and occasionally sugar.

By any standard the work is extremely arduous. Women assigned to road construction must dig level roadbeds, position cobblestones within them, and secure the rocks with sand and gravel. All this hard labor can be

The Adventist Development Relief Agency (ADRA) and the mayor's office advertise their civic virtue

easily ruined if a truck drives over a half-completed street. Similarly, when the final outcome does not meet the specifications of ADRA technicians, the crews must redo the work. Women who are not assigned to road crews may be delegated the task of digging rocks from the banks of the contaminated Río Seco. El Alto has long mined the river for the cobblestones used in city streets, and the rocks no longer lie near the surface. Workers must unearth them with picks and shovels and then hoist them onto trucks. The workers suffer from a variety of job-related injuries, such as strained backs and pulled muscles, but neither the state nor ADRA provides them with health care or insurance.

The conditions for receiving food handouts in El Alto were not always so onerous. Before 1992 a series of mothers' clubs operated by the Catholic charity Caritas distributed the food handouts from the P.L. 480 program, which had no work requirement. Women simply gathered once a month to receive a food allotment. But as the welfare debate heated up in the United States, and U.S. welfare recipients were obliged to work in order to receive benefits, U.S. government-sponsored programs in Bolivia adopted a similar "get-tough" policy. Beginning in the early 1990s, food-aid beneficiaries had to participate in the Food-for-Work program, and neighborhood work brigades replaced approximately 115 mothers' clubs as the organizational form through which food was distributed. The food ration that workers received, according to one USAID official, was initially not even large enough to replace the calories that the workers expended in a day of work, but this problem, he insisted, was eventually eliminated.

The Food-for-Work program has served as a prototype for the decentralized approach to poverty alleviation embodied in the 1994 Popular Participation Law (Beasley 1992), and USAID and ADRA functionaries like to boast that the program is an example of neighborhood people empowering themselves. According to two individuals with intimate knowledge of the program, Food-for-Work "shows that democratic initiatives can have an immediate and dramatic result—a better life for poor people—brought about by better public goods and services because the poor participate in the process" (Sleeper and Patterson 1995:4). Such paens to democracy clearly seek to establish the legitimacy of unwaged female labor by invoking platitudes about popular "participation." When I asked a USAID bureaucrat to explain the absence of wages for women workers, he replied that wages would only encourage men to compete for the "jobs." Men, he felt, were irresponsible, and unlike women they were not conscientious about providing food for their families and were likely to spend wages on alcohol.

Clearly, USAID and ADRA bureaucrats and state functionaries value the participation of poor women in the Food-for-Work program because of their contribution to the efficient implementation of various public works projects. "Popular participation," however, is a vicious discourse that masks the growing dislocation between the arenas in which people (especially women) participate and the arenas in which decisions about their lives are made. Participation is not, after all, an end in itself. It should generate a greater capacity for women to make important decisions that affect their lives. Poor indigenous women are among the most powerless people in El Alto, and, rather than building ties between them and popular organizations, Food-for-Work creates clientelistic ties between women and the state, USAID, and ADRA while further entrenching class, gender, and ethnic divisions in El Alto.

Although Food-for-Work takes advantage of the unpaid labor of the poorest women in the city, microcredit programs target the cash surpluses that can still be extracted from other, slightly better-off people—once again, primarily women. These programs represent a new form of popular discipline that, through high interest rates and indebtedness, siphon surplus out of poor neighborhoods and provides a means for dominant groups to turn a profit on poverty. Microcredit schemes also appeal to the state because, like Food-for-Work, they are a low-cost substitute for public investment in health, education, and infrastructure, and the forms of organization associated with them offer a nonthreatening alternative to real collective organization.

During the 1990s, following the widely heralded success of the Grameen Bank of Bangladesh, credit schemes for "microentrepreneurs" exploded in the Third World, and El Alto was no exception. By 1995 at least six organizations offered "microcredit" to residents of the city, and in the space of only a few years they were loaning money to thousands of borrowers and enjoying considerable prosperity. The champions of microcredit argued that the lack of access to credit trapped people in poverty—not labor exploitation, low prices for crafts and agricultural commodities, or national debts and their associated austerity programs—and they claimed to "empower" the poor by extending high-interest loans to them.[9] Indeed, empowerment, or the lack of empowerment, was a constant refrain that I heard from microcredit managers, whose ultimate message to El Alto's poor was that credit holds the key to a prosperous and successful life.

A variety of international organizations finances microcredit programs in El Alto: USAID, for example, is a major supporter of three organizations—Bancosol, Promujer, and the Centro de Servicios Integrados para el Desarrollo Urbano (PROA); the Inter-American Development Bank lends major financial support to three others; and the Dutch, German, Swiss, and Swedish governments provide funding as well. A number of prominent Bolivian entrepreneurs have also invested their capital in these lucrative ventures. Although the particulars of microcredit vary from organization to organization, all the programs have certain features in common. The schemes loan money—from as little as $20 to several thousand dollars—to borrowers, who are usually organized into groups of eight to fifteen people. The borrowers are overwhelmingly women, who use the loans to finance petty commerce activities, and they pay monthly interest rates that, in 1995, ran from 3 to 6 percent.

The German-backed Procrédito, for example, is a major lender in the city, and it is similar to other programs. From 1992 to 1994 the organization made more than thirty thousand loans to people who resided primarily in El Alto and La Paz. Seventy percent of the loans were for less than $500, and 63 percent of the loans supported commerce or service activities. Although men accounted for more than one-third of the borrowers, women were by far the majority (63 percent), yet they tended to receive smaller loans than men.[10] For the backers of Procrédito the program's most salient statistic was the low rate of loan delinquency: by the end of 1994 only 1.5 percent of the loans were delinquent by eight days or more.

Procrédito's competitors can boast similar figures, and they all point to low delinquency rates as evidence of the unqualified success of small-scale lending. The poor, they claim to skeptical colleagues in the stodgy commercial banking sector, are creditworthy, and the banks can profit from these loans. This growing realization is responsible, in part, for the transition to for-profit institutions that some development NGOs, which specialize in microcredit lending, are making.[11] Yet even though some of El Alto's poor have indeed proved themselves good risks, they have been forced to do so at a high cost to themselves and others. A closer examination of microcredit schemes belies the fervent claims of popular empowerment so effusively espoused by microcredit enthusiasts. The schemes have engineered new ways to make money on the backs of the poor and implemented novel forms of social control that weigh heavily on low-income borrowers and nonborrowers alike.

Bancosol—the preeminent microfinancier—is the best example of this process. Founded in 1988 as a USAID-affiliated NGO called PRODEM (Programa de Apoyo de la Microempresa), which specialized in loans to small-scale urban entrepreneurs, it evolved into a for-profit banking institution within four years. During this transition, prominent well-situated La Paz businessmen used international development aid, and free-market rhetoric about transforming the poor into small-scale entrepreneurs, to build a lucrative private enterprise.[12] Between 1992 and 1994 Bancosol's clientele more than doubled, and women came to represent 85 percent of the bank's more than thirty thousand borrowers (Rivera Cusicanqui 1996).

Bancosol attracted clients with interest rates slightly below the usurious rates charged by lenders in the city's informal economy. But as it made the transition from NGO to private bank, its interest rates jumped from 3 percent to 6 percent monthly (Rivera Cusicanqui 1996).[13] This rate spike, however, did not affect the bank's rapid expansion. Bancosol enjoyed monopsony status for a period, and the demand for credit was so acute among the thousands of people pushed into increasingly competitive petty commercial activities that clients continued to flock to the organization even after competitors appeared.

The growth and expansion of microcredit lenders have created a credit market in La Paz and El Alto that is rigidly segmented by class and ethnicity. Middle- and upper-class whites have always been able to obtain loans from La Paz's major commercial banks by mortgaging a piece of property and presenting letters of recommendation, and the interest rates are somewhat lower than those found in the microcredit sector. Commercial banks, however, have refused to lend money to the legions of rural immigrants and poor urbanites who populate the city, and this is precisely the clientele that Bancosol and other microcredit lenders have captured so successfully. As a result, La Paz and El Alto now have two credit markets: one for whites, the other for cholos and "Indians" (Rivera Cusicanqui 1996).

The conditions that microcredit lenders have established for receiving a loan are quite different than those found in the mainstream private sector. Unlike the major commercial banks, Bancosol does not ask for collateral or letters of recommendation from potential borrowers. It substitutes these guarantees with self-regulation based on the model of a "solidarity group," which all clients must join. A solidarity group consists of five to eight people who are held collectively responsible for loan repayment and control each other through subtle threats and informal sanctions. Moral pressure, gossip about an individual's self-worth, and shame from not making payments are all means by which the demands of the institution mold an individual's behavior. In this way microcredit institutions distort and appropriate the concept of solidarity—once associated with the struggles of the Left—and make it synonymous with debt repayment.

Lenders, however, do not place all their faith in the self-regulation of borrowers. They also hire and train dozens of male employees to ensure that solidarity operates effectively among group members. The credit man-

agers that Bancosol employs are overwhelmingly mestizos who have grad-
uated from the public university with degrees in accounting, economics,
and business administration. They understand the social relationships and
cultural practices of the largely female clientele whom they supervise, and
the bank links their salary bonuses to the women's timely repayment of
debt. Bancosol claims that the unique managerial requirements of microcredit lending, and the higher transaction costs of many small loans, justify the institution's high interest rates, but Rivera Cusicanqui argues that
higher interest rates unnecessarily punish these clients and facilitate the administrative control necessary to discipline an unruly immigrant population (Rivera Cusicanqui 1996).

While Bancosol and other microcredit lenders have contributed to the
emergence of a highly unequal credit market divided along class and ethnic lines, they have also aggravated forms of oppression among subaltern
peoples in the city. Microcredit aggravates processes of differentiation between relatively better-off borrowers, who can manage the pressures of
debt repayment, and the poorest residents, who cannot. This begins with
the selection of credit beneficiaries. Lenders require that potential clients
demonstrate that they possess a relatively stable business. Procrédito,
whose loan prerequisites are similar to Bancosol's, expects clients to own a
house or a store, operate a business for at least one year, and have no out-
standing debts. These requirements favor longtime urban residents, who
are more likely to have established economic activities in the city, and they
discriminate against renters and recent immigrants, who are less secure
economically and more "Indian."

For borrowers the pressure to repay loans can strain forms of mutual assistance based on friendship, kin, and fictive kin ties that are often crucial
to survival. Among the vendors of the huge 16 de Julio market, for example, individual economic interests and opportunism are tightly interwoven
with reciprocal relationships based on some degree of trust. These reciprocal relationships include patron-client interactions and the moral constraints that temper them, as well as the exchange of information and assistance among equals. They are best exemplified by *casera* relationships in
which two people—a buyer and a seller—do business with each other on
a regular basis. The buyer, in exchange for loyalty to a particular seller, receives high quality goods at fair prices. Although caseras may not be social
equals, they depend on each other a great deal, and their relationships facilitate the circulation of enormous quantities of goods based on verbal
agreements and promises of future payments.

The circulation of goods, however, takes place in a precarious economic environment. Income from vending is already low, and seasonal fluctuations and broader economic trends also influence earnings in unpredictable ways. In addition, as discussed in chapter 4, the street markets are saturated with vendors, who must compete intensely to make a minimal income. As a result, when lenders pressure microcredit borrowers with nonnegotiable demands for debt repayment, these demands often stretch to the breaking point far-reaching social relationships that link rural dwellers and urban residents, as well as the destitute and the slightly better-off. This in turn can lead not only to greater exploitation among individual debtors but also to the increasing appropriation of resources, such as unpaid labor, from the weaker members of these complex relationships (e.g., rural dwellers, children, and recent immigrants). The women who can most effectively manipulate microcredit are likely to be married, well established in the city, and able to rely on the help of extended families. Rivera Cusicanqui notes that "indebtedness to Bancosol only results in a viable capitalization strategy for the most established operations and those that are most adept at extracting an unpaid surplus from their networks of reciprocity. The capacity for repayment depends on flows of free labor and the subsidy of the city by the countryside" (1996: 281).

Finally, microcredit programs embody forms of cultural discrimination. This, as we have seen, begins with the tendency to favor established longtime urban residents—the so-called cholas—over their more "Indian" counterparts, and to control them with male mestizo administrators, but it has other manifestations as well. A civilizing agenda is especially pronounced at Promujer, a microcredit lender that withholds loans until female clients can prove their worth as mothers and business administrators.

Promujer has operated in El Alto since 1990 and is heavily supported by USAID. Women who wish to receive credit must participate in a one-year program of five courses, or modules, that purport to teach them the basics of successful mothering and business development. The first three modules emphasize self-esteem, maternal and child health care, and childhood development, but they do not include abortion services, education about human immunodeficiency virus (HIV), or contraception counseling. The fourth module moves the women into instruction in basic business skills, based on the erroneous assumption that those who work in the city's markets are unable to manage money or comprehend the meaning of price fluctuations and economic cycles. Once the women have completed this module, Promujer finally allows them to form communal banks, which are similar to Bancosol's solidarity groups, and receive credit. Promujer's director stresses the importance of these modules for female development. The women, she asserts, "for their own lack of 'empowerment,' do not know what they are capable of" [*Por su propia falta de 'empowerment,' ellas no saben de lo que son capaces*]. She also boasts that while "Bancosol has clients [*clientes*], Promujer has associates [*socias*]."

In this way Promujer reduces female empowerment to little more than a cliché. It is severed from any discussion of gendered relations of power and the collective disempowerment of women and men that economic structural adjustment measures set in motion. To the extent that empowerment has any meaning for these women at all, the message is that emancipation comes from having as much money as possible and conforming to Western stereotypes of appropriate female behavior. Yet as long as international development organizations like Promujer continue to place the blame for poverty on poor women and their cultural practices—a practice that has parallels with the debates about poverty and the demonization of African American women in the urban United States (Williams 1994)—empowerment, by any definition, is likely to remain beyond the grasp of most women.

NGOs and the Left: Defining New Priorities

The flood of "neoliberal" NGOs, the money channeled to them by international development agencies, and the dominance of neoliberalism generated an identity crisis among other NGOs of the erstwhile Left, and even imagining a different kind of social order became more difficult. Left-leaning NGOs struggled to redefine themselves vis-à-vis their neoliberal rivals and began a desperate search for alternative development strategies, a process that created new divisions within them and frequently produced dramatic personnel reorganizations. In the early 1990s, for example, 140 of the oldest Catholic and Left-leaning NGOs, funded primarily from Europe, became affiliated with a national umbrella organization called the Coordinadora Nacional de Redes (CNR) and adopted the label "Instituciones Privadas de Desarrollo Social" (IPDS) (private social development institutions) to define member organizations. By so doing, the CNR distanced itself from NGOs that distributed food handouts and those tied to USAID, which called themselves "private volunteer organizations" (PVOs). It also sought to create a clearer and more positive-sounding appellation for its members.[14] A private social development organization, according to the CNR, initiated long-term development projects, rejected neoliberal reforms, and sought to change the status quo (Pinelo 1992). But directors of these organizations acknowledged that they were not posing a coherent alternative to neoliberalism but merely trying to combat its worst effects on the poor.

Their programs began to concentrate on providing services, income-generating schemes, and microenterprise development plans that were often indistinguishable from the projects advanced by competitors. The organizations signed agreements with the state to shoulder the burden of providing service in particular areas of the country where the state no longer operated or, in some cases, where it had never had a significant presence. Their activities, however, became concentrated primarily along the La Paz–El Alto–Cochabamba–Santa Cruz axis, where in the early 1990s two-thirds of the NGOs in Bolivia operated (Dewez 1991), and the emergence of a variety of NGO networks did little to better coordinate programs nationwide. All NGOs—old and new—increasingly addressed social problems in ways that closely followed the World Bank's recommendations for the reorganization of the state apparatus. In 1995 the approximately forty NGOs of El Alto offered services to local people in three basic domains: primary health care, education (technical training and literacy), and small business development via microcredit. Four NGOs also focused on home construction and improvement. Health and education were areas that the state, prompted by the World Bank, had increasingly abandoned, and business development—particularly among several USAID-linked NGOs—reflected the prevailing dogma about the best way to reactivate the Bolivian economy.

As international donors turned their attention to the newly democratized countries of Eastern Europe in the early 1990s, competition between NGOs for development dollars intensified, and the differences between them largely disappeared. Yet even as the differences between development NGOs were more difficult to discern and NGO-state relations grew ever more cooperative, tensions persisted between NGOs and the state. NGOs, especially those controlled by rival political parties, became threatening to state agencies, which were themselves highly dependent on funds from international donors. State officials coveted NGO monies for their own projects and for distribution among political allies, and they were legitimately concerned with the large sums flowing to NGOs without any national accountability.

These tensions were particularly apparent during the administration of President Jaime Paz Zamora (1989–1993), when the government hinted about imposing a tax on foreign funds channeled to NGOs and threatened to directly intervene in their financial affairs. It also created a national

NGO registry and a subsecretariat within the Ministry of Planning and Coordination to coordinate NGO activities, but these regulatory attempts met with little success. Only a fraction of the NGOs active in the country registered with the government, and several international NGOs did not even maintain national offices in Bolivia. Attempts to pass laws governing the behavior of NGOs in Bolivia continued, but NGO-state tensions eased—but did not entirely disappear—with the departure of Paz Zamora from the presidency.

For example, Flavio Clavijo, the CONDEPA mayor of El Alto, viewed NGOs as a power base for his political rivals, particularly those in the Movimiento Bolivia Libre (MBL). Unlike the MBL, however, CONDEPA never developed an NGO strategy to advance its agenda. The mayor believed NGO directors in El Alto used foreign aid for personal enrichment, and he was highly critical of almost all.[15] Yet the mayor, like the Bolivian state in general, coveted NGO money while tolerating NGOs because they provided a minimal level of social services and helped to maintain political stability during a period of shrinking state resources. Consequently, he could not afford to completely alienate them.

One facet of this rivalry emerged during an interview that I conducted with the mayor in 1994. Before beginning the interview, I carefully explained to him that I was an anthropology professor from American University, a private institution in Washington, D.C., and that I planned to write a book about El Alto. I also told him that I was particularly interested in his opinions of the NGOs operating in the city. He then proceeded to delineate his objections to NGOs, which included their failure to account publicly for the funds received from international organizations and their unwillingness to cooperate with his office. His harshest remarks, however, were directed at one very prominent and progressive NGO, and particularly its director, a woman from a renowned La Paz family closely tied to the MBL. Although he had no concrete evidence, the mayor claimed that this woman was totally corrupt. He said that she had enriched herself with money earmarked for the poor, and one need only look at the automobiles and real estate that she had accumulated to appreciate this fact.

These slanderous remarks, I quickly discovered, were not only for my ears. They were also directed to the U.S. embassy and more generally the U.S. government, which is a potentially fecund source of financial assistance. The mayor had mistakenly assumed that I was associated with the embassy, perhaps because of my affiliation with a university called "American" that was located in the U.S. capital. His error became apparent when he assured me at the end of the interview that if I, or "any of my colleagues from the embassy," wanted a second interview, he would be more than happy to talk with us. The mayor appeared to believe that, through me, he could curry favor with the U.S. government and discredit a rival at the same time.

Despite these tensions between the mayor's office and El Alto NGOs, the central government embarked on an unprecedented period of cooperation with NGOs after the 1993 presidential election of MNR leader Gonzalo Sánchez de Lozada. The MNR, MIR, and MBL were among the political parties that comprised the ruling coalition, and the state recruited an unusually large number of individuals from the NGO sector into important positions in the state bureaucracy.[16] For example, dozens of former NGO staff members filled jobs in a new "super" ministry—the Ministry of Human Development—which, in a nod to social diversity, included subsecretariats assigned to gender, ethnic, and generational issues; the heads of these subsecretariats were all former NGO directors.

By the mid-1990s, then, the economic crisis had generated a plethora of NGOs assigned the task of poverty alleviation as state agencies retrenched. Meanwhile, the fall of socialism and the neoliberal juggernaut had contributed to the organization of a new, albeit uneasy, consensus among Left-leaning and neoliberal NGOs and between them and the Bolivian state. The number of NGOs expanded, however, not only because of the erosion of the survival possibilities of peasants and immigrants and the threat to political instability that their growing immiseration posed to dominant groups. NGOs were also a response to the new vulnerabilities that plagued middle-class professionals, who were faced with declining living standards and the shrinkage of state agencies that once employed them. Indeed, the availability of international funding made it possible for some individuals who enjoyed the right connections to gain access to resources and to establish new NGOs in a time of economic austerity. It also opened up limited opportunities for popular organizations and some of the poor. As different groups and individuals contended for access to international funding and a few managed to establish new global connections, tensions arose among them, as chapter 8 explores.

8 · Global Connections

You still don't have an NGO? C'mon, c'mon. Get with it! If you work in development, you must have an NGO. It's the wave of the '90s. . . . Don't fool yourself, colleague. . . . For those that lost time studying philosophy, social sciences, history, international relations, law, pedagogy, political economy, anthropology, journalism, ecology, and things that are no good for selling fried chicken, there is nothing left but a good NGO.

—Gino Lofredo, "Hágase rico en los 90," *Chasqui*

Founding an NGO, or securing a job with one, became an increasingly attractive employment option for many middle-class professionals in the 1980s and 1990s. In the midst of the worst economic crisis in a generation, cultivating international connections and establishing an NGO enabled some professionals to reestablish a modicum of social and economic stability. Successful NGO entrepreneurs even benefited from the economic crisis, because structural adjustment policies drove more people into greater poverty and prompted aid agencies to channel money to NGOs to mitigate the suffering. They were thus able to position themselves to speak on behalf of the poor, who were generally less successful in gaining access to development aid.

This chapter examines how the increase in foreign development funding via NGOs offers some people and popular organizations the opportunity to obtain resources and establish ties to powerful international "aid," or "cooperation," agencies.[1] Specifically, it analyzes the often contentious relationships between middle-class professionals of the erstwhile Left and poor alteños as they contend with each other for access to international funding. It also considers the tensions that emerge among the poor when NGOs incorporate some in their activities and exclude others.

I first argue that progressive NGOs—despite their stated good intentions—are not strengthening independent popular organizations to represent disempowered constituencies. On the contrary, the spread of NGOs has opened up new avenues of social mobility for some members of the professional middle class who have been threatened by declining living standards and in some cases downsized from the state sector. NGOs have reinforced their ability to speak for disempowered constituencies, and this facility has increasingly tied the NGOs to the policy agendas of international development agencies.

I then demonstrate that NGOs have also created new, albeit limited, opportunities for some urban poor who live in the right places, have the right connections, and satisfy the criteria for appropriate beneficiaries set by international aid agencies. As popular groups organize in response to the availability of international funding, they frequently distance themselves from others whose economic circumstances do not improve and who cannot be incorporated in the small-scale projects of many NGOs. This not only creates cleavages between the NGO sector and unincorporated constituencies but may also aggravate problems of representation within popular organizations that ally with NGOs.

As the poor resituate themselves within a changing political and economic context, the distinctions between some NGOs and popular organizations frequently blur. This generally happens in two ways: an NGO creates a popular organization, which then becomes an example of the NGO's alliance with the poor, or an organization that emerges from a grassroots initiative takes on NGO-like characteristics as it seeks international financial support for its projects. The shifting and blurring of organizational forms raise questions about how the NGOs have affected the strategies of resistance and the ability of impoverished alteños to represent themselves.

Middle-Class Professionals and NGOs

Although Bolivia's economic crisis and the post-1985 neoliberal reforms weighed most heavily on the poor, middle-class professionals did not escape unscathed. The rampant inflation of the early 1980s devalued their earnings, and the subsequent shrinkage of state agencies reduced a major source of middle-class jobs. Between 1985 and 1991 the proportion of the Bolivian population employed by the state fell from 24 percent to 17 percent (CEDLA-ILDIS 1994), and salaries from public sector jobs were usually significantly lower than those for comparable positions in the private sector. The economic depression of the 1980s was particularly unsettling to professionals who had lived abroad during the dictatorships or who had benefited from scholarship programs to study in foreign universities. When they returned to Bolivia, they faced a drastic decline in the living standards that they had enjoyed in Mexico, the United States, and Europe. The proliferation of NGOs, however, presented new possibilities, but neither establishing an NGO nor securing a job with one was a simple matter.

Technical skills were never enough. The "personal recommendation," or, as one person stated more bluntly, a *patrón*, was crucial, and race and gender always shaped the ways that patronage networks operated locally. With few exceptions, Aymara professionals experienced little success in founding NGOs. They were more likely to acquire work as "popular educators" within NGOs because of their knowledge of Aymara. These jobs demanded a high degree of contact with NGO beneficiaries, but they ranked fairly low in the hierarchy of positions available within the organizations. Knowledge of a foreign language, such as English, German, French, or Dutch, was more important for aspiring professionals seeking to make their way in the world of development NGOs, and those who could operate in transnational social contexts held a distinct advantage over those who could not. To a greater degree than their Aymara counterparts, white middle-class professionals had lived for months or years in foreign countries, where they established contacts with foundations and development organizations, became fluent in the languages of the host countries, and acquired university degrees, which were more prestigious than those earned in Bolivia. They also gained an understanding of the cultural practices, beliefs, and idiosyncrasies of foreign nationals. In Bolivia they parlayed these cultural understandings and international connections, as well as technical skills and family and party loyalties, into the creation of a series of fledgling NGOs or jobs within NGOs.

The size of NGO staffs in El Alto ranged from a handful of people to several dozen employees. With only a few exceptions, the professionals did not live in the city, although most "support staff" (e.g., secretaries, popular educators, and drivers) did. Professionals either commuted to offices in El Alto on a daily basis from the lower elevations of La Paz, or they came to the city from La Paz–based headquarters when specific activities required their presence. They generally held contracts of varying duration, and, although most were Bolivian nationals, a significant number were foreigners—primarily Europeans and North Americans.

Bolivia attracted foreign citizens for a number of reasons. Living in the country—at least for a while—was an adventure. Some were attracted by the perceived exoticism of Bolivia's indigenous peoples, and most—especially the Dutch and the Scandinavians—were committed to addressing the severe social and economic problems that plagued the country. Good jobs were scarce at home, and working with an NGO gave them a chance to develop professional skills and enhance the attractiveness of their résumés for future European and North American employers. The foreigners generally negotiated contracts directly with development organizations in their home countries and worked with NGOs in Bolivia as "volunteers" or "advisers." They also received a series of benefits that their Bolivian counterparts did not enjoy, such as housing, health insurance, payment in U.S. dollars, and expense-paid trips home every year. When their contracts were completed, these individuals typically returned home or received new assignments in different countries or other parts of Bolivia. Only a few settled permanently in Bolivia. The latter were primarily European women who married local men and who had grown up in multicultural environments.

Unlike most of their foreign counterparts, Bolivian NGO staff members were concerned with making careers for themselves locally, because they considered La Paz to be home. They were generally more attuned to the subtleties of local politics and culture than their foreign colleagues, and, unlike most of those colleagues, they had usually been politically active at some point in their lives, bringing their activist concerns to the NGOs that they joined or founded. By the late 1980s and 1990s, however, they were emphasizing the professional, rather than the political, importance of their work. This was partly the result of shifts within NGOs and the international development arena.

By the late 1980s NGOs were beginning to upgrade the technical and administrative capabilities of their staffs, because they needed to sharpen their competitive edges vis-à-vis other NGOs. The concern with professionalism also emerged because European funding agencies had grown more conservative. With the return of civilian rule in Bolivia these agencies were no longer interested in supporting overtly partisan causes and started to make more rigorous demands of their clients, who operated in an ever more competitive funding environment. The NGOs wanted quantifiable project results and required much tighter accounting procedures. In addition, a domestic debate about the role of NGOs in Bolivian society emerged in the early 1990s, as the government of Jaime Paz Zamora raised questions about NGO funding, control, and accountability, and as some popular organizations began to criticize NGO behavior. One director commented to me that, "formerly, concepts like efficiency and competitiveness were sins to us, but now they are very important here."

Although NGOs continued to contrast their projects to the bureaucratic and ineffective programs of the state, they also presented their initiatives as contributions to broad improvements in social welfare and progressive change that transcended the divisive and opportunistic activities of the political parties. By adopting the appearance of political neutrality, the NGOs sought to legitimize themselves and their organizations to international financial entities and to Bolivian society in general. In El Alto, however, this apolitical stance inadvertently exacerbated alteños' alienation from the traditional political parties, which local people widely viewed as venal, corrupt, and unable to represent the interests of poor city residents.[2]

Most urban dwellers had expected the traditional political parties to improve the standard of living in the aftermath of military rule, but when elected leaders decreed unpopular economic measures and abused state power for personal enrichment, people became disillusioned with the political process. Similarly, many activists grew pessimistic about the prospects for meaningful social change. They often withdrew from the parties and frequently affiliated with NGOs; this behavior both reflected and reproduced a widespread cynicism. Some NGOs shared this disaffection and distanced themselves from the parties.

A public forum convened by a prominent El Alto NGO in October 1994 exemplifies the efforts of many NGOs to transcend the fractious infighting of local political parties. The purpose of the forum was to inform residents about the recently passed Popular Participation Law and its implications for El Alto. A staff member presided over the event and began the meeting by carefully distancing himself and the NGO from any association with the parties. He further emphasized that the NGO was sponsoring the event as a community service and that it wanted to encourage greater political participation—in any party—by city dwellers. About sixty people listened intently; most were members of neighborhood committees, civic organizations, youth groups, and women's organizations, and all had some experience with the parties.

The NGO representative began his analysis of the law by stating that it constituted a new way of relating to the state, one that was less paternalistic than in the past and that gave more power to local groups to set forth their demands. The law was giving to the citizenry the responsibility for creating livable neighborhoods in El Alto, he said, so that instead of continuing to make demands, people could become "active subjects" in the resolution of their problems. He then carefully elaborated both the perceived benefits and disadvantages of what the law would likely entail for El Alto. On the positive side, he explained that the law for the first time recognized the existence of historically marginalized local organizations and gave them more power to determine their future. This was particularly important in the countryside, where the state had long denied the legitimacy of indigenous *ayllus*.[3] By empowering ayllus, as well as urban neighborhood committees and other grassroots organizations, the law embraced the cultural diversity of Bolivia and acknowledged that the old discourse about *mestizaje* effaced important cultural differences.[4] He added that the law mandated the assignation of state resources to municipalities on the basis of population and that, theoretically, this would benefit El Alto.

On the negative side, he continued, the law posed a problem of representation. El Alto's numerous neighborhood committees would constitute what the law described as "territorial base organizations" (OTBs), the local entities charged by the state with initiating development projects, providing services, and so forth. In many neighborhoods, however, the committees were corrupt, ineffective, and unrepresentative of the needs of local people; moreover, political parties frequently controlled the organizations and manipulated them for partisan purposes. The speaker added that the country needed another law to control the parties, and many people in the audience nodded enthusiastic agreement.

In relation to the problems of representation, he said that the OTBs could fragment social life and undermine, rather than advance, local initiatives. How, he asked, were small-scale entities going to make broader alliances and connections? The danger was that territorial concerns would take precedence over broad-based solidarity. He also noted that, although the law recognized different cultural traditions, people must bear in mind that "the traditional" had long contributed to the marginalization of indigenous peoples, especially women. He summarized his presentation by stating that the law might offer some new openings for popular expression, but it contained significant dangers and pitfalls.

In the discussion that followed, the NGO representative urged those present to take control of the neighborhood committees so that the parties could not manipulate them. He cited a local example to drive home his point. Residents of the neighborhood, he said, had recently asked the mayor's office for help in transforming a garbage dump into a plaza for children, but local officials presented a budget for the project with excessive costs. The NGO then decided to take over the project and build the plaza with the help of residents. Together they eliminated the garbage dump and built the plaza for a fraction of the cost estimated by local officials, but the mayor took the credit for the plaza in a report on the accomplishments of his administration.

Throughout the meeting the NGO representative consistently placed the organization outside the realm of local politics and characterized it as solely concerned with informing citizens of their rights and improving living conditions in El Alto for everyone. He advanced his seemingly bal-

anced presentation of the law within a general understanding that whatever its strengths and weaknesses, the Popular Participation Law was now
the law, and the time for protesting it was essentially over. Local people, he
stressed, had to find the best ways to accommodate their interests within
the state's parameters.

The reality, however, was somewhat more complicated. Far from being
above the rough-and-tumble of local political struggles, the NGO was a
major actor. On the eve of the Popular Participation Law's passage, the
NGO had reorganized its programs so that it could exercise more power
with the municipal government once the law went into effect. It did so by
concentrating in one villa of particular strategic political importance a
number of programs that had been spread out across the city. And, although the NGO moved to accommodate the new law in late 1994 and
1995, the mayor's office and CONDEPA were still refusing to recognize
the law and were blocking the creation of OTBs in the city. The CON-
DEPistas, who basically controlled the municipality of El Alto, saw the law
as an attempt by the coalition of ruling parties to wrest control of the city
from them. Thus mutual antipathy shaped the relationship between
CONDEPA and the NGO, which many people identified as aligned with
the Movimiento Bolivia Libre (MBL), CONDEPA's political rival.

Although the NGO's apolitical self-representation did not always convince local people, it was central to the success that NGOs—old and new,
neoliberal and not-so-neoliberal—enjoyed with international donor agencies. By the mid-1990s NGOs had captured considerable foreign financial
support and assumed a much more dominant position as the representatives of the poor. As a director of Coordinadora Nacional de Redes (CNR),
the NGO umbrella organization, explained: "During the dictatorship,
NGOs were not seen as actors in their own right. They were supposed to
support the popular movement, which was understood as peasants, the
COB and so forth. With the return of democracy and the weakening of
the popular movement, NGOs began to act more independently and take
the lead in proposing solutions to problems."

The relationship between middle-class professionals, NGOs, and political parties was in fact quite fluid and complex, belying the simplistic and
self-serving public representations. Although some NGOs remained
closely affiliated with particular parties, this was not always the case. The
consolidation of international funding connections frequently enabled individuals and groups to challenge party orthodoxy and to renegotiate their
positions within party patronage networks or break with the parties altogether. Daily contact with the poor also moved some middle-class profes-

sionals to question rigid political dogma and to understand social life in more nuanced and complex ways. This was the case, for example, with some female professionals who were in touch with the broad currents of international feminism and who founded several NGOs in El Alto. To capture financial aid for a series of feminist projects these women capitalized on a growing concern with gender among international development organizations. By so doing, they not only secured employment for themselves but also used international ties to advance a domestic debate about gender that was not on the agendas of the political parties of either the Left or the Right.

For example, Paula Cuéllar and a friend, Mireya Balcázar, created an NGO in 1982 after the restoration of civilian rule allowed them to return from exile. Cuéllar had worked with women and children in a poor neighborhood of La Paz, and Balcázar had been involved with Catholic Church activities in El Alto. Both women were self-described feminists, and before the 1980 military coup d'état preempted their efforts and drove them into exile, they had been active in the Movimiento de Izquierda Revolucionaria (MIR).

They were drawn to the MIR because it was the only party at the time with a clearly defined position on women. Yet, according to Cuéllar, the MIR's stance on women was never entirely satisfactory. The party did not seriously engage the feminist issues of the day, and it was, she told me, "more interested in women's votes and the presence of women at rallies than in addressing the particular concerns of women." While in exile, Cuéllar and Balcázar reassessed their relationship with the MIR, and when they returned to Bolivia, the two women decided to establish a feminist NGO that dealt specifically with the concerns of poor urban women.

The organization began modestly with a $5,000 grant from Christian Aid, a British agency run by Anglican friars. The NGO operated out of a small room that Balcázar's mother loaned them for an office and almost immediately encountered problems with the MIR, which viewed the feminist example as a threat. The leadership asked Cuéllar and Balcázar, who still maintained ties to the party, to close the organization, but the women decided to leave the MIR instead. Cuéllar said, "We told [the MIR] to go to hell."

During the next fifteen years the NGO prospered and became one of the most successful agencies of its kind in El Alto. In 1995 twenty-five professionals worked for the organization, and many former employees had moved into a variety of staff positions elsewhere. Some had jumped to different NGOs. Others, like Cuéllar herself, made their living as independent consultants for both state agencies and private development organizations, and a few had found employment in the Ministry of Human Development after 1993. The NGO's top-level directors were ideologically identified with the MBL, although not everyone belonged to the MBL or even other political parties, and the NGO obtained a steady stream of financial support from a variety of liberal European development organizations that were eager to fund projects focused on women.

As the organization expanded and consolidated, it deemphasized the "movement issues" that spurred its creation and focused more on "development" and the elaboration of income-generating projects. When I interviewed Cuéllar in 1995, she was not completely comfortable with this transition, but to account for it she pointed to the devastating effect of the economic crisis on poor women. She argued that the economy created a pressing need to respond to deepening poverty in concrete material ways. To raise money for projects Cuéllar and other staff members engaged in the increasingly competitive, and continuous, practice of writing proposals and submitting them to international aid agencies for consideration. In some cases, the projects were quite creative, and when implemented they were generally well received by local beneficiaries. A library, for example, offered a variety of books and study space for neighborhood children; a radio station broadcast news and educational programs; a women's soccer tournament drew women into leisure activities outside the home; and courses on baking and sewing attracted many women, who were encouraged to create their own "microenterprises." The success of these and other projects won the praise and the largesse of development agency representatives, who periodically visited El Alto. The NGO eventually became so successful that it enjoyed the relative luxury of operating on a five-year plan, whereas some of its less fortunate competitors struggled to survive on a project-by-project basis.

Yet as staff members adopted the concepts and concerns that informed official policy and the prevailing development discourse—for example, microenterprise development—their political prescriptions grew increasingly ambiguous. Small-scale projects, rather than broad-based protest and the creation of popular alliances, had become the order of the day. Although the NGO did, and continues, to contribute to improvements in living standards for some local people within its newly circumscribed sphere of influence, the organization could not extend its achievements beyond a relatively small constituency. The approach reflected a new, and perhaps more realistic, assessment of the balance of power, but it increasingly constituted less of a challenge, or an alternative, to dominant neoliberalism.

NGO-sponsored women's soccer league

The achievements of this NGO demonstrate how some professionals positioned themselves between international development agencies and local people to become the representatives of the poor. By so doing, the NGO professionals considerably strengthened their own position vis-à-vis international organizations and the state. They also managed to successfully contend with national political parties in furthering their programs and agendas by representing themselves as disinterested professionals detached from the rude partisan squabbles that occupied the parties. Rather than being one actor within a broad-based popular alliance of unions, citizen groups, and some political parties, however, the NGO and others like it were increasingly becoming the most powerful act in town.

NGOs and Grassroots Organizations

With the weakening of labor and popular organizations in the wake of structural adjustment, poor Bolivians had greater difficulty representing and defending their interests vis-à-vis the state. Some people, however, could appeal to international agencies through NGOs for support for their agendas. NGOs could circumvent the state, but unlike many state officials, they were not accountable to local people. This made it relatively easy to encourage some organizational forms and actively ignore others. Indeed, the popular organizations that NGOs supported frequently lacked concrete political agendas or visions for social change.

In the late 1980s and early 1990s, for example, when the Caritas mothers' clubs still controlled food handouts in the city, several emerging European-financed NGOs that lacked organized constituencies among El Alto's poor targeted the clubs in the hope of winning the women over to another agenda. They typically tried to capture the groups with their own programs and then reorient them around different agendas that frequently stressed the rights of women and placed considerable emphasis on consciousness-raising seminars and discussions about timely issues. Yet many women in these clubs had little interest, or time, for consciousness-raising programs. Nor were they particularly motivated by the sincere efforts of some NGOs to strengthen popular organizations and encourage greater citizen participation in local politics. Most had to confront a much more fundamental question: how to cope with the depressing daily realities that economic structural adjustment and grinding poverty forced on them. The clubs and the NGOs offered a partial answer for some by expanding their repertoire of temporary survival tactics, but very poor women, who hardly ever enjoyed "leisure time," could not spare the time necessary to become politically active. To dedicate themselves to politics, such women required concrete and immediate material remuneration for their efforts.[5]

Genera Cusicanqui is a rural immigrant who moves easily in the world of El Alto's development NGOs, and she is also a longtime organizer of mothers' clubs with Caritas. In 1995 she was earning $47 per month and receiving other benefits from work with a variety of NGOs, because her husband—a local police officer—could not support her and their seven children on a monthly salary of $165. Cusicanqui turned the patio of her home into an NGO-sponsored day care center during the morning. She also participated in a garden project sponsored by the same NGO; it provided her with fresh vegetables and a small income from their sale. Three afternoons a week she traveled to the headquarters of another NGO, where she attended leadership courses. Part of the attraction of the courses, she told me, was the transportation stipend given to participants. Cusicanqui considered it part of her salary and chose to walk to the classes rather than spend the money. Finally, Cusicanqui advertised a low-cost housing program for still another NGO, and in exchange for her efforts the NGO gave her materials to construct a bathroom in her house.

The extent to which Genera Cusicanqui drew on NGOs to satisfy her family's needs was unusual, but the way in which she did so was not. As part of their ongoing struggles to survive, some alteños periodically harnessed the flow of goods and benefits from foreign-financed development programs. When the NGO programs ended, or shifted to other areas, people like Cusicanqui generally returned to the limited means that they controlled and had never entirely abandoned. This typically involved the astute use and constant re-creation of their own social networks.

Consequently, NGOs had to offer some concrete material incentive to ensure the participation of these women in their more ambitious educational and consciousness-raising programs. NGOs actually grew less by supporting preexisting popular organizations than by creating new ones through the offer of economic aid, and they were thus never able to completely escape from the clientelism that they condemned. Moreover, whereas local people turned to NGOs for economic largesse, the NGOs needed the groups to justify their development activities to international donor agencies. Clientelism toward those below was thus important for maintaining the flow of funding from donor agencies in Europe and the United States. Indeed, despite their much proclaimed "autonomy," NGOs were deeply immersed in upward- and downward-directed clientelistic relationships.

As NGOs spread throughout the city, they frequently found themselves competing with each other and with political parties for constituents. The nature of this competition was not the same throughout the city. NGOs were virtually absent in some neighborhoods, while as many as ten organizations operated projects in others. Similarly, some villas were more strategically important for the parties. A number of political parties and NGOs operated in the Villa 16 de Julio, where some of the chaos, rivalry, and confusion that shaped their interactions with local people was apparent when I visited an adult literacy class.

The class was sponsored by an NGO that specialized in adult education and consisted of about thirty Aymara women whom I met through Leonarda Alea, a math teacher with the NGO. Alea allowed me to sit in on her math class, but I soon discovered that another NGO and a political party had also laid claim to the group. As we entered the classroom and Alea introduced me to the women, I recognized Angélica, an MNR militant whom I had met the previous day at a mothers' club meeting. She greeted me and immediately began to complain about that meeting. Angélica asserted that the Federación de Amas de Casa was claiming her club for itself, and she stated indignantly that "I organized that group." She went on to explain that because of her efforts, the women had managed to save about 400 bolivianos ($80) for various group activities. This money, according to Angélica, was then taken by the leaders of the Federación de Amas de Casa, who claimed that the money represented unpaid dues. Angélica was clearly furious.

After listening to her complaints, I took a seat among the women who had started gathering for Alea's math class, but what ensued more closely approximated a three-ring circus than an adult education course. As Alea began her class, she was able to maintain the attention of only those seated closest to her, because Angélica had initiated a political meeting at the other end of the room. Angélica was announcing that food donations would soon arrive from Bolivia's first lady, the wife of MNR president Gonzalo Sánchez de Lozada, and Angélica proceeded to call out the names of the women—nominal MNR members—who were eligible to receive them. An argument developed as some women expressed skepticism about the long-promised food that never seemed to actually arrive. As the debate heated up and became mixed with Alea's frustrated efforts to teach double-digit addition, three representatives from another NGO entered the room and greeted everyone loudly. Undaunted by the activities already under-way, they began calling out names and distributing certificates to women who had recently completed a primary health care course sponsored by their institution.

After everyone had finished, I left with Alea and asked her how she felt about the class. She expressed frustration at the distractions and the disor-ganization of the meeting. She said that even though the party and NGO representatives had tried previously to divide the afternoon into discrete time slots for each organization, the women had no respect for time and simply wandered in and out. They were, she said ruefully, really only there for the food donations.

It would be an error to assume that NGOs are simply imposing them-selves on local people. In a desperately poor city, where people frequently have no alternative means to help themselves, residents frequently welcome NGOs into El Alto's neighborhoods, and they maintain cordial long-term relationships with many well-meaning staff members.[6] Yet because of their localized approach to poverty alleviation, NGOs cannot include everyone, and their programs may create divisions as people compete for access to their benefits.

Consider, for instance, a day care program initiated by an NGO in 1987 during the depths of the economic crisis. The NGO decided to sup-port poor women, who were working longer hours outside the home, by promoting a series of neighborhood day care centers. It acquired several lo-cales and then taught neighborhood women the basic principles of early childhood education through a series of classes and group discussions. The plan was for the women to eventually take over the centers and manage them as neighborhood resources. Before the centers could be handed over to the communities, however, problems arose. The NGO allowed some women who participated in the courses and had completed some prerequisites to work in the centers on a volunteer basis. The NGO provided them with small transportation subsidies to reach the centers from their homes and allowed them to bring their children, who, along with the mothers, received a hearty lunch and afternoon snack. From the NGOs' perspective, these women were volunteering their time to help others like themselves—women who had to work long hours during the day and who had no place to leave their children.

Child in NGO-sponsored day care program

The women not selected as volunteers, however, had a very different view of the situation. They felt excluded from an attractive employment niche, one that provided meals for women and their children at a time when the crisis left them hungry and unable to feed their families. Along with representatives of some neighborhood committees, these women proposed to the NGO that local women rotate through the centers, so that more people could have access to the free meals that accompanied the "jobs." An NGO staff member, who reflected on the conflict several years later, remarked somewhat ruefully that the women had not shared his enthusiasm for early childhood education and had viewed the centers, now defunct, primarily as a source of subsistence.

The NGO boom has indeed opened new opportunities for some urban poor. Fashionably exotic groups, such as women's and indigenous peoples' organizations, have been most successful in attracting NGO attention and support.[7] Yet as individuals and groups acquire international funding, forging horizontal ties becomes a complicated endeavor. The experience of Fernando Mejía and his wife, Estela Escandón, illustrate this phenomenon.

Both Mejía and Escandón were born in the Catavi-Siglo XX mining complex, where they and their families were intimately involved with the labor movement. Mejía was a mine worker for years and was deeply involved with the union. Escandón's father had been a national labor leader until he was killed in a mysterious automobile accident, and her mother was a founding member of the Housewives Committee of Siglo XX, which fought for women's and workers' rights during the dictatorships. Mejía and Escandón were forced into exile because of their political activism.

In 1976, for example, the Banzer regime took Mejía prisoner and shipped him and several other Bolivian political prisoners to Chile, where the men were placed in a southern prison camp with victims of General Augusto Pinochet's reign of terror. Mejía and a small group of companions managed to escape, and with the assistance of the Chilean underground they sought asylum in the Dutch embassy in Santiago. The men were eventually granted Dutch visas and left Chile for Holland, where Mejía remained in exile for a year and a half. He returned to Bolivia in 1978, when the fall of Banzer and a tenuous democratic opening made it safe for him to do so. Democracy, however, was never consolidated, and the 1980 military coup d'état forced him and his wife to return to Holland. This time Mejía remained for six years.

During their residency in Holland, Mejía made contacts with Dutch citizens involved with development in Third World nations and with solidarity causes. He also learned Dutch and acquired a university degree.

When he finally returned to Bolivia in 1986, it was not to work in the mine, because, as he said, "The situation had changed, and I had a profession." Indeed, Paz Estenssoro had just issued Supreme Decree 21060, the state operated mines were closing, and unemployed miners and their families were streaming into El Alto. Mejía discovered that not only working conditions had changed in Bolivia. Many of his friends and associates were different as well. Mutual hostility often poisoned the relations between those who had remained behind and suffered in Bolivia and those who had left and prospered in exile. The former were often envious of what they perceived as the self-serving accomplishments of returned exiles. The exiles, for their part, were suspicious of the political commitments and alliances of the people who stayed. Mejía's friends told him that he should have remained in Europe, because Bolivia had no jobs. As Mejía explained, "The situation in Bolivia had changed. All of my friends—compañeros from work, political associates—asked me what I was doing, why I had come back. Even my family asked me why I returned. They thought that I was very 'irregular'—imprisoned, exiled, here, there. But I came back because I had finished studying and gotten a job in Holland to work in Bolivia. My return had to be well planned, and it was."

Mejía had landed a one-year contract with a Dutch NGO that specialized in fitting disabled individuals with prostheses. After he fulfilled his contractual obligations, he and Escandón, who had earned a pharmacology degree in Eastern Europe, then returned to Holland. They went with their own ideas for projects to support displaced miners, and they came back to Bolivia with financial support for a soup kitchen and an auto repair shop in the city. Husband and wife eventually parlayed these projects into two NGOs. Escandón's organization targeted women in El Alto who had been forced out of the mining communities, and Mejía's NGO supported peasant communities in the surrounding countryside, as well as displaced miners in El Alto. Mejía and Escandón were among the few NGO professionals who lived in El Alto, and their institutions enjoyed a relatively constant stream of international support.

Fernando Mejía and Estela Escandón illustrate how some former members of the working class could establish and use international connections to their own advantage. These connections helped the couple to weather the social and economic difficulties of repatriation, and, more important, they enabled the pair to move out of the working class at a time when working people confronted serious economic problems.

Several anthropologists have described the stereotypic ways in which various Third World activists represent themselves and their causes to foreign funding agencies in order to garner political and economic support. Brysk (1996), Conklin (1997), and Jackson (1995), for example, discuss how South American indigenous peoples use political strategies that rely on representations of "authentic Indianness" that conform to Western clichés about them. Edelman (1991) documents a similar phenomenon among Costa Rican peasants, who understand and use European perceptions of peasants as quaint rustics to advance their own agendas. Estela Escandón and Fernando Mejía, however, did not make use of such stereotypical representations as they appealed to and negotiated with European funding agencies. To do so could have been counterproductive. The cliché of the Bolivian tin miner—militant, Marxist, revolutionary, and organized—had a certain romantic appeal for segments of the Left, but it was much too radical for most funding organizations in the 1980s. The cold war was not over, and the miners were on the defensive but not completely defeated. The miners' militancy and the danger that they posed to the status quo had not receded into the past. Furthermore, most international development organizations had never embraced an agenda that made a priority of the social and economic problems of laborers.

Thus Mejía and Escandón did not play on their "authenticity" as mine workers, yet they did not deny their past, either. They courted potential funders with many of the same organizing skills that they had learned in the labor movement—patience, analysis, persuasion, and sociability. They could talk from personal experience about the situation in the mining communities, and they were well aware of the problems that confronted residents of El Alto. They also understood the broader political and economic ramifications of neoliberal policies, and they could operate effectively within the world of NGO cultural politics. When, for example, European development agency representatives visited El Alto, Mejía and Escandón would invite them to lunch and serve wine, rather than the more typical soda, with the meal.

As Mejía and Escandón consolidated their NGOs and international contacts, however, they faced growing criticism from former mine workers, who struggled to secure employment and survive amid the harsh conditions of the city. These people were enormously suspicious of the motivations and means by which the couple actually succeeded. Many ex-miners, for example, singled out Estela Escandón as an example of opportunism and corruption in their discussion with me about NGOs. Some insisted that she used development funds to build her home. Others claimed that she was only concerned with personal advancement. Still others pointed to a failed bid for local political office as an MBL candidate to illustrate her political opportunism and hypocrisy. None of these individuals offered any proof to substantiate their claims.

El Alto was indeed rife with individual opportunism and corruption. Yet who had the right to speak for whom was not at all clear. Charges of embezzlement, rumors of corruption, and accusations of opportunism surfaced in situations in which the visible advances of some people contrasted with the plight of others from similar backgrounds who had been left behind. Escandón's NGO also raised expectations among local people—especially women from the mining camps—that were beyond her capacity and the capacity of her organization to address. These critiques by local people spoke to the inequality that separated them from the largely middle-class professionals who staffed the NGOs, and they reflected the divisive effects of economic clientelism on grassroots constituencies.

Such complaints were by no means directed at Estela Escandón alone. They were also advanced against the directors of NGOs in other parts of the city by many ordinary people and the leaders of popular organizations. Usually, the latter had participated in NGO programs, but they often resented NGO clientelism and coveted NGO monies for their own activities. They reproached staff members for developing projects in the name of the poor and using development aid to finance comfortable lifestyles. A local female leader claimed that "there are many NGOs that receive money in our name and do projects that we know nothing about" (UNITAS 1991:79). Similarly, during a meeting organized by six El Alto NGOs in 1992, local women criticized the NGOs' consciousness-raising programs. They explained that the NGOs permitted women only to "reflect and become conscious of our problems" but excluded them from the planning, execution, and evaluation of programs (Comité Interinstitucional 1992).

Several popular organizations and their leaders have tried to circumvent established NGOs and assert their own claims to international funding because of their suspicions and critiques of the established NGOs. Doing so, however, is never easy. The leaders of popular organizations recognize that they usually need advice, as well as financial assistance, to carry out their duties, which are often new to them. Forging alliances with more powerful, better-connected professionals from the white middle class can offer them a certain amount of security, but these ties can also bring humiliating forms of dependency, and they may raise questions among constituents about a leader's honesty and commitment to their concerns. Similarly, as popular organizations assert their claims on international financial aid, the distinctions between NGOs and grassroots organizations become less clear cut. The case studies that follow demonstrate how the boundaries between

NGOs and popular organizations are increasingly blurred, as impoverished groups try to gain access to new kinds of resources.

The Pachamama Center and the Sole Federation of Popular Women's Organizations of El Alto

In 1995 the Pachamama Center operated a handicraft project involving about thirty groups of women in a number of El Alto villas. The groups, which consisted of five to twenty women, produced alpaca scarves, hats, and gloves; leather handbags; and small dolls for export and sale to tourists through a retail outlet that the center managed in La Paz. The project began in 1991, with funding from the Catholic Church, and the Pachamama Center grew up along with it. Some of the first groups that participated in the program were Caritas mothers' clubs, but when food handouts stopped flowing to the clubs in the early 1990s, the groups either dissolved or looked for other sources of institutional support. Those that became affiliated with the Pachamama Center were often seeking a means to minimally satisfy some of their household needs, but the small group of progressive Bolivian women and European volunteers who staffed the center had other ideas.

Although the immediate goal of the handicraft project was to provide poor women with an income, the long-term objective was much more ambitious. Project personnel hoped to strengthen a women's federation—the Sole Federation of Popular Women's Organizations of El Alto—that the NGO helped to establish among the El Alto artisan groups and a few La Paz–based cooperatives. The purpose of the federation, according to Pachamama's director, was to defend the social, economic, and political rights of poor women and not, she stated emphatically, to serve a few beneficiaries in the insular fashion of an NGO.

To this end, the NGO required every participant to attend popular education courses as part of the program. The individual groups met once a week for two to three hours with a staff member to read the Bible and relate biblical themes to members' lives and the goals of the federation. These sessions drew on the pedagogical teachings of Paulo Freire and were modeled on the Christian base communities promoted by the progressive wing of the Catholic Church in many parts of Latin America.[8] The staff of the center hoped that these groups would produce community leaders and attract more participants, thus expanding the size, scope, and potential influence of the federation.

Members of handicraft project

Since its inception the federation has achieved a semiautonomous existence from the center. It organizes events and makes public pronouncements that appear in the local press on a range of issues that affect women. Yet despite the federation's activities, it represents a relatively small, inward-looking group of local women who have little interest in becoming part of a broad inclusive organization. Because of the highly competitive market for local crafts, members of the artisan groups are more interested in defending their positions within the craft program than in expanding the federation's membership.[9]

While working with one group of five women, for example, a European staff volunteer constantly chided the participants for not recruiting more women into the program, but her entreaties were usually met with uncomfortable silences or unconvincing excuses. The women understood the center's limited ability to market their products rapidly and at a high price: the tourist season in La Paz lasted from mid-July through late September, and many vendors competed for the tourists' dollars. The center also did not have a well-established international marketing network; it relied on a few unreliable contacts to place products during the Christmas and New Year holidays. The artisans knew that additional participants in the hand-icraft program would lower their earnings and threaten the already narrow market niche that they had carved out for themselves. Members therefore quite naturally sought to protect themselves by limiting the number of beneficiaries.

Women's determination to protect their limited prerogatives also ex-tended beyond these small groups. In October 1994 the federation partic-ipated in a march that it organized with the help of the Pachamama Cen-ter to celebrate Bolivian Women's Day and the anniversary of the federation. The center's staff encouraged members of the individual artisan groups to take part in the march, which other residents of El Alto perceived as an "NGO event." Approximately five hundred women from the federa-tion and other El Alto–based NGOs participated, because, as many stated, it was important to speak out in support of women's rights. Yet in private conversations and murmured discussions before the event, some women made it clear that they felt that a failure to participate would jeopardize their relationship to the center. Some even believed that they would be fined for not taking part.[10] These beliefs left many of the center's staff members aghast.

As participants in the crafts project defended their limited claims to re-sources, their organization, with its ties to the Pachamama Center and beyond, to the Catholic Church, more closely resembled an NGO that provided project support to a limited number of beneficiaries than a broad-based representative organization that supported women's rights. Through these alliances some women secured—at least momentarily—a minimal income for themselves. Yet the part-time insecure nature of the work and the piece rates they received hardly made this an adequate source of in-come; indeed, the work mirrored in many ways the industrial homework and production systems described in other Third World settings (e.g., Ben-ería and Roldán 1987; Seabrook 1996). In at least one villa women aban-doned the handicraft program altogether in 1995, because piecework for a La Paz–based Korean contractor was more attractive.

By 1995, with funding for the Pachamama program drawing to a close and no new benefactor in sight, the center decided to shift its emphasis after acknowledging that the artisan groups had become closed cliques that were not blossoming into a broader popular movement. Staff members decided to place their energies behind a series of technical training courses for women at the center's headquarters; these courses would teach the fundamentals of sewing and knitting so that poor women would have a marketable skill. Such efforts, however, did not address the low prices that artisans receive for their products or the labor issues that urban workers face. For workers—particularly women—low wages, limited employment opportunities, insecure working conditions, and lack of benefits constitute major impediments to improving their livelihoods.

Not surprisingly, the punishing discipline of the free market was, at least momentarily, overwhelming for the women of the federation. Small-scale projects, rather than broad-based protest, appealed to them because of the intense competition that characterized the struggle for survival in El Alto, and because NGOs like the Pachamama Center offered the opportunities to a limited number of beneficiaries. Developing ties to a broader constituency remained problematic in this context, and the federation continued to operate less as the combative popular organization envisioned by staff members of the Pachamama Center than as an NGO geared to the needs of a limited number of aid recipients.

The National Federation of Household Workers

Unlike the El Alto women's federation, the National Federation of Household Workers has wavered between two different strategies of struggle and organization. The federation is an umbrella organization that links local domestic workers' unions in several Bolivian cities; it is affiliated with a Latin America–based confederation of domestic workers. The federation's dilemma is whether union members should seek closer ties with and project support from numerous La Paz–based NGOs that focus on gender issues, or whether the federation should concentrate on building union membership and promoting domestic workers' rights independent of NGOs. These questions have engaged the membership with varying degrees of intensity for several years. The answers have not been easy or straightforward.

Although the chapters of the National Federation of Household Workers—established during the 1990s—were not born from an NGO, the current membership and the national leaders in La Paz are attracted by the possibilities that international financial support offers their federation. When the federation has established relationships with NGOs, however, they have often been tense and filled with mutual misunderstandings. The domestic workers have an abiding mistrust of the NGOs and the people who staff them, because they and members of other popular organizations believe that NGO staff members are basically corrupt and use foreign aid to support extravagant lifestyles. They are also highly suspicious of the intentions of the middle-class women who work in NGOs, because these women have domestic workers in their own homes, and relationships with them can be extremely demeaning.[11]

These misgivings have attenuated the union's contact with NGOs. At the same time, however, the domestic workers recognize that they cannot realistically sustain an organization with local contributions, such as membership dues, and they know that NGOs can provide badly needed financial assistance. They appreciate that the conditions demanded by NGOs are usually less onerous than the demands made by political parties, which have made occasional overtures to the women, but union leaders know that they must also reach out to popular organizations for solidarity and support. They have sometimes turned to the COB for guidance, but the COB's male leadership basically ignores them (see Gill 1994:126–29). Like the female staff members of the NGOs, male unionists employ servants in their households. "Unionists are terrible employers," said one member of the domestic workers' union. "They are so hypocritical with their worker speeches."[12] The domestic workers also resent the COB's failure to attend their events or even acknowledge their invitations, and they unfavorably compare the labor leaders with President Gonzalo Sánchez de Lozada, whose office regularly responds to their invitations with thank-you letters that explain why the president's busy schedule precludes his attendance. But more important than the COB's lack of etiquette is its overall weakness vis-à-vis the state and its inability to develop a strategy that incorporates the gender and ethnic diversity of the working class. Because of these problems, the domestic workers have increasingly, albeit hesitantly, turned to international organizations and their NGO intermediaries for collaboration and financial support.

In addition to financial backing for their daily activities, union leaders need advice about how to carry out some of their duties. Certain leadership responsibilities may be new for them and involve dealing with people and organizations that appear strange and unfamiliar, especially to those who have little experience in leadership positions. The leaders know that NGOs can often provide useful counsel. The guidance the leaders need may range from an explanation about how to operate a fax machine to advice about coordinating a national meeting to recommendations for acquiring the services of professionals, such as lawyers or social scientists.

Leaders, however, fear that behind the advice and the stated good intentions of many NGO staff members are unspoken agendas.[13] Because of these fears the unionists may remain aloof and try to learn little by little, or they may wait until they personally encounter someone in whom they can place their trust.[14]

When they do engage NGOs, they may do so as a defensive move designed to control the ability of these increasingly powerful organizations to speak on their behalf. In 1995, for example, union members hesitantly accepted the invitation of an NGO to participate in a video about domestic service that would be part of a project to sensitize employers about the needs and feelings of servants. The unionists questioned the NGO's ability to represent their concerns and feared that the organization would exploit them by using the video to raise money in Europe for staff members' salaries. After much internal debate the rank-and-file eventually assented when they realized that the NGO planned to go ahead with the project with or without their participation.

NGOs have in fact not been the best allies. A proposed law to regulate domestic service did not receive the critical scrutiny from feminist NGOs that it deserved. The proposed law mandated a minimum ten-hour workday for live-in domestic workers, even though other sectors of the labor force had won the right to an eight-hour workday decades earlier. The argument in support of a longer day for live-in servants was that the extra hours were a form of compensation to employers who provide food and lodging for peasant girls with no other means of support in the city. This was a position commonly advanced by employers, but in 1995 it started to be articulated by the Subsecretariat of Gender—a section of the Ministry of Human Development that is developing the legislation and is staffed almost entirely by middle-class women from the NGO sector.

After assessing the balance of forces, the federation grudgingly supported this legislation, because leaders reasoned that a law—any law—was better than nothing at all. In private, however, they were quick to condemn the provision for a ten-hour day, pointing out that employers do not allow the servants to use their rooms as if they were private quarters. Federation leaders noted that employers strictly control visitors and reserve the right to store mops, brooms, and other household items in the servants' quarters. Moreover, in many cases domestic workers did not even have their own rooms and were obliged to sleep on kitchen floors.

Leaders understood that their organization did not have the organizational and political strength to push forward alternative legislation, and in the absence of stronger support from organized labor, they had few allies in their struggles for better working conditions. Consequently, they cautiously engaged NGOs in the hope of benefiting from the financial support that these organizations could provide. As they did so, the vision and the possibility of forging a strong union that fights for better conditions for working women faded from view, and the union increasingly adopted the project-centered focus of an NGO.

NGOs have assumed the right to represent some impoverished groups to the state and international funding organizations. They have done so by creating grassroots organizations and collaborating with preexisting groups to support specific kinds of initiatives. Although the NGO boom has benefited some women who are positioned to take advantage of the new opportunities offered by economic restructuring, it has thus far done little to strengthen the ability of disadvantaged constituencies to organize politically and fight against neoliberalism. The NGO boom has aggravated the rifts and fragmentation that divide people from each other, as some people manage to resituate themselves within emerging configurations of power, while others see new possibilities and old ways of surviving closed to them.

Equally problematic is that the NGOs have not backed the struggles of politically organized public school teachers. During the 1995 strike, examined in chapter 5, NGOs based in El Alto and La Paz neither supported the labor movement nor spoke out against the detention of leaders, the suspension of the right to assemble, and the police repression. For NGOs and their international patrons, public school teachers were too culturally mundane. They manifested none of the exoticism of indigenous peoples or the trendiness of gender; indeed, they were frequently criticized by middle-class professionals in the NGOs for being alienated from their own culture and constituting a hindrance to the reform of public education. But more important than teachers' cultural ambivalence was that public support for workers' rights—especially those of state workers who belong to one of the most radical unions in Bolivia—was never on the agendas of the NGOs. Such a display of solidarity could alienate them from their international patrons, and this was a risk that NGOs were not willing to take. In addition, NGO directors, who were primarily social democrats, were reticent about collaborating with Trotskyists.

When asked about support from NGOs, teacher Alex Morales, head of education and culture for El Alto's Central Obrera Regional (COR), the local chapter of the COB, said that NGOs not only failed to participate in the demonstrations that preceded the imposition of martial law but did not even display symbolic solidarity through the publication of statements in the newspapers.[15] Indeed, the director of a La Paz NGO most noted for its work in the public education system limited himself to writing a series of editorials in a national newspaper that addressed technical aspects of the educational reform, but the editorials never mentioned the strike or the demands of the teachers.[16] In addition, the director of another NGO, which specializes in the production of radio programs in health and mathematics for elementary school children, felt comfortable broadcasting the programs during the strike. "The teachers know that we support them," he said awkwardly, "but we have to honor our contract with the radio station." Such statements and practices illustrate the difference between NGOs' self-representation as the advocates of "civil society" and their actual practice when groups of working people dared to challenge neoliberalism and the Bolivian state.

9 · El Alto, the State, and the Capitalist Imperium

In a Barsotti cartoon published in the *New Yorker*, two workers are looking into the distance and one comments to the other: "There, there it is again—the invisible hand of the marketplace giving us the finger." They, like working people in El Alto, understand that capitalist processes are rather more concrete and destructive than the notion of an invisible hand suggests, and, after more than a decade of economic restructuring—and getting the proverbial finger from national and international policy makers—El Alto continues to provide an instructive example of what is wrong with the global economic order. Although neoliberalism has not caused all the city's misery, the free-market reforms of the last fifteen years are both aggravating and undermining old forms of capitalist oppression while simultaneously creating new ones.

To understand the consequences of these processes for the poor of El Alto, in this book I have turned an ethnographic lens on changing forms of state rule, and this perspective has delineated how the state, in the midst of global, political, and economic restructuring, appears in and disappears from the lives of ordinary people in the city. I have also explored how diverse alteños, as they become poorer, contend not only with the state but with each other and a variety of NGOs to get what they need to continue to live. I have argued that as the state increasingly shuns "the nation" and nation-building projects to attend to the claims of global creditors, it fails to deal with the demands of ordinary people for decent jobs, health care, education, and a range of other services. The ensuing crisis has threatened the domestic legitimacy of the state and prompted neoliberal policy makers to adopt a number of strategies to fortify the state's authority. The strategies include the decentralization of some power to local entities, the surrendering of social service provision to a plethora of nominally private NGOs, and the deployment of new discourses about "popular participation." Yet even as the state retrenches from its social welfare responsibilities, it is reemerging in defense of capitalist privilege and refurbished militarism. The state has sold numerous public resources (transportation and telecommunications companies, pension funds, mines, etc.) to private firms, often at artificially low prices, while the armed forces continue to enjoy substantial power. The military apparatus has weathered the downsizing and privatization of public institutions better than those charged with the distribution of social services, even though it too has experienced a limited reorganization. As the state's policies push more people into poverty, the state increasingly calls upon the army and militarized police forces to repress the so-called dangerous classes and to control the widespread alienation from the retreating state.

This reconfiguration of state power has broad implications for daily life in El Alto and other impoverished Third World cities undergoing similar transformations. As the state ignores the worsening plight of the urban poor, survival turns almost entirely on the social relationships that people are able to construct themselves, but in El Alto men and women—ruined peasants, ex-miners, schoolteachers, displaced urbanites from La Paz—are too poor to provide each other with all the resources they need. What has been done to them—and what they in turn are often forced to do to each other—gives rise to a complex array of tensions that people cannot resolve on their own. Unemployment and forced migration frequently disrupt the fragile social bonds that hold households together; mass landlordism divides the very poor from the slightly better-off; rampant real estate speculation and selling the same lot to more than one set of buyers at a time pits residents against each other; the saturation of the informal economy with desperate vendors forces people to compete for declining returns; and clientelistic relationships with more powerful groups and individuals reproduce the growing social fragmentation.

My grim account appears to offer little hope of a more comfortable egalitarian future for residents of the city, because the political and economic supports for a benevolent capitalism have always been fragile, and, increasingly, they seem to no longer exist. The historical moment considered by this book is reactionary in every sense, and it is therefore easy to agree with Ellen Meiksins Woods, who concludes at the end of her study of democracy and capitalism that "the lesson we may be obliged to draw from our current economic and political condition is that a humane, 'social,' truly democratic and equitable capitalism is more unrealistically utopian than socialism" (1995:293).

The experiences of Bolivian tin miners certainly support this assertion. The closure of state mines pushed workers out of jobs, forced them from their communities, and dealt a heavy blow to the labor movement. Miners now scratch out a living with Aymara immigrants on the streets of El Alto. The relationships and understandings that guided their class struggles in the mining centers are not always useful in the city, where miners encounter each other less as "workers" than as "self-employed" individuals. The omnipresence of the state is vastly diminished in their daily lives, and because of the debilitation of the union, advancing their claims in broader political arenas is extremely difficult. Former miners must resituate themselves against state power and the power of the International Monetary Fund. Yet this is not easy, because their very identity has changed. Men and women from the mining communities are faced with the daunting task of rebuilding a series of social relationships with their Aymara neighbors, who suffer from many of the same humiliations and restrictions imposed on the kinds of lives that people can have.

How they deal with the state and global financial institutions depends to a considerable degree on how they remember, forget, and even separate themselves from past experiences, as they shape a future in the context of present uncertainties. Yet, as we have seen, former miners are having considerable difficulty overcoming the fragmentation of social life in El Alto. What lessons might they still draw from past experiences that could serve as a resource for future struggles? How much of an alternative vision of social life do they have to create anew from contemporary life circumstances? And what kinds of lessons will children draw from the experiences of social rupture, migration, and loss? The answers to these questions are extremely important in Latin America, where popular movements and the Left are widely viewed as having failed to achieve many of their objectives.[1] As living conditions continue to deteriorate for those on the bottom, miners are finding it increasing difficult to incorporate their experiences of collective struggle into narratives of resilience and survival, much less a vision of a better world. Nevertheless, the memory of their struggles remains alive in the city, where it animates the teachers' battle against the Educational Reform Law.

Public school teachers understand what happened to the miners, and they now worry that the state will dispose of them in the same way. Some even describe the neoliberal assault on public education as another *reloca-*

lización, the official euphemism for the massive firing of miners. They mean, of course, the loss of their jobs—a class relocation—not a physical process of removal. Neoliberalism does indeed threaten the future of public education and the job security of teachers. It also heightens long-standing tensions between parents and teachers that are difficult to address within the confines of El Alto's poverty.

For parents, education represents one of the very few routes out of poverty for their children, and they take it very seriously. They are therefore justifiably angered by teachers who view the teaching profession less as an opportunity to educate children than as a vehicle for social and economic mobility. And parents are appropriately annoyed by teachers who distance themselves from their cultural and social origins and treat students and parents like second-class citizens. The Educational Reform Law offers these parents the hope of improving the quality of education through greater local control of teachers and schools, and we should not be surprised that some parents view the state as an ally in their efforts to make teachers accountable to students. Nevertheless, the tantalizing promises of the educational reform—including bilingual education and updated teaching methodologies—come packaged with an assault on teachers' job security, and the state is not offering additional educational funding, which is likely to come from extra fees charged to parents.

Teachers, for their part, are the products of the impoverished system in which they work. Faced with low pay and diminishing job security, they are hard pressed to deliver a quality education. Burnout and high attrition rates are indicative of some of the problems that they must confront, and even the best, most committed teachers cannot properly educate hungry malnourished children crammed into overcrowded classrooms. Most understand parental concerns because they too are parents, but they correctly argue that reforming El Alto's inadequate public education system should not happen at the expense of their job security.

Looking at the antagonisms that emerge among alteños in the context of neoliberal restructuring is not to state simply that social life is divided, impoverished, and disorganized because of the actions of the state and the IMF. The point is too well known to need further elaboration. Exploring the ruptures that divide alteños from each other is, rather, to think seriously about social and historical change among subjugated people. It is to consider how collective organizing becomes more difficult within a shifting framework of incorporation into and dislocation from national and international circuits of power. It is to think about how people with very few resources struggle to retain a sense of humanity and self-worth in the context of serious constraints imposed by others who are not accountable to them. As Gerald Sider has remarked: "Divisions and ruptures can . . . be an impetus for mobilization and a source of strength within ongoing confrontations, for they give to exploited and oppressed classes and communities a partly autonomous historical dynamic: continuing and changing social relations to one another which, despite their complex origins, come to be partly their own" (1996:76). Rather than delineating a context of defeat and passive resignation, or simply romanticizing resistance of the "everyday" kind, we must attend to the complexity of local experiences and the ways in which pain, loss, and desperation shape daily life.

Although it is impossible to foresee the outcome of these processes, the specific material conditions that people encounter govern to a very large extent what is, and is not, feasible at particular historical junctures. Creating a politics that addresses the eroding material basis of social life, bridges the divisions among local people, and respects cultural heterogeneity— even as people are re-creating and transforming cultural differences—is perhaps the biggest challenge that alteños and other Latin Americans face. Although the destruction of the miners' union undermined the principles of one form of class solidarity, it opened possibilities for new alliances between former miners and Aymara immigrants in El Alto, as both groups increasingly encountered the same dismal working conditions on the streets of the city. Moreover, the ongoing battle between public school teachers and the state suggests that more traditional forms of class politics are still alive. Yet it is not clear that alteños will be able to defend and broaden the key principles of egalitarianism and solidarity that have informed popular struggles.

Developing alliances between grassroots organizations and sympathetic international constituencies is clearly important, because alteños need new political connections to advance their claims in national and international arenas. They also need financial support in order to do so. We have seen that it is unrealistic to expect impoverished people to sustain themselves and their organizations on the inadequate resources that are available to them. Creating ties to mainstream political parties has not always been a viable alternative, either. Affiliating with mainstream parties frequently robs local people of their autonomy and leaves them feeling manipulated, deceived, and even more marginalized.

Although NGOs appear to present alternatives to the parties and the state, the proliferation of NGOs also poses a series of pitfalls for local residents. Some people can seize on the opportunities offered by the NGOs and initiate, or take part in, projects that provide them with relief from the city's grinding poverty. By so doing, they effectively bypass the state and establish ties with local elites and global institutions that open new pathways of class mobility for them. Such opportunities, however, tend to be available only to those individuals who fulfill the NGO criteria for appropriate beneficiaries. As these and other people organize in response to international funding, they frequently abandon broad-based collective organizing for the more immediate rewards of narrowly defined projects that benefit only them and a handful of other individuals. Consequently, everyone in need of assistance is not included in the numerous disconnected microprojects purveyed by the NGOs, and the life circumstances of those not served deteriorate or fail to improve. NGO programs are an inadequate substitute for a broad, democratically managed urban development plan, and they tend to aggravate processes of differentiation and fragmentation in the city.

Although NGOs incorporate some of El Alto's poor in new national and global networks, the organizations are primarily controlled by middle-class professionals, who are their ultimate beneficiaries. NGOs have become an important employment option for the professional middle class at a time when economic crisis and the retrenchment of state agencies are eroding a traditional source of middle-class jobs. As professionals lay claim to "development" resources, they bolster their own economic fortunes, and, by portraying themselves as the representatives of the poor, they strengthen their position vis-à-vis the state and international funding agencies. Such self-serving portrayals offend many would-be beneficiaries in El Alto who disagree with how they are represented to international agencies by NGO staff members and who want to control NGO funds for their own projects.

NGOs that emerged from progressive movements insist that supporting a broadly defined "popular movement" is one of their primary objectives. Yet as neoliberalism wears into the next millennium, the nature of this commitment is ever more problematic. The opposition of public school teachers to the Educational Reform Law was not, and is not, supported by NGOs, even though the teachers moved to the forefront of popular resistance to neoliberalism in the aftermath of the mining debacle. Given the neoliberal assault on the labor movement—and the earlier repression by military dictatorships—it is remarkable that a combative union continues to exist in Bolivia. Yet despite their tenacity, teachers are contradictory figures for most NGO directors. Teachers display none of the exoticism of other kinds of NGO beneficiaries, and the Trotskyist union leadership offends the social democratic sensibilities of most NGO directors, who characterize its confrontational politics as a practice of a bygone era. Thus the growth of NGOs in El Alto has been based less on the support of preexisting popular organizations than on the creation of new ones.

This does not have to be the case. Although Bolivia has been notable for the size, strength, and militancy of its popular movements, progressive NGOs can still play a more positive role in supporting grassroots organizations in both national and international arenas. They can also play some positive role in articulating the concerns of unrepresented sectors and contributing to improvements in well-being. To do so, however, they must first critically engage neoliberal state policies and reexamine their own relationship to the state, as well as their shifting ties to local people. They must then begin to conceptualize more daring projects of coordinated action and political cooperation among the popular Lefts in all countries of the Americas.

Although the relationship between development NGOs and local people is problematic, the NGO-ization of El Alto has also generated new problems and possibilities for the state. Striping away state-supported social services and entitlements is a central activity of neoliberal policy makers everywhere, but it generates intense public controversy. Passing off the provision of these services to nominally private NGOs is part of an exercise in state legitimation. NGOs palliate the worst effects of state policies on the poor and fill some of the gap left by the state. One result, however, is that state institutions are now even less available and accountable to poor citizens than in 1985, when economic restructuring began. NGOs have simultaneously occupied a larger political space in the city. The most successful NGOs now threaten the very legitimacy that the state sought to restore. This is not because the organizations challenge the state's existence, as some did during the military dictatorships. Rather, neoliberal NGOs and those that accommodated to neoliberalism are providing services that the state no longer offers, or only provides badly, and they claim to be doing so more efficiently than public agencies and in the spirit of nonpartisan professionalism. In addition, the large sums of development dollars that flow into NGO coffers without any local accountability further aggravate the challenge that NGOs pose to the state.[2]

Thus in 1993, when the Sánchez de Lozada administration invited NGOs to engage its vision of popular participation and appointed individuals from the NGO sector to government posts, it was trying to reassert its control over social life and to incorporate NGOs more directly under its tutelage while ceding some local planning to NGOs and grassroots organizations. Whether the state is able to accomplish this task remains to be seen. In the 1990s the growing political convergence of the Bolivian state and development NGOs is less the result of the state's regulation of the latter than the increasing control exercised over both by global financial institutions.

We should therefore not concur immediately with anthropologist James Ferguson, who asserts, based on an analysis of a World Bank development project in Lesotho, that "the 'development apparatus' . . . is a machine for reinforcing and expanding the exercise of bureaucratic state power" (1994:255). To do so glosses over the complex reconfiguring of state power that is underway in Bolivia and elsewhere. Ferguson's otherwise insightful analysis misses the ways that neoliberals target the public sector for reduction; indeed, reconfiguring the public sector is the primary goal of neoliberal development theory. Because his investigation is based on Foucauldian conceptualizations of decentered power and relies on discourse analysis, he does not appreciate the diverse ways that state institutions are participating in (or vanishing from) the process of global economic restructuring, and he overlooks the ways that poor people incorporate themselves in new networks of power that bypass the state.[3]

Manuel Castells has suggested that the state is increasingly one of many nodes in a broader network of global power (1997:304). This observation is less novel for impoverished, dependent Third World countries than for European and North American states, but it is indicative of how states' control over territory, goods, and people is changing. We have seen how microcredit programs in El Alto represent the frontier of a new form of surplus extraction pioneered by international development banks and domestic entrepreneurs that operate beyond the control of the state. But we have also seen how the state, through exploitative food-for-work programs, is gaining access and control over the labor of poor women to subsidize public works projects in the city. Rather than simply expanding state power, "the development apparatus" is constitutive of the complex ways that the state is being reconfigured and the ways its relationship to ordinary people is being transformed. The state's ultimate success in redefining its legitimacy will turn on an ability to engage the concrete material needs of impoverished citizens, a likelihood that seems ever more remote.

Even though the Bolivian state has lost control over many aspects of social and economic policy, its military apparatus remains key to the enforcement of the very order that neoliberal policies are actively undermining. Indeed, the armed forces constitute the guardian of the country's nominal, and increasingly militarized, democracy (NACLA 1998). While antinarcotics police forces loom most prominently, the traditional armed forces, marginalized from the war on drugs by their own corruption, survive under neoliberalism because of enduring and deepening social tensions. The army in particular remains little more than an internal enforcer of the domestic status quo, as it has failed to define a new mission related to external defense.

Seeking to craft a new role for themselves in the post–cold war world, some sectors of the military have turned haltingly to development and civic action programs in order to strengthen the legitimacy of the armed forces. As the burden of compulsory military service has shifted from the state to poor recruits and their families, many young men complain that entering the army is a waste of time, because they learn few of the skills promised by the institution. Military development programs address these complaints by claiming to educate recruits and to use them to address the country's poverty. Such initiatives, however, obscure the distinctions between civilian and military arenas at a time when state-sponsored civilian social service agencies are retrenching, but the military programs enjoy considerable support from poor people, who are increasingly unable to turn to other public entities for assistance. Indeed, the military remains the most powerful, and increasingly the only viable, state entity in Bolivia.

Compulsory military service, perhaps more than any other arena of social life, reflects the collusions, antagonisms, and accommodations that shape daily life in contemporary El Alto. Even though the military brutalizes men and obliges them to subsidize its activities, young men enter military service voluntarily because it is one of the few opportunities available to them to cope with their own social marginalization. Military service symbolizes certain rights to citizenship and confers others. It also enables poor men to challenge their social exclusion through the assertion of a sense of masculinity cultivated in the armed forces. Yet poor men's use of military service for self-affirmation is also tied to collusion with dominant uses of the male poor and linked to relationships of inequality between dominated men and women and even among different kinds of men. Young men never become true citizens after their stint in the armed forces, and military development schemes cannot manage or absorb the difficulties that their families face. Moreover, even if the military programs were widely available, they likely would aggravate existing inequalities among the poor.

Although nobody ventures predictions nowadays about the end of capitalism, no social system lasts forever, and the relative brevity of the neoliberal project suggests that triumphalist claims about a glorious "New World Order" are premature. Yet the collapse of communism, and particularly the crumbling of the Cuban Revolution, means that impoverished peoples of the Americas can now be treated with even less prudence than in the past. This point was brought home to me when I returned to Bolivia in 1997 and encountered Fernando Mendoza, a mine worker I had interviewed. Mendoza had just turned fifty and on the day after his birthday quickly petitioned the government for his monthly retirement pension. He explained that if he waited, the enactment of a new social security law would disqualify him for fifteen years. The law, passed after the privatization of the social security system, changed the official retirement age from fifty to sixty-five—more than six years beyond the life expectancy of the average Bolivian, and even further beyond the life expectancy of miners, who suffer from a variety of respiratory ailments related to work in the mines.

The brutality of contemporary neoliberalism is not limited to Bolivia. For example, growing inequalities and the concentration of landownership in Brazil sparked the Landless Workers' Movement, which has generated a national debate about agrarian reform. Neoliberalism and social justice issues also animate the Zapatistas in Mexico. The same forces that make social life so untenable in El Alto and Latin America wreak havoc in other parts of the Third World, as well as in U.S. cities. They also invade the defended precincts of the U.S. middle class and middle classes elsewhere and threaten the fragile privileges that depend on the continued exploitation of immigrants, minorities, and other working people. The similarities compel us to acknowledge that our futures are more closely intertwined than many would like to believe, and the particulars of geography are no guarantee against oppression and loss. As this book goes to press, thousands of people protest the secretive, antidemocratic global trade talks sponsored by the World Trade Organization (WTO) in Seattle. Demonstrators demand that the WTO stop undermining health, labor, and environmental protections around the world. To sustain and encourage these and other struggles that are likely to develop, a truly democratic and popular internationalism must be high on the agenda for the coming years.

Notes

1. Introduction

1. Although the "Chicago Boys" is a label used to describe the group of Chilean economists educated at the University of Chicago who orchestrated Chile's turn to neoliberalism, "the Boys" is a more general label that has been used to designate their counterparts in other Andean countries. See Conaghan, Malloy, and Abugatas (1990).

2. See, for example, Davidoff and Hall (1987) for a discussion of gender and religion in the formation of the British middle class.

3. A number of anthropological and historical studies within the Marxist tradition have not received the scholarly attention that they deserve. See, for example, Sider (1986) for an interesting theoretical discussion of the dynamics of class and culture and Steadman (1986) on class and gender. See also the debate between Patrick Joyce (1996) and Geoff Ely and Keith Nield (1996).

4. Cholo is an amorphous category that represents the vast social distance between two other salient racial divisions in Bolivian society: "indio," or Indian, and "blanco," or white. Because distinctions and boundaries between indios and cholos, and cholos and blancos, are so nebulous, Bolivians frequently contest these designations. All translations from the Spanish are my own.

5. See the collection of articles edited by Sider and Smith (1997) for more discussion of differentiation and class; see also Sider (1993).

6. Mendoza's classic novel describes social conditions in Llallagua, a major mining center, at the turn of the century.

7. See Conaghan and Malloy (1994) and Vilas (1997) for discussions of decentralization and political participation in the Andes and elsewhere.

8. Although the term *nongovernmental organization* could refer to the commercial private sector, scholars typically use the term to describe nonprofit, national, and international organizations.

9. There is considerable debate in the literature about what actually constitutes an NGO. See, for example, Arellano-López and Petras (1994) and Graham (1992).

10. See also "Imperialism," the 1993 special issue of *Radical History Review*, for scholarly debate about the contemporary relevance of imperialism as an analytic category.

11. For example, after Sánchez de Lozada became president in 1993, Bolivians often complimented me and other North Americans by observing that we spoke Spanish better than the president. These comments were less a reflection of our facility with the language than of Sánchez de Lozada's heavy accent and abysmal grammatical mistakes.

12. See Edelman (1997) for a comparative discussion of nineteenth-century liberalism and twentieth-century neoliberalism in Central America.

13. Current research on Latin America includes some important studies of processes of state formation. See, for example, Alonso (1995), Nugent (1997), Joseph and Nugent (1994), Smith (1990b), and Urban and Sherzer (1991).

14. Much of the discussion of coercion and consent draws on Antonio Gramsci's discussions of hegemony, a ongoing contested process that, for Gramsci, defined the limits of the possible at particular historical junctures (Gramsci 1971).

15. Much of the research on so-called new social movements, for example, overstates the autonomy of urban popular movements, frequently idealizes "civil society" as a realm of democratic popular organizing and identity formation separate from the state (e.g., Escóbar and Alvarez 1992; Jelin 1990), and separates "cultural politics" from material and historical processes (Alvarez, Dagnino, and Escóbar 1998). Social movements, however, forge alliances with other actors, particularly states. These alliances shift over time and have enormous significance for how people understand their problems and act on them. Local leaders may also choose to participate in state projects, and their democratic intentions cannot always be assumed. For a critique of new social movement research, see Calhoun (1993) and Edelman (1999).

16. See Held (1991) for more discussion on the fate of democracy and the state in the increasingly interconnected global system.

17. See Roseberry (1994) for a critical discussion of some of Corrigan and Sayer's ideas and their relevance for understanding processes of state formation in Mexico.

18. See Wilson (1987) and Lewis (1966).

19. Bourgois's book won an award from the profession, and Nugent described it as an "impressive and important book" in the *American Ethnologist* (1996:687). It generated a certain amount of positive attention in the popular media, but prompted academic reviewers and journalists on both the Left and the Right to condemn the author. Lassalle and O'Dougherty (1997) accuse him of corroborating racist stereotypes, albeit inadvertently. Di Leonardo describes Bourgois's book as "yellow journalism" (1998:349), and Adam Schatz (1995:836–39) excoriates Bourgois for similar reasons in the *Nation*. Right-wing reviewer Richard Bernstein, however, chides Bourgois in the *New York Times* for worrying that "he might be seen as fostering prejudicial images of the poor" and dismisses Bourgois's attempts to discuss institutional racism in New York. According to Bernstein, Bourgois is unable to entertain the possibility that crack dealers "might simply be bad" (1995:C19).

20. See William Roseberry's discussion of the research on Latin American peasants (1993) for a useful summary of the definitions of and the debates surrounding the agrarian question.

21. See, for example, the four-volume work on La Paz by Xavier Albó, Tomás Greaves, and Godofredo Sandoval, *Chukiyawu: La cara Aymara de La Paz* (1981, 1982, 1983, 1987), as well as Silvia Rivera Cusicanqui's work on microcredit operations in La Paz and El Alto (1996). Recent research by North Americans on La Paz includes the Buechlers' work on small-scale manufacturing (Buechler and Buechler 1992) and my ethnography on female domestic service (Gill 1994).

22. Marc Edelman (1996:43) also makes this observation in his research on a transnational peasant movement.

2. City of the Future

1. In this regard, La Paz resembles other cities in North and South America. See, for example, Davis (1990) on Los Angeles and Caldeira (1996) on Rio de Janeiro. Yet La Paz has not reached the violent extremes that these authors describe.

2. A 1996 survey of urban dwellers that included residents of El Alto found that 87 percent of the nearly one thousand people questioned believed that common delinquency was on the rise ("La corrupción" 1996:1).

3. This is a marked contrast to the neighboring Brazilian cities of Rio de Janeiro and Sao Paulo, where the urban police forces engage in extrajudicial executions and forcibly "disappear" civilians (Human Rights Watch/Americas 1997). The use of *disappear* as an active verb came into use in Latin America during the era of military dictatorships in the 1970s and 1980s. "To disappear" refers to the way that people were kidnaped and murdered by military and paramilitary death squads, who subsequently denied any knowledge of the victims' whereabouts.

4. For more discussion of the growth of a transnational working class in several Asian cities, see Seabrook (1996).

5. See Gill (1987) for a discussion of the emergence of large-scale commercial agriculture in eastern Bolivia and its consequences for peasant migrants from the highland and valley regions of the country.

6. See Albó and Preiswerk (1986) for a detailed description of Gran Poder.

7. See Hansen (1994) for a discussion of the used clothing trade in Zambia.

3. Adjusting Poverty

1. This fear of hospitals is very common among poor Bolivians. See also Scheper-Hughes (1992:246–49) for a discussion of the "everyday violence" of hospital clinics in Northeast Brazil.

2. A large anthropological literature examines these monstrous beings. For Bolivia see Wachtel (1994), Rivera Cusicanqui (1990:113–14), Weismantel (1998), and Crandon-Malamud (1991). For accounts in other parts of the Andes, see Brown and Fernández (1991:143–63) on the Peruvian Amazon, Taussig (1987:221–41) on Colombia, and Ansión (1989) on the Peruvian highlands.

3. The municipal government provisionally recognized the claims of residents to their lots in Villa Pedro Domingo Murillo, and the developer was jailed on charges of tax fraud.

4. See Sider and Smith (1997) for a useful discussion of experience and silence.

4. Miners and the Politics of Revanchism

1. See Barrios de Chungara (1978) for an interesting discussion of gender relationships in the mining communities. Barrios de Chungara—the wife of a tin miner—describes how in 1961 miners' wives organized a housewives' committee to support the struggles of their husbands. Nevertheless, male workers jeered the women and told them to return to the kitchen.

2. June Nash's classic book on the San José mine (1979) demonstrates how solidarity was crafted by the rituals and practices that gave meaning to workers' experiences and collective oppression.

3. See Godoy (1990) for a discussion of the very different kinds of working conditions that prevailed in numerous small-scale mines scattered about the countryside of northern Potosí department.

4. For years successive governments—civilian and military—did not invest in modernized equipment or the exploration of new reserves. Governments alternately used mineral revenues to subsidize agroindustrial development in the eastern lowlands or to service the foreign debt, accumulated in the 1970s during the regime of General Hugo Banzer.

5. At this writing, the government has still refused to equalize redundancy payments to former miners.

6. See Arauco Lemaitre and Romero Bedregal (1987) for an analysis of the destinations of ex-miners.

7. I am using the term *classy* in much the same way that Steedman (1986:23) uses it to describe female weavers from northern England.

8. See Carolyn Steedman (1986) for an interesting discussion of children and class.

9. See Katherine Verdery (1996:168–203) for a discussion of pyramid investment schemes in postsocialist Romania. Verdery argues that these schemes arose in Romania and other postsocialist Eastern European societies in the wake of economic restructuring and the transition to capitalism. By enriching a few and impoverishing many, they became important new instruments of class formation.

10. Díaz turned to other economic pursuits to earn a living. She worked for a time in a civic action program dubbed "Food for Work," which provides surplus U.S. grain through the U.S. Agency for International Development. That program required her to work on road construction projects in exchange for payment in food. She also knitted sweaters on a part-time basis for export businesses and participated in various NGO programs designed to generate income among poor women.

11. See Steve Striffler (1999) for an interesting discussion of economic restructuring in the Ecuadorean banana industry. Striffler demonstrates how the shift from plantation-based production to contract farming undermined the ability of people to identify as workers.

12. See "Terminó conflicto" (1992).

5. School Discipline

1. These figures represent salaries paid in 1995.

2. See Luykx (1999) for an interesting discussion of a normal school in La Paz department and the education of rural schoolteachers.

3. For a discussion of the long-term consequences of similar educational reforms, see Collins and Lear's discussion of the Chilean reform, which was initiated fourteen years before the 1994 Bolivian Educational Reform Law (Collins and Lear 1995). The Chilean reform has generated many of the outcomes that Bolivian teachers fear.

4. Teacher resistance eventually forced the state to rescind this part of the law.

5. For years peasants in the coca-growing region of the Chapare have been waging a battle with the government and the United States over their right to grow coca leaf. Their protests were a major factor in the government's decision to impose martial law.

6. I visited one jailed leader in La Paz's filthy and overcrowded San Pedro prison. Shortly after his imprisonment, this individual began to experience acute facial paralysis, but despite his obviously serious condition, he was not given any medical assistance.

6. The Military and Daily Life

1. *Low-intensity democracy* is a term that I have borrowed from Robinson (1996:4).

2. This is similar to the process that Lovell and Stiehm (1989) describe for the U.S. military.

3. The allegedly civilizing influence of military service is less important in the predominantly mestizo lowlands. This may have some bearing on the higher rate of draft evasion in this part of the country.

4. Not surprisingly, the parallels between this aspect of the Bolivian military and that described for the U.S. military by Arkin and Dobrofsky (1990) are strong.

5. Although the resolution sent tremors through the military establishment, no widespread draft evasion occurred in 1990, and in subsequent years the CSUTCB did not press the antidraft campaign.

6. See, for example, "Valle" (1986), "Presupuesto de FF.AA." (1986), and "Reforma del presupuesto" (1986).

7. See "No habrá aumentos en FF.AA." (1989), "Si no se aumentaba" (1989), "El anterior gobierno" (1989).

8. See "Reservistas del altiplano" (1992).

9. Men have other legal ways to acquire a military book without actually serving in the armed forces. Physical disabilities and family situations in which the son is the sole supporter of elderly parents exempt men from service. University students are also allowed to postpone service until the completion of their studies, at which time they must enlist for one year at the rank of "honorary subofficer." They receive payment in accord with that rank and are employed as professionals. Engineers, for example, might teach; doctors provide medical services, and so forth. Student deferments are obviously not an option for poor men, who cannot afford the cost in time and money of a university education.

10. These tales of suffering also rarely acknowledge the considerable sacrifices made by their mothers and other family members, who bring food and clothing to them during their tour of duty.

11. See Sider (1993:203–207) for similar assertions by Native Americans in the United States.

12. The tradition of *Viernes de Soltero,* or Bachelor Fridays, among urban middle-

class bureaucrats and workers, both married and single, is part of a broader social and cultural arena in which sexual subordination and the reaffirmation of certain kinds of masculinity occur. Men typically gather to drink, talk, and bond with each other.

13. See Stern (1995:151–88) for additional discussion of the social construction of masculinity in colonial Mexico.

14. The official did so during a period of repressive military dictatorship, when, as a young man, he was part of the political opposition. Yet for partisan political purposes, right-wing politicians—who in many cases had also avoided military service, albeit, perhaps, in a legally recognized way—fanned the scandal surrounding his falsified military booklet. Ex-recruits know that political leaders of the Right and Left routinely use their class and ethnic privileges to avoid service and still manage to find gainful employment. They thus had little sympathy for the individual enveloped in the scandal.

15. See Linda Rennie Forcey (1987:117–35) for more discussion of how women in the United States encourage sons to enlist in the armed forces so that they can shift some of the enormous responsibility for the young men's welfare to the state.

16. See "Reforma del presupuesto" (1986). Numerous conscripts whom I interviewed about military service dispute Valle's assertions. The vast majority of these recruits did not learn how to read and write during their year of compulsory military service.

17. See "Empieza plan de alfabetización" (1991).

18. See Emily Martin (1987). The comparison between the violent imagery used to instruct troops and the benign ways that nuclear scientists talk about making bombs is also noteworthy. See, for example, Gusterson (1998) and Cohn (1987).

19. The actual sums spent by the U.S. Defense Department on civic actions programs in Bolivia are:

1996	$21,300
1997	$148,849
1998	$159,900

These figures appear small because the Defense Department considers them "incidental" to the much greater expense associated with troop and equipment deployment, which are not factored into the costs of civic action initiatives (Latin American Working Group 1998).

7. Power Lines

1. "Ruidosa marcha de cacerolas" (1995).

2. Those NGOs that operated during the dictatorships typically adopted a low public profile. One organization, for example, changed its name to a more technocratic-sounding appellation and did not post a sign on its offices. Similarly, its programs, which were primarily centered in the countryside, deemphasized consciousness-raising activities and concentrated on protecting a popular political base during a time of extreme political and economic hardship.

3. The career of former vice president Víctor Hugo Cárdenas (1993–1997) embodied this shift. During the 1970s and 1980s Cárdenas was a participant and then a leader of an Aymara peasant movement known as Katarismo. He was simultaneously affiliated with a church-based NGO, which provided him with political cover to a con-

siderable extent. With the return of civilian rule he left the NGO and dedicated himself to more open political organizing.

4. Castañeda (1993:237–66) discusses the fragmentation of the Left's basic paradigm throughout Latin America during the 1980s.

5. International organizations established similar funds in other Latin American countries for the same reasons.

6. Castañeda (1993) describes similar processes in other parts of Latin America. Paradoxically, little evidence existed to support such an assumption in Bolivia, where private enterprise has long counted on state subsidies and protection.

7. See Laura MacDonald (1997) for a discussion of a similar USAID strategy in Costa Rica, where it promoted NGOs as a private sector alternative to so-called state paternalism.

8. Elson (1992:41) points out that men are freer than women to migrate in search of work. She also suggests that the increase of female-headed households in much of the Third World shows that migration can be a cover for desertion, which further depletes the resources available to women. Also, see her article for a general discussion of the importance of unpaid female labor for structural adjustment programs.

The P.L. 480 program is a long-standing U.S. government program that distributes surplus produce to Third World countries. Although the program is ostensibly a form of "development aid," it undermines independent wheat producers in many parts of Latin America and props up prices for U.S. farmers.

9. When they spoke of empowerment, these individuals frequently used the English word *empower* or the Spanish *potenciar.*

10. Although 63 percent of the borrowers were women, they received only 56 percent of the total amount that Procrédito disbursed.

11. Wahl (1997) argues that NGOs take on only those responsibilities that are insufficiently lucrative to attract the commercial sector, such as social and environmental concerns. He believes that, because NGOs do not contend with the private sector, they risk becoming politically irrelevant on the world stage and being excluded from key arenas of decision making. In Bolivia the move from nonprofit NGO to for-profit banking institutions suggests that some NGOs are quite willing to advocate capitalist policies and that they are less adverse to the commercial private sector than Wahl implies.

12. Bancosol president Fernando Romero was in a good position to lead this effort. Born in the lowland city of Santa Cruz in 1941, Romero received a master's degree in industrial administration from the Massachusetts Institute of Technology. He subsequently became a leading agroindustrialist in the department of Santa Cruz. He was the president of the state-operated sugar mill UNAGRO and led the cattle ranchers' association (Unión Agrícola Ganadera). He was also the director of the conservative La Paz daily *La Razón* and headed the World Bank–sponsored Social Emergency Fund from 1985 to 1988.

13. This was at a time when interest rates worldwide were declining.

14. The decision to adopt the label "IPDS" emerged in a context of growing confusion within the government, Bolivian society, and among NGOs about what an NGO actually was. The debate surrounding labels and definitions was, and is, interesting, because of the way it illustrates processes of association and distancing among these organizations and the state. It is important to note, however, that the decision to

call themselves "instituciones *privadas*" (private institutions) was a considered one. "Private institutions" appealed to the political agendas of international funding agencies, and the designation had no associations with the oppositional politics of the past associated with the label "nongovernmental organization." Yet, because most received funding from government agencies, they were at best only nominally private organizations.

15. Unlike the MBL, CONDEPA has never developed a political strategy based on the use of NGOs to mobilize a constituency; rather, CONDEPA's charismatic leader, Carlos Palenque, specialized in using radio and television to gain a following. Palenque owned a radio and television station in La Paz and used his enormously popular program, *Tribuna libre del pueblo*, to maintain a national political presence (see chapter 2).

16. This was a reversal of the usual process of downsizing state functionaries into the NGO sector. See Arellano-López and Petras (1994).

8. Global Connections

1. *Aid* is the adjective used in the United States to describe the activities of development organizations, whereas European funders prefer the less paternalistic *cooperation.*

2. Martin Scurrah (1995) develops this point in a useful article on Peru. See also Ferguson (1994) for an interesting discussion of the depoliticization associated with a World Bank development project in Lesotho.

3. Ayllus are extended kin groups.

4. After the 1952 revolution the Bolivian state sought to downplay racial and ethnic differences in order to construct a national identity, one in which people identified as Bolivians, rather than as whites, "Indians," and so forth. To this end, it touted the mixed racial and cultural heritage of the population. The notion of racial mixing is referred to as mestizaje.

5. Judith Adler Hellman (1994) makes a similar point about the political participation of poor Mexican women who are also being buffeted by free-market reforms.

6. It is important to remember that this openness to NGOs is constantly manufactured through the everyday violence of state policy, for example, the unemployment and dislocations generated by structural adjustment. Local people have few other choices.

7. See Brysk (1996), Conklin (1997), and Jackson (1995).

8. The Vatican has increasingly spoken out against the progressive church in Latin America and, together with conservative local clergy, has rolled back or dismantled the base community movement. Pope John Paul II has sought to keep the poor and disenfranchised within the Catholic fold by making an unprecedented number of trips to the Third World and by sanctifying more individuals from poor communities. See Sheehan (1997) for a discussion of this papal practice.

9. See Page-Reeves (1998) for a discussion of the world market for hand-knit alpaca sweaters and the difficulties posed for cooperative knitting groups in Cochabamba, Bolivia.

10. The women's worries were not unwarranted. Fining people who fail to participate in marches, or withholding largesse, such as food handouts, are typical practices of political parties and some unions.

11. One federation leader is actually the former employee of an NGO director and describes the woman as one of the worst employers that she ever had.

12. This point was driven home to me during the reception for the Spanish version of my book *Precarious Dependencies*. The reception was organized by the domestic workers' union and coincided with the inauguration of its new center. The union leader hand-delivered an invitation to the charismatic founder and long-time leader of the COB, Juan Lechín Oquendo. She was met at the door by Lechín's maid, who promised to give the invitation to "Don Juan," but at the appointed time nobody was particularly surprised that Don Juan was not able to make it, although his maid did.

13. Aymara anthropologist Estéban Ticona (1996) notes the problems that professional "advisers" pose for a Bolivian peasant confederation—the Confederación Sindical Única de Trabajadores Campesinos de Bolivia (CSUTCB). He also writes that "it is noteworthy that indigenous professionals and peasants are not advisors. The only exception is Constantino Lima [an indigenous leader] . . . when the CSUTCB was born" (Ticona 1996:48).

14. For example, I became a confidant of two leaders after the publication in Bolivia of my book *Precarious Dependencies*. A seemingly powerful gringa who was clearly sympathetic with their cause but neither an NGO staff member nor a disinterested COB functionary, I was sought out by these leaders on several occasions. They not only complained to me about the problems that they faced with NGOs but also sought my advice on several issues. In one instance they had hired a professional to analyze the data from a questionnaire about domestic service that the union had distributed among its membership. The leaders were not satisfied with the individual's work but had already paid her half of a fairly substantial fee for her services. They worried that the study would never be completed and that the rank-and-file would accuse them of embezzling the money.

15. Morales was one of several labor leaders imprisoned after the enactment of the state of siege.

16. See Aguirre Ledezma 1995a, 1995b.

9. El Alto, the State, and the Capitalist Imperium

1. See Striffler (1998) for an interesting consideration of these issues in Ecuador.

2. The large amount of money channeled to NGOs in the late 1980s and early 1990s is unlikely to continue. Cutbacks are likely as European and North American governments turn their attention to East Europe and the former Soviet republics. By the mid-1990s the NGO boom in Bolivia did appear to be leveling off.

3. Other postmodernist discourse-centered analyses that seek to "deconstruct" development suffer from similar shortcomings. See, for example, Escobar (1995).

References

Abrams, Philip. 1988. "Notes on the Difficulty of Studying the State." *Journal of Historical Sociology* 1(1):58–89.

Aguirre Ledezma, Noel. 1995a. "Reformas en la educación alternativa." *Presencia*, May 3, p. 2.

———. 1995b. "La reforma educativa y algunas condiciones para su viabilidad." *Presencia*, May 11, p. 2.

Albó, Xavier, Tomás Greaves, and Godofredo Sandóval. 1981. *Chukiyawu: La cara Aymara de La Paz: El paso a la ciudad*, vol. 1. Cuaderno de Investigación, no. 20. La Paz: Centro de Investigación y Promoción del Campesino.

———. 1982. *Chukiyawu: La cara Aymara de La Paz: Una odisea: Buscar pega*, vol. 2. Cuaderno de Investigación, no. 22. La Paz: Centro de Investigación y Promoción del Campesino.

———. 1983. *Chukiyawu: La cara Aymara de La Paz: Cabalgando entre dos mundos*, vol. 3. Cuaderno de Investigación, no. 24. La Paz: Centro de Investigación y Promoción del Campesino.

———. 1987. *Chukiyawu: La cara Aymara de La Paz: Nuevos lazos con el campo*, vol. 4. Cuaderno de Investigación, no. 29. La Paz: Centro de Investigación y Promoción del Campesino.

Albó, Xavier and Matías Preiswork. 1986. *Los señores del gran poder*. La Paz: Centro de Teología Popular.

Alonso, Ana Mara. 1995. *Thread of Blood: Colonialism, Revolution, and Gender on Mexico's Northern Frontier*. Tucson: University of Arizona Press.

Alvarez, Sonia, Evelina Dagnino, and Arturo Escobar, eds. 1998. *Culture of Politics, Politics of Culture: Re-Visioning Latin American Social Movements*. Boulder, Colo.: Westview.

Ansión, Juan, ed. 1989. *Pishtacos: De verdugos a sacaojos*. Lima: Tarea.

Appadurai, Arjun. 1990. "Disjuncture and Difference in the Global Cultural Economy." *Public Culture* 2(2):1–23.

Arauco Lemaitre, Isabel and Hugo Romero Bedregal. 1987. "Bolivia: Estudio sobre el minero relocalizado." Report issued by Fondo Social de Emergencia, La Paz.

Arellano-López, Sonia and James Petras. 1994. "Non-Governmental Organizations and Poverty Alleviation in Bolivia." *Development and Change* 25: 555–68.

Arkin, William and Lynne R. Dobrofsky. 1990. "Military Socialization and Masculinity." In Francesca M. Cancian and James William Gibson, eds., *Making War, Making Peace: The Social Foundations of Violent Conflict*, pp. 68–78. Belmont, Calif.: Wadsworth.

Arze Aguirre, René Danilo. 1987. *Guerra y conflictos sociales: El caso rural boliviano durante la campaña del Chaco*. La Paz: Centro de Estudios Sobre la Realidad Económica y Social.

Barrios de Chungara, Domitila. 1978. *Let Me Speak: The Autobiography of a Bolivian Mining Woman*. Edited by Moema Vieser. New York: Monthly Review Press.

Beasley, Anne. 1992. A Description of the Title II Program and Its Impact on Beneficiaries. USAID manuscript, La Paz, Bolivia.

Bebbington, Anthony and Graham Thiele, eds. 1993. *Nongovernmental Organizations and the State in Latin America: Rethinking Roles in Sustainable Agricultural Development*. New York: Routledge.

Benería, Lourdes and Martha Roldán. 1987. *The Crossroads of Class and Gender: Industrial Homework, Subcontracting, and Household Dynamics in Mexico*. Chicago: University of Chicago Press.

Bernstein, Richard. 1995. "Entering the Minds of a City's Young Drug Dealers." *New York Times*, December 27, p. C19.

Bourgois, Philippe. 1995. *In Search of Respect: Selling Crack in El Barrio*. New York: Cambridge University Press.

Bratton, Michael. 1988. "Beyond the State: Civil Society and Associational Life in Africa." *World Politics* 41(3):407–30.

Brown, Michael F. and Eduardo Fernández. 1991. *War of Shadows: The Struggle for Utopia in the Peruvian Amazon*. Berkeley: University of California Press.

Broyles, William Jr. 1990. "Why Men Love War." In Francesca M. Cancian and James William Gibson, eds., *Making War, Making Peace: The Social Foundations of Violent Conflict*, pp. 29–37. Belmont, Calif.: Wadsworth.

Brysk, Alison. 1996. "Turning Weakness into Strength: The Internationalization of Indian Rights." *Latin American Perspectives* 23(2):38–57.

Buechler, Hans and Judith-Maria Buechler. 1992. *Manufacturing Against the Odds: Small-Scale Producers in an Andean City*. Boulder, Colo.: Westview.

Caldeira, Teresa. 1996. "Fortified Enclaves: The New Urban Segregation." *Public Culture* 8(2):303–28.

Calhoun, Craig. 1993. "'New Social Movements' of the Early Nineteenth Century." *Social Science History* 17(3):385–427.

Carroll, Thomas F. 1992. *Intermediary NGOs: The Supporting Link in Grassroots Development*. West Hartford, Conn.: Kumarian Press.

Castañeda, Jorge G. 1993. *Utopia Unarmed: The Latin American Left After the Cold War*. New York: Knopf.

Castells, Manuel. 1997. *The Information Age: Economy, Society, and Culture*. Vol. 2: *The Power of Identity*. Malden, Mass.: Blackwell.

CEDLA/ILDIS (Centro de Estudios para el Desarrollo Laboral y Agrario/Instituto Latinoamericano de Investigaciones Sociales). 1994. *Informe social 1: Balance de indicadores sociales*. La Paz: CEDLA/ILDIS.

Cernea, Michael. 1989. "Nongovernmental Organizations and Local Development." *Regional Development Dialogue* 10(2):117–42.

Clark, Ann Marie. 1995. "Nongovernmental Organizations and Their Influence on International Society." *Journal of International Affairs* 48(2):507–25.

Codina, Gabriel. 1994. "Los rostros de la reforma educativa." *Cuarto Intermedio* 33: 26–45.

Cohn, Carol. 1987. "Sex and Death in the Rational World of Defense Intellectuals." *Signs* 12(4):687–718.

Collins, Joseph and John Lear. 1995. *Chile's Free-Market Miracle: A Second Look*. Oakland, Calif.: Institute for Food and Development Policy.

Comité Interinstitucional de la Mujer en El Alto. 1992. Propuesta para la creación de la Comisión de la Mujer en la H.A.M.E.A. El Alto. Conclusiones del Seminario Taller. La Paz.

Conaghan, Catherine M. and James M. Malloy. 1994. *Unsettling Statecraft: Democracy and Neoliberalism in the Central Andes*. Pittsburgh: University of Pittsburgh Press.

Conaghan, Catherine M., James M. Malloy, and Luis A. Abugatas. 1990. "Business and the 'Boys': The Politics of Neoliberalism in the Central Andes." *Latin American Research Review* 25(2):3–30.

Conklin, Beth A. 1997. "Body Paint, Feathers, and VCRs: Aesthetics and Authenticity in Amazonian Activism." *American Ethnologist* 24(4):711–37.

Corrigan, Philip and Derek Sayer. 1987. *The Great Arch: English State Formation as Cultural Revolution*. London: Basil Blackwell.

Crandon-Malamud, Libbet. 1991. *From the Fat of Our Souls: Social Change, Political Process, and Medical Pluralism in Bolivia*. Berkeley: University of California Press.

Davidoff, Leonore and Catherine Hall. 1987. *Family Fortunes: Men and Women of the English Middle Class, 1780–1850*. Chicago: University of Chicago Press.

Davis, Mike. 1990. *City of Quartz: Excavating the Future in Los Angeles*. London: Verso.

Dewez, Philippe. 1991. Bolivia: La relación estado-organizaciones nogubernamentales. Commission of European Communities. Manuscript.

di Leonardo, Micaela. 1998. *Exotics at Home: Anthropologies, Others, American Modernity*. Chicago: University of Chicago Press.

Dunkerley, James. 1992. "Political Transition and Economic Stablization: Bolivia, 1982–1989." In James Dunkerley, ed., *Political Suicide in Latin America and Other Essays*, pp. 173–243. London: Verso,

ECLAC (Economic Commission for Latin America and the Caribbean). 1992. *El pérfil de la pobreza en América Latina y el Caribe*. Santiago, Chile: ECLAC

——. 1996. *Statistical Yearbook for Latin America and the Caribbean*. Santiago, Chile: ECLAC.

Edelman, Marc. 1991. "Shifting Legitimacies and Economic Change: The State and

Contemporary Costa Rican Peasant Movements." *Peasant Studies* 18(4):221–49.

———. 1996. "Reconceptualizing and Reconstituting Peasant Struggles: A New Social Movement in Central America." *Radical History Review* 65 (spring):27–47.

———. 1997. "Notes on Liberalism, Neo- and Not-so-Neo-: Central America in the Late Nineteenth and Late-Twentieth Centuries." Paper presented at the Twentieth International Congress of the Latin American Studies Association, April 17–19, Guadalajara, Mexico.

———. 1999. *Peasants Against Globalization: Rural Social Movements in Costa Rica.* Palto Alto, Calif.: Stanford University Press.

Edwards, Michael and David Hulme, eds. 1996. *Beyond the Magic Bullet: NGO Performance and Accountability in the Post–Cold War World.* West Hartford, Conn.: Kumarian Press.

"El anterior gobierno dejó a FF.AA. sin presupuesto." 1989. *Los Tiempos.* November 1.

Elson, Diane. 1992. "From Survival Strategies to Transformation Strategies: Women's Needs and Structural Adjustment." In Lourdes Benería and Shelley Feldman, eds., *Unequal Burden: Economic Crisis, Persistent Poverty and Women's Work*, pp. 26–48. Boulder, Colo.: Westview.

Ely, Geoff and Keith Nield. 1996. "Starting Over: The Present, the Post-Modern, and the Moment in Social History." *Social History* 20(3):355–64.

"Empieza plan de alfabetización en las fuerzas armadas." 1991. *Presencia,* November 6.

Enloe, Cynthia. 1980. *Ethnic Soldiers: State Security in Divided Societies.* Athens: University of Georgia Press.

Escobar, Arturo. 1995. *Encountering Development: The Making and Unmaking of the Third World.* Princeton, N.J.: Princeton University Press.

Escobar, Arturo and Sonia E. Alvarez, eds. 1992. *The Making of Social Movements in Latin America: Identity, Strategy, and Democracy.* Boulder, Colo.: Westview.

Ferguson, James. 1994. *The Anti-Politics Machine: "Development," Depoliticization, and Bureaucratic Power in Lesotho.* Minneapolis: University of Minnesota Press.

Fisher, William. 1997. "Doing Good? The Politics and Antipolitics of NGO Practices." *Annual Review of Anthropology* 26: 439–64.

Forcey, Linda Rennie. 1987. *Mothers and Sons.* New York: Praeger.

Fowler, Alan. 1991. "The Role of NGOs in Changing State-Society Relations: Perspectives from Eastern and Southern South Africa." *Development Policy Review* 9: 53–84.

Franko, Patrice. 1994. "De Facto Demilitarization: Budget-Driven Downsizing in Latin America." *Journal of Interamerican Studies and World Affairs* 36(1):37–73.

Gilbert, Alan. 1994. *The Latin American City.* London: Latin America Bureau.

Gill, Lesley. 1985. "Rural Cooperatives and Peasant Differentiation: A Bolivian Case Study." In Barry L. Isaac, ed., *Research in Economic Anthropology*, vol. 7, pp. 225–50. Greenwich, Conn.: JAI Press.

———. 1987. *Peasants, Entrepreneurs, and Social Change: Frontier Development in Lowland Bolivia.* Boulder, Colo.: Westview.

———. 1994. *Precarious Dependencies: Gender, Class, and Domestic Service in Bolivia.* New York: Columbia University Press.

Glatthaar, Joseph T. 1990. *Forged in Battle: The Civil War Alliance of Black Soldiers and White Officers.* New York: Collier MacMillan.

Gledhill, John. 1995. *Neoliberalism, Trasnationalization, and Rural Poverty: A Case Study of Michoacán, Mexico.* Boulder, Colo.: Westview.

Glick-Schiller, Nina, Linda Basch, and Cristina Blanc-Szanton. 1992. "Transnationalism: A New Analytic Framework for Understanding Migration." *Annals of the New York Academy of Science* 645: 1–24.

Godoy, Ricardo. 1990. *Mining and Agriculture in Highland Bolivia: Ecology, History, and Commerce Among the Jukumanis.* Tucson: University of Arizona Press.

Gould, Jeffrey. 1990. *To Lead as Equals: Rural Protest and Political Consciousness in Chinandega, Nicaragua, 1912–1979.* Chapel Hill: University of North Carolina Press.

Graham, Carol. 1992. "The Politics of Protecting the Poor During Adjustment: Bolivia's Social Emergency Fund." *World Development* 20(9):1233–51.

Gramsci, Antonio. 1971. *Sections from the Prison Notebooks.* Edited and translated by Quintin Hoare and Geoffrey Nowell Smith. New York: International Publishers.

Green, Linda. 1999. *Fear as a Way of Life: Mayan Widows in Rural Guatemala.* New York: Columbia University Press.

Gusterson, Hugh. 1998. *Nuclear Rites: A Weapons Laboratory at the End of the Cold War.* Berkeley: University of California Press.

Gutmann, Matthew. 1996. *The Meanings of Macho: Being a Man in Mexico City.* Berkeley: University of California Press.

Hansen, Karen. 1994. "Dealing with Used Clothing: Salaula and the Construction of Identity in Zambia's Third Republic." *Public Culture* 6(2):503–23.

Hannerz, Ulf. 1992. *Cultural Complexity: Studies in the Social Organization of Meaning.* New York: Columbia University Press.

Harris, Olivia and Xavier Albó. 1984. *Monteras y guardatojos: Campesinos y mineros en el norte de Potosí.* Cuaderno de Investigación, no. 26. La Paz: Centro de Investigación y Promoción del Campesino.

Harvey, David. 1993. "Class Relations, Social Justice, and the Politics of Difference." In Judith Squires, ed., *Principled Positions*, pp. 41–66. London: Wishart.

Harvey, Neil. 1998. *The Chiapas Rebellion: The Struggle for Land and Democracy.* Durham, N.C.: Duke University Press.

Held, David. 1991. "Democracy, the Nation-State, and the Global System." In David Held, ed., *Political Theory and the Modern State*, pp. 197–235. Oxford: Polity Press.

Hellman, Judith Adler. 1994. *Mexican Lives.* New York: New Press.

Henwood, Doug. 1997. *Wall Street.* New York: Verso.

Hudson, Rex A. and Dennis M. Hanratty, eds. 1991. *Bolivia: A Country Study.* Washington, D.C.: Library of Congress.

Human Rights Watch/Americas. 1996. "Bolivia Under Pressure: Human Rights Violations and Coca Eradication." Report. New York.

——. 1997. "Police Brutality in Urban Brazil." Report. New York.

"Imperialism: A Useful Category of Historical Analysis?" 1993. Special issue of *Radical History Review*, no. 57 (fall).

INE (Instituto Nacional de Estadística). 1992. "Censo nacional de población y vivienda." Report. La Paz, Bolivia.

Jackson, Jean. 1995. "Culture, Genuine and Spurious: The Politics of Indianness in the Vaupés, Colombia." *American Ethnologist* 22(1):3–27.

Jelin, Elizabeth, ed. 1990. *Women and Social Change in Latin America.* London: Zed.

Joseph, Gilbert M. and Daniel Nugent, eds. 1994. *Everyday Forms of State Formation: Revolution and the Negotiation of Rule in Modern Mexico.* Durham, N.C.: Duke University Press.

Joyce, Patrick. 1996. "The End of Social History." *Social History* 20(1):73–91.

Justicia y Paz. 1975. "La masacre del valle." Report. La Paz.

Kearney, Michael. 1991. "Borders and Boundaries of State and Self at the End of Empire." *Journal of Historical Sociology* 4(1):52–74.

——. 1995. "The Local and the Global: The Anthropology of Globalization and Transnationalism." *Annual Review of Anthropology* 24: 547–65.

Klein, Herbert S. 1982. *Bolivia: The Evolution of a Multi-Ethnic Society.* New York: Oxford University Press.

Klubock, Thomas Miller. 1998. "From Welfare Capitalism to the Free Market in Chile: Gender, Culture, and Politics in the Copper Mines." In Gilbert M. Joseph, Catherine C. LeGrand, and Ricardo D. Salvatore, eds., *Close Encounters of Empire: Writing the Cultural History of U.S.–Latin American Relations,* pp. 369–99. Durham, N.C.: Duke University Press.

Kowarick, Lúcio. 1994. "Introduction." In Lúcio Kowarick, ed., *Social Struggles and the City: The Case of Sao Paulo,* pp. 31–40. New York: Monthly Review Press.

"La corrupción y delincuencia van en ascenso." 1996. *Presencia,* May 26, p. 1.

Lagos, Maria. 1994. *Autonomy and Power: The Dynamics of Class and Culture in Rural Bolivia.* Philadelphia: University of Pennsylvania Press.

Lancaster, Roger. 1992. *Life Is Hard: Machismo, Danger, and the Intimacy of Power in Nicaragua.* Berkeley: University of California Press.

Landim, Leilah. 1987. "Non-governmental Organizations in Latin America." Supplement to *World Development* 15: 29–38.

Lassalle, Yvonne M. and Maureen O'Dougherty. 1997. "In Search of Weeping Worlds: Economies of Agency and Politics of Representation in the Ethnography of Inequality." *Radical History Review* 69 (spring):243–60.

Latin America Bureau. 1987. *The Great Tin Crash: Bolivia and the World Tin Market.* London: Latin America Bureau.

Latin America Working Group. 1998. "Just the Facts: A Civilian's Guide to U.S. Defense and Security Assistance to Latin America and the Caribbean." Washington, D.C.

Leeds, Elizabeth. 1996. "Cocaine and Parallel Politics in the Brazilian Urban Periphery: Constraints on Local-Level Democratization." *Latin American Research Review* 31(3):47–84.

Léons, Madeline Barbara and Harry Sanabria. 1997. *Coca, Cocaine, and the Bolivian Reality.* Albany: State University of New York Press.

Levenson-Estrada, Deborah. 1994. *Trade Unionists Against Terror: Guatemala City, 1954–1985.* Chapel Hill, N.C.: Duke University Press.

Lewis, Oscar. 1966. *La Vida: A Puerto Rican Family in the Culture of Poverty—San Juan and New York.* New York: Random House.

Linebaugh, Peter. 1992. *The London Hanged: Crime and Civil Society in the Eighteenth Century*. London: Cambridge University Press.

Little, Peter and Michael Painter. 1995. "Discourse, Politics, and the Development Process." *American Ethnologist* 22(3):602–608.

Lofredo, Gino. 1991. "Hágase rico en los 90." *Chasqui*, no. 39: 1–5.

Lovell, John P. and Judith Hicks Stiehm. 1989. "Military Service and Political Socialization." In Roberta S. Siegel, ed., *Political Learning in Adulthood*, pp. 172–202. Chicago: University of Chicago Press.

Luykx, Aurolyn. 1999. *The Citizen Factory: Schooling and Cultural Production in Bolivia*. Albany: State University of New York Press.

MacDonald, Laura. 1997. *Supporting Civil Society: The Political Role of Non-Governmental Organizations in Central America*. New York: St. Martin's.

Marcus, George. 1995. "Ethnography in/of the World System: The Emergence of Multi-Sited Ethnography." *Annual Review of Anthropology* 24: 95–117.

Martin, Emily. 1987. *The Woman in the Body: A Cultural Analysis of Reproduction*. Boston: Beacon.

MDH/SNS (Ministerio de Desarrollo Humano y Secretaría Nacional de Salud). 1994. "Plan de instrucción del soldado: 'Centinela de la salud'" Report. La Paz.

Moore, Michael. 1990. *Roger and Me*. Burbank, Calif.: Dog Eat Dog Films/Warner Home Video. Videocassette.

Morales, Rolando. 1994. "Lineamientos para aliviar la pobreza urbana: El caso de la cuidad de El Alto, La Paz, Bolivia." Report issued by Programa de Gestión Urbana of La Paz, Habitat, and United Nations.

NACLA (North American Congress on Latin America). 1998. "Militarized Democracy in the Americas." NACLA *Report on the Americas* 32(3):15–43.

Nash, June. 1979. *We Eat the Mines and the Mines Eat Us: Dependency and Exploitation in Bolivian Tin Mines*. New York: Columbia University Press.

——. 1992. "Interpreting Social Movements: Bolivian Resistance to Economic Conditions Imposed by the International Monetary Fund." *American Ethnologist* 19(2):275–93.

——. 1994a. "El declive de las minas nacionalizadas y la política neoliberal en Bolivia." Paper presented at the Cursos de Verano de la Universidad Hispanoamericana de la Rabida, August 1–5, 1994, La Rabida, Spain.

——. 1994b. "Global Integration and Subsistence Security." *American Anthropologist* 96(1):7–30.

"No había aumentos en FF.AA." 1989. *Presencia*, January 11.

Nugent, David. 1996. Review of *In Search of Respect*. *American Ethnologist* 24(3):685–87.

——. 1997. *Modernity at the Edge of Empire: State, Individual, and Nation in the Northern Peruvian Andes, 1885–1935*. Palo Alto, Calif.: Stanford University Press.

Page-Reeves, Janet. 1998. "Alpaca Sweater Design and Marketing: Problems and Prospects for Cooperative Knitting Organizations in Bolivia." *Human Organization* 57(1):83–93.

Palmer, Brian. 1994. *Goodyear Invades the Backcountry: The Corporate Takeover of a Rural Town*. New York: Monthly Review Press.

Pérez, Elizardo. 1992. *Warisata.* La Paz: HISBOL/CERES.

Pinelo, José. 1992. Las IPDS en el contexto nacional. Manuscript. La Paz, Bolivia.

"Presupuesto de FF.AA. No pudo ser ejecutado." 1986. *Los Tiempos,* December 19.

"Reforma del presupuesto recorta $b. 30 billiones a gastos de defensa." 1986. *Presencia,* November 10.

"Religiosos denuncian abusos en el reclutamiento militar." 1987. *Presencia,* July 19.

"Reservistas del altiplano no regresan aún a sus hogares." 1992. *Presencia,* February 13.

Ritchey-Vance, Marion. 1990. *The Art of Association: NGOs and Civil Society in Colombia.* Arlington, Va.: Interamerican Foundation.

Rivera Cusicanqui, Silvia. 1990. "Liberal Democracy and Ayllu Democracy in Bolivia: The Case of Northern Potosí." *Journal of Development Studies* 20(4):97–121.

———. 1996. "Trabajo de mujeres: Explotación capitalista y opresión colonial entre las migrantes Aymaras de La Paz y El Alto, Bolivia." In Silvia Rivera Cusicanqui, ed., *Ser mujer indígena, chola o birlocha en la Bolivia postcolonial de los años 90,* pp. 163–300. La Paz, Bolivia: Ministerio de Desarrollo Humano, Subsecretaría de Asuntos de Génaro.

Robinson, William J. 1996. *Promoting Polyarchy: Globalization, U.S. Intervention, and Hegemony.* Cambridge, U.K.: Cambridge University Press.

Roseberry, William. 1993. "Beyond the Agrarian Question in Latin America." In Frederick Cooper, Alan Isaacman, Florencia Mallon, William Roseberry, and Steve J. Stern, eds., *Confronting Historical Paradigms: Peasants, Labor, and the Capitalist World System in Africa and Latin America,* pp. 318–68. Madison: University of Wisconsin Press.

———. 1994. "Hegemony and the Language of Contention." In Gilbert M. Joseph and Daniel Nugent, eds., *Everyday Forms of State Formation: Revolution and the Negotiation of Rule in Modern Mexico,* pp. 355–66. Chapel Hill, N.C.: Duke University Press.

"Ruidosa marcha de cacerolas reclamó aumento de salarios." 1995. *Presencia,* March 9.

Sandóval, Godofredo. 1992. *Las ONGs y los caminos del desarrollo.* La Paz: JICA/CEP.

Sandóval, Godofredo and M. Fernanda Sostres. 1989. *La Ciudad prometida: Pobladores y organizaciones sociales en El Alto.* La Paz: Systema/ILDIS.

Sandóval, Godofredo, Jose Antonio Péres, and Cristina Mejía. 1989. "Impacto institucional del FSE." Report issued by Systema, La Paz.

Sayer, Derek. 1994. "Everyday Forms of State Formation: Some Dissident Remarks on Hegemony." In Gilbert M. Joseph and Daniel Nugent, eds., *Everyday Forms of State Formation: Revolution and the Negotiation of Rule in Modern Mexico,* pp. 367–79. Durham, N.C.: Duke University Press.

Schatz, Adam. 1995. "Among the Dispossessed." *Nation,* December 25, pp. 836–39.

Scheper-Hughes, Nancy. 1992. *Death Without Weeping: The Violence of Everyday Life.* Berkeley: University of California Press.

Schirmer, Jennifer. 1998. *The Guatemalan Military Project: A Violence Called Democracy.* Philadelphia: University of Pennsylvania Press.

Scurrah, Martin J. 1995. "The Politics of Anti-Politics: NGOs and Democracy in Peru." *Journal of Iberian and Latin American Studies* (Victoria, Australia) 1(1–2): 128–40.

Seabrook, Jeremy. 1996. *In the Cities of the South: Scenes from a Developing World.* London: Verso.

"Se denuncia persecución de la policia militar a estudiantes." 1988. *Presencia,* July 18.

Segal, David. 1989. *Recruiting for Uncle Sam: Citizenship and Military Manpower Policy.* Lawrence: University of Kansas Press.

Sheehan, Elizabeth. 1997. The Political Economy of Sanctity: Making Catholic Saints for the Third Millenium. Manuscript.

Sider, Gerald. 1986. *Culture and Class in Anthropology and History.* Cambridge, U.K.: Cambridge University Press.

———. 1993. *Lumbee Indian Histories: Race, Ethnicity, and Indian Identity in the Southern United States.* New York: Cambridge University Press.

———. 1996. "Cleansing History: Lawrence, Massachusetts, the Strike for Four Loaves of Bread and No Roses, and the Anthropology of Working-Class Consciousness." *Radical History Review* 65 (spring):48–83.

Sider, Gerald and Gavin Smith, eds. 1997. *Between History and Histories: The Making of Silences and Commemorations.* Toronto: University of Toronto Press.

"Si no se aumentaba presupuesto de defensa, los cuarteles se cerraban." 1989. *Hoy,* November 2.

Sleeper, Jonathan A. and Charles Patterson. 1995. "How a PL-480 Title II Food Program Supports Neighborhood Empowerment." Report issued by USAID, La Paz, Bolivia.

Smith, Carol. 1990a. "The Militarization of Civil Society in Guatemala: Economic Reorganization as a Continuation of War." *Latin American Perspectives* 17(4):8–41.

Smith, Carol, ed. 1990b. *Guatemalan Indians and the State: 1540–1988.* Austin: University of Texas Press.

Steedman, Carolyn. 1986. *Landscape for a Good Woman.* London: Virago Press.

Stern, Steve J. 1995. *The Secret History of Gender: Women, Men, and Power in Late Colonial Mexico.* Chapel Hill: University of North Carolina Press.

Stoler, Ann Laura and Frederick Cooper. 1997. "Between Metropole and Colony: Rethinking a Research Agenda." In Federick Cooper and Ann Laura Stoler, eds., *Tensions of Empire: Colonial Cultures in a Bourgeois World,* pp. 1–58. Berkeley: University of California Press.

Striffler, Steve. 1998. "Communists, Communists Everywhere: Forgetting the Past and Living with History in Ecuador." Paper presented to the Cultural Pluralism Seminar, Columbia University Seminars, November 16, New York City.

———. 1999. "Wedded to Work: Class Struggles and Gendered Identities in the Restructuring of the Ecuadorian Banana Industry." *Identities* 6(1):91–120.

Subsecretaría de Asuntos de Género. 1994. "Las cifras de la violencia registrada en El Alto." Report issued by the Ministerio de Desarrollo Humano, La Paz, Bolivia.

Taussig, Michael. 1987. *Shamanism, Colonialism, and the Wild Man: A Study in Terror and Healing.* Chicago: University of Chicago Press.

"Terminó conflictos con mineros relocalizados." 1992. *Hoy,* August 22.

Thompson, Edward P. 1978. "Eighteenth-Century English Society: Class Struggle Without Class." *Social History* 3(2):133–65.

———. 1993. "The Moral Economy Reviewed." In E. P. Thompson, ed., *Customs in*

Common: Studies in Traditional Popular Culture, pp. 259–351. New York: New Press.

Ticona, Estebán. 1996. "CSUTCB: Trayectoria y Desafíos. Informe especial." Report issued by Centro de Información y Documentación (CEDOIN), La Paz, Bolivia.

UNAS (Unidad de Apoyo y Seguimiento a la Reforma Educativa). 1994. "Registro de docentes y personal administrativo." Report. La Paz, Bolivia.

UNITAS (Unión Nacional de Instituciones para el Trabajo de Acción Social). 1991. *La revuelta de las nacionalidades.* La Paz: UNITAS.

Urban, Greg and Joel Sherzer. 1991. *Nation-States and Indians in Latin America.* Austin: University of Texas Press.

"Valle: Presupuesto de las FF.AA. fue reducido en 46 por ciento." 1986. *Hoy*, February 8.

Van Niekerk, Nico. 1992. "La cooperación internacional y la persistencia de la pobreza en los Andes bolivianos." Report issued by UNITAS/MCTH, La Paz, Bolivia.

Verdery, Katherine. 1996. *What Was Socialism, and What Comes Next?* Princeton, N.J.: Princeton University Press.

Vidaurre, Janette. 1994. "Conscripts for Health." *World Health Forum* 15: 345–47.

Vilas, Carlos. 1993. "The Hour of Civil Society." NACLA *Report on the Americas* 27(2):38–42.

———. 1997. "Participation, Inequality, and the Whereabouts of Democracy." In Douglas A. Chalmers, Carlos M. Vilas, Katherine Hite, Scott B. Martin, Kerianne Piester, and Monique Segarra, eds., *The New Politics of Inequality in Latin America*, pp. 3–42. New York: Oxford University Press.

Volk, Steven. 1975. "Class, Union, Party: The Development of a Revolutionary Union Movement in Bolivia (1905–1952)." *Science and Society* 39(1&2):26–43, 180–98.

Wachtel, Nathan. 1994. *Gods and Vampires: Return to Chipaya.* Chicago: University of Chicago Press.

Wahl, Peter. 1997. "Tendencias globales y sociedad civil internacional: Una ongización de la política mundial?" *Nueva Sociedad* 149: 42–50.

Weber, Eugen. 1976. *Peasants into Frenchmen.* Palo Alto, Calif.: Stanford University Press.

Weismantel, Mary. 1998. "White Cannibals: Fantasies of Racial Violence in the Andes." *Identities* 4:9–43.

Williams, Brett. 1994. "Babies and Banks: The Reproductive Underclass and the Raced, Gendered Masking of Debt." In Steven Gregory and Roger Sanjek, eds., *Race*, pp. 348–65. New Brunswick, N.J.: Rutgers University Press.

Wilson, William Julius. 1987. *The Truly Disadvantaged: The Inner City, the Underclass, and Public Policy.* Chicago: University of Chicago Press.

Winn, Peter. 1986. *Weavers of Revolution: The Yarur Workers and Chile's Road to Socialism.* New York: Oxford University Press.

Womack, John. 1968. *Zapata and the Mexican Revolution.* New York: Knopf.

Wood, Ellen Meiksins. 1995. *Democracy Against Capitalism: Renewing Historical Materialism.* New York: Cambridge University Press.

World Development. 1987. Special Issue on NGOs, vol. 15 (supplement).

Index